Business Result

Pre-intermediate | Student's Book

David Grant, Jane Hudson & Robert McLarty

Interactive Workbook material
by Gareth Davies, Chris Speck & Shaun Wilden

D1207992

OXFORD
UNIVERSITY PRESS

Contents

VIDEO : This section of the unit has a video clip linked to the topic.

Introduction

Welcome to *Business Result Pre-intermediate*. In this book you will find:

| 16 units | Practice files | Information files | Audio scripts |
| Interactive Workbook on DVD-ROM |

What's in a unit?

Starting point
- an introduction to the unit
- discussion questions

Working with words
- reading and listening about the world of work
- new words and phrases that you can use in your work
- practise the new words in speaking activities

Language at work
- grammar lessons in real work situations
- helps you communicate better
- practise grammar in the classroom in speaking activities
- for more practice go to the *Practice file*

Practically speaking
- essential words and phrases for general use
- helps you sound more natural when you speak English

Business communication
- key expressions for exchanging information, socializing, presenting, and meetings
- real work situations
- *Key expressions* list in every unit

Case study / Activity
- authentic case study, or activity
- improve your fluency
- practise the language from the unit

What's in the *Practice file*?

Written exercises on the key language in
- *Working with words*
- *Business communication*
- *Language at work*

plus a language reference section with more grammar explanations.

Use the *Practice file*
- in class to check your understanding
- after class for extra practice.

Follow the links to the *Practice file* in each unit

>> For more exercises, go to **Practice file 3** on page 106.

What's the *Interactive Workbook* on DVD-ROM?

The *Interactive Workbook* lets you practise the language from the *Student's Book*. It also helps you test your own progress. Use it at home or in the office to practise the language you learn in class.

Exercises and Tests
- practise key language with interactive exercises
- check your progress with unit tests

Glossary
- check the meaning of over 400 words and phrases
- listen to the words and add your translation

Phrasebank
- listen to the key expressions from the *Student's Book*
- learn new phrases for telephoning, exchanging information, socializing, travel, presenting, and meetings
- create your personal phrasebook

Email
- learn useful phrases for writing emails
- copy example emails to use at work

Listen again
- listen again to the *Student's Book* audio, or download to your MP3 player

Video
- Watch a video clip related to a section in the unit. Every unit has a video clip which recycles and extends the language of the unit.
- Complete the interactive exercises while you watch the video clips
- This icon **VIDEO** shows you the section of the unit that the video relates to. Watch the video after you have completed the work in the *Student's Book*.

(i) >> Interactive Workbook >>

Fast-track option

If you are on a short course, you can do the fast-track option. For each unit, do *Language at work*, *Practically speaking*, and *Business communication* in class. You can do the other sections in your own time if you wish.

How to use Business Result Pre-intermediate | A complete blended learning package

Student's Book | Main unit

In class: Learn vocabulary, grammar, and expressions with listening, reading, and speaking activities.

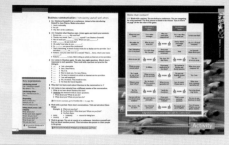

In class or self-study: When you see this, go to the *Practice files* at the **back of the book**.

» For more exercises, go to the **Practice files**.

Self-study: When you see this, go to the *Interactive Workbook* on your **DVD-ROM**.

ⓘ » Interactive Workbook »

Student's Book | Practice file

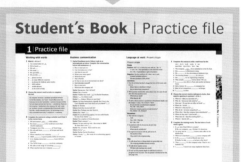

Business Result online

Self-study: You can access the *Business Result website* by either following the prompts on your **CD-ROM**, or by going to **www.oup.com/elt/result**

Interactive exercises:
- Working with words
- Business communication

Reference material:
- Tips on writing
- Glossaries
- *Student's Book* grammar explanations
- Practice file answer key

and more …

Interactive Workbook

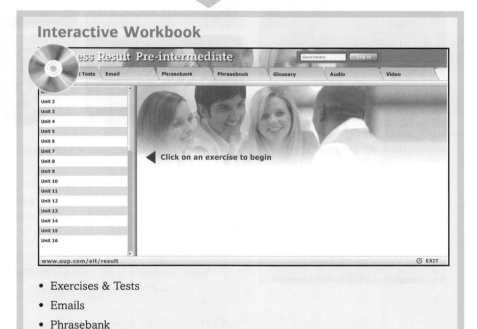

- Exercises & Tests
- Emails
- Phrasebank
- Personal phrasebook
- Glossary
- *Student's Book* audio
- Video with interactive exercises

1 | Companies

Learning objectives in this unit

- Talking about what companies do
- Talking about your company using the present simple
- Making polite requests
- Introducing yourself and others

Activity

- Make that contact!

Starting point

1 Look at the pictures on this page. What do you know about these companies?

2 Do you think it's better to work for a large or a small company?

3 What kind of company do you work for?

Working with words | Company facts

1 **Read these descriptions of some companies. Complete their names.**

1 This company **provide**s many different Internet services, including news, online shopping, and email. Most of its **sales** come from advertising on its website. Its head office is in Sunnyvale, California.

Y __ __ __ __

2 This company **produce**s tyres for cars and other vehicles. It **is based** in France, but it has more than 125,000 **employee**s all over the world. It is also well known for its red and green travel guides.

M __ __ __ __ __ __ __

3 This northern European company operates in the retail market. It **specialize**s in low-price products, including furniture, bathrooms, and kitchens.

I __ __ __

4 It's a **subsidiary** of the European Aeronautic Defence and Space Company (EADS). The company makes planes for the commercial aircraft market, where its main **competitor** is Boeing.

A __ __ __ __ __

5 This company makes many different electrical and electronic products, such as TVs, computers, and mobile phones. It is South Korea's largest company and exporter.

S __ __ __ __ __ __

2 Complete these sentences with the words in **bold** in **1**.

1 Some companies make or _____ goods.

2 Other companies _____ or offer services.

3 If you _____ in a particular product or service, it's your main activity.

4 If you work for a company, you are an _____.

5 If your head office is in a particular city, your company _____ _____ there.

6 If you work in a _____, your company is part of a bigger group.

7 If you sell a lot of products, your _____ are very good.

8 If another company operates in the same market as you, it is your _____.

>> For more exercises, go to **Practice file 1** on page 102.

3 Work with a partner. Make sentences using the words in the table.

Gazprom	produces / makes …
Pirelli	specializes in …
AOL	operates in …
Mitsubishi	provides / offers …
Volkswagen	sells …
UNICEF	's competitors are …

4 01▷ An employee is talking about her company. Listen and complete the information in the table.

Name of company	BESAM
Products	[1]A _____ [2]d _____ mechanisms: locks and [3]s _____ systems
Group	Assa Abloy
Nationality	[4]S _____
Number of employees	[5]_____,000
Sales	[6]€ _____ billion
Number of subsidiaries	[7]_____ in 40 countries
Other information	Main [8]c _____ are the Eastern Company, Ingersoll-Rand, and Master Lock

5 Work with a partner. Talk about Besam, using some or all of these phrases and the information in **4**.

It's a(n) … company / organization.

It's a subsidiary of …   Its head office is …

It makes / produces …   It provides / offers …

It has … employees   It operates in …

It is based in …   It specializes in …

Its main competitors are …   It has sales of …

6 Now talk about your company using the phrases in **5**.

ⓘ >> Interactive Workbook >> Glossary

Language at work | Present simple

1 Work with a partner. Ask and answer these questions.

1 Do you work for a multinational company?
2 Is it a new company?
3 What does it do?
4 Does it operate in many countries?
5 Where do you work?

2 Match the questions in 1 to answers a–e.

a Yes, it does. ___
b It provides engineering services to the car industry. ___
c I have an office in London and another in Tokyo. ___
d Yes, I do. ___
e No, it isn't. ___

3 We use the present simple to talk about general facts or regular actions. Find examples in 1 and 2 for each of these rules.

1 In the third person singular (*he / she / it*), the verb ends in *-s* or *-es*.
   Example: _____
2 With *I / you / we / they*, there is no final *-s*.
   Example: _____
3 In most questions, use *do* with *I / you / we / they* and *does* with *he / she / it*.
   Example: _____
4 Don't use *do* and *does* in questions with the verb *to be*.
   Example: _____

>> For more information and exercises, go to **Practice file 1** on page 103.

4 Read the text. Discuss the questions with a partner.

When you see the name Nestlé, perhaps you think of breakfast cereals, Nescafé instant coffee, or Nespresso machines. But what else do you know about the company? What other products does it sell, and where? How many people work for the company and why do they like working there? What does the company do to protect the environment?

Listen to *Nestlé in Focus* tonight at 8.00 p.m. to get answers to these and many other questions.

5 Work with a partner. Make questions about Nestlé using the prompts below.
   Example: How old is the company?
1 How old / company?
2 What products / company / specialize in?
3 What / its annual sales?
4 Where / its head office?
5 How many factories / have?
6 company / sell / products / all five continents?
7 How many people / employ?
8 What / offer / its employees?
9 company / a lot of work in the community?
10 How / protect the environment?

Tip | Questions with prepositions
In a question with a preposition, the preposition is usually the last word, not the first.
   *Where is he **from**?*
   *Who do you work **for**?*
   *What market do you sell **in**?*

6 02▷ **Match answers a–j to questions 1–10 in 5. Then listen to the radio programme and check.**

a 780. ____

b More than 140 years old. ____

c Yes, it does. ____

d 276,000. ____

e More than 107 billion Swiss francs. ____

f Many possibilities for training. ____

g Yes, it gives money and other help. ____

h Food and beverages. ____

i Vevey, Switzerland. ____

j By using less water, energy and packaging. ____

7 **Make sentences about Nestlé, using the questions in 5 and answers in 6.**

Example: *The company is more than 140 years old.*

8 **Work with a partner. Ask and answer the questions in 5 about your company.**

9 **Work with a different partner. Tell them about your first partner's company.**

Practically speaking | How to make polite requests

1 **Complete these questions with *I* or *you*.**

1 Could ____ speak to you for a moment?

2 Can ____ tell me your name?

3 Can ____ have another drink, please?

4 Could ____ call me again tomorrow?

5 Would ____ repeat that, please?

6 Could ____ help me for a moment?

2 03▷ **Work with a partner. Match the questions in 1 to responses a–f below. Listen and check your answers. Then practise the conversations.**

a Yes, sorry. The reference is 1256 K. ____

b Yes, of course. ____

c I'm afraid I'm on holiday. ____

d Sorry, but I'm very busy. ____

e Certainly. Same again? ____

f Sure. It's Woody Neilson. ____

3 **Work with a partner. Take turns to make and respond to requests, using the verbs in brackets.**

Example: *Can I have your telephone number, please?*

1 I want your telephone number. (have)

2 I want your address. (give)

3 I don't understand you. (speak more slowly)

4 I need your signature on this document. (sign)

5 I need two chairs for my table. You have two free chairs at your table. (take)

6 I don't have time to speak to you now. (talk later)

7 I need your pen to sign the visitor's book. (borrow)

8 I didn't hear what you said. (say)

Tip | *can, could,* and *would*

Could and *would* are generally more polite and formal than *can*.

Would is not used with *I*:
  Could I speak to you?
  NOT ~~Would I speak to you?~~

Business communication | Introducing yourself and others

1 04▷ **Gianluca Donatelli is at a conference. Listen to him introducing himself to Jana Frkova. Make notes about**
  1 Jana's nationality
  2 her job
  3 why she's at the conference.

2 05▷ **Complete what Gianluca says. Listen and check your answers.**
  1 Excuse me. _____ this seat free?
  2 Thanks very much. Can I _____ myself? I'm Gianluca Donatelli.
  3 Nice to meet you _____, Jana. Where are you _____?
  4 And _____ do you work for?
  5 Oh really? And what do you _____?
  6 So _____ are you at this conference?
  7 That's interesting. A friend of mine works for an Italian service provider. Can I introduce _____ to _____?
  8 Roberto. Can you come here for a minute? This is … Sorry, what's your name _____?
  9 Roberto. _____ is Jana. She's writing an article on Internet service providers.

3 05▷ **Listen to Gianluca again. He asks Jana eight questions. Match Jana's responses to each question. Then work with a partner and practise the dialogue.**
  1 _c_   a I am a journalist.
  2 ___   b Jana. Jana Frkova.
  3 ___   c Yes, it is.
  4 ___   d Nice to meet you. I am Jana Frkova.
  5 ___   e I'm here to research an article on Internet service providers.
  6 ___   f I am self-employed.
  7 ___   g Yes, of course. That would be nice.
  8 ___   h I'm from the Czech Republic.

4 **Why don't we learn much about Gianluca in the conversation in 1?**

5 06▷ **Listen to two extracts from a different version of the conversation.**
  1 What do we learn about Gianluca this time?
  2 Underline the stressed words in Jana's questions.
    1 What about you? What do you do?
    2 What about you? What are you here for?

  ▷▷ For more exercises, go to **Practice file 1** on page 102.

6 **Work with a partner. Have short conversations. Talk and ask about these things.**
  Example: **A** *Where are you from?*
  B *I'm from Spain. What about you? Where are you from?*
  A *I'm from Japan.*
  • name   • company   • reason for being here
  • country   • job

7 **Work in groups. You are at a party at a conference. Introduce yourself and find out about another person. Then introduce this person to other people in the group.**

  ⓘ ▷▷ Interactive Workbook ▷▷ **Email** and ▷▷ **Exercises and Tests**

Make that contact!

07▷ Work with a partner. You are both at a conference. You are competing for a big customer. The first person to finish is the winner. Turn to File 01 on page 135 for the rules of the game.

Turn to File 01 on page 135 for the rules of the game.

PLAYER A Start			PLAYER B Start	
Where are you from?	I'm a sales manager.	Who are your main competitors?	Yes, I am. Nice to meet you.	Is this seat free?
We make car windows.	Who do you work for?	JOKER	Sorry, what's your name again?	No, it's a French company.
Can I introduce you to my boss?	It's 1263 Gray Rd, Carmel.	Does your company operate in Europe?	Italy	I'm Spanish. What about you?
How do you do?	JOKER	Yes, sure. It's Jan Olsen.	JOKER	Yes, it's 07 45 32 19 66.
What are your annual sales?	In Milan.	How many employees do you have?	We operate in Europe and North America.	What does your company do?
No, I work in one of our subsidiaries.	What services do you provide?	JOKER	Do you use English in your job?	Yes, I am.
Where's your head office?	No, we don't. We're a service company.	What do you specialize in?	Yes, of course. Please take it.	What does your company specialize in?
No, I'm American.	JOKER	I work for Goodyear.	JOKER	I'm in the Hotel Cap Verde.
Can you tell me your hotel room number?	My wife? She's a journalist.	Does your company have a website?	That's a very personal question!	Do you do any business in Asia?
Yes, we do / No, we don't.	Can I borrow your pen?	JOKER	You speak very good English!	Yes, of course. I'll give you my phone number.

Congratulations! You made contact with the customer first!

Activity

2 | Contacts

Starting point

1 **At work, who do you usually speak to**
   1 by phone?
   2 face-to-face?

2 **Do you prefer communicating with people by email or on the phone?**

3 **How much of your day do you spend**
   1 speaking with people?
   2 working alone?

Working with words | Describing your job and job contacts

1 **What do these people do in their work?**
   1 a retail buyer
   2 a public relations officer
   3 an occupational psychologist

2 **Read the text quickly and compare your answers to 1.**

1 Sara – Retail Buyer

I work for a supermarket chain. My job **involves** buying prepared salads and vegetables from local and national *suppliers*. I also **take part** in different logistics projects. For example, at the moment we're working with an external *consultant*. He's looking at ways to get our salads and vegetables to the supermarket shelves more quickly.

2 Benjamin – Public Relations Officer

I work for the police, but I'm not a policeman. A lot of my work **consists of** answering questions from journalists when the police are in the news. I'm also **involved in** a new project to attract new people to the police force. For this, I'm working with senior police officers and with outside *employment agencies*.

3 Heidi – Occupational Psychologist

I'm self-employed. Basically, I **deal with** problems of relations between *staff*. At the moment, for example, I'm doing a study on virtual teamwork for one of my industrial *customers*. They work with many *subcontractors* all over the world, and their managers want to communicate better with their *colleagues* abroad. I work a lot with *training organizations* which provide the courses my customers need.

3 Read the text again and complete the table.

Which person or people ...	Sara	Benjamin	Heidi
work(s) on problems of communication?			
work(s) with people outside the company?			
work(s) with products?			
works with companies, but not for a company?			

4 Work with a partner. Match the words in *italics* in the text to definitions a–h.
   a companies which sell their products to you _____
   b organizations which find new employees for you _____
   c companies which do work for you which you can't do yourself _____
   d people who work in the same company as you _____
   e organizations which offer courses to company employees _____
   f a person from outside a company who gives expert advice _____
   g companies which buy your products _____
   h all the people who work for a company _____

5 Work with a partner. Which people or organizations do you have contact with in your job?

6 08▷ Sang Chun is talking about his job in a software company. Listen and tick (✓) the people that he works with and the jobs that he does.

People	Jobs
Customers	Answering calls
Suppliers	Visiting
Sales reps	Developing new programs
Programmers	Discussing old programs

7 08▷ Complete this description of Sang Chun's job with a form of the phrases in **bold** from the text in **2**. Listen again and check your answers.

   Main job

   This _____ _____ answering calls from customers who are having problems with their software. It also _____ working with sales reps from time to time.

   Other tasks

   He isn't _____ _____ developing *new* programs. But when programmers are preparing new versions of *old* products, he _____ _____ in the discussions.

   Typical problems

   He _____ _____ installation issues, password problems, bugs, etc.

   ≫ For more exercises, go to **Practice File 2** on page 104.

8 Work with a partner. Tell your partner about your job. What is similar to your partner's job, and what is different?
   • Main job
   • Other tasks (projects, etc.)
   • Typical problems
   • People you work with inside and outside the company

Tip | verb / adjective + preposition + -*ing*
When a verb follows a preposition, it always ends with -*ing*.
   *My job consists **of** answer**ing** the phone to customers.*
   *He's involved **in** develop**ing** new software.*

Language at work | Present continuous

1 **Work with a partner. Answer these questions.**

1 What do you do?
2 What are you working on this week?
3 What are you doing at the moment?

2 **Match the questions in 1 to answers a–c.**

a I'm looking at ways to get our products to customers more quickly. ___
b Basically, my job consists of answering customer calls. ___
c I'm trying to improve my English. ___

3 **In 2, sentences a and c are in the present continuous and sentence b is in the present simple. Which tense do we use to talk about**

1 a present action? _____
2 a temporary project? _____
3 a general fact or regular action? _____

4 **Complete this rule about the present continuous.**

The *present continuous* is formed with the verb _____ + *-ing* form.

5 **Work with a partner. Look at these signs. Where would you see them?**

a
Lift out of order
Please use stairs

b
ACCESS DENIED
Please check password
and try again.

c
MEETING IN
PROGRESS.
DO NOT DISTURB.

d
➡ Automatic reply: I am out
of the office until 19th March.

6 **09▷ Listen to two conversations and match them with two of the signs in 5.**

1 ___
2 ___

7 **09▷ Complete conversation 1 with the present continuous form of the verbs in the list. Then listen again and check your answers.**

have   accept   try   speak   work

A Who _____ I _____ to?
B Sorry, this is Nadira. I _____ _____ to access my customer files, but the computer _____ _____ my password.
A … There's a problem with the server.
B _____ somebody _____ on it at the moment?
A Yes, *I* am. But it's not easy, because I'm on my own here. Everybody else _____ _____ lunch.

8 09▷ **Work with a partner. Listen to conversation 2 again. Have a conversation using the prompts below.**

A Excuse me.

B What? Meeting!

A Who?

B A supplier. New prices. Why / disturb?

A Somebody / room.

B This room / every Monday.

A Sales Director / priority.

B He / wait / now?

A Yes.

B OK. I / leave.

>> For more information and exercises, go to **Practice File 2** on page 105.

9 **Work with a partner. Take turns to ask and answer questions, using the present simple or present continuous form of the prompts below.**

- speak / English at work?
- travel / a lot for your work?
- travel / anywhere this week?
- sometimes / work / special projects?
- do / any other training courses at the moment?

- receive / any visitors / this week?
- boss / work / every day?
- he / she / work / today?
- he / she / travel / a lot for work?
- he / she / travel / this week?

ⓘ >> Interactive Workbook >> **Email**

Practically speaking | How to say phone numbers and spell names

1 10▷ **Listen and write the phone numbers you hear.**

1 The code for England is _____.

2 My mobile number is _____.

2 **Work with a partner. Say your home, work, and mobile phone numbers to your partner. Write down what your partner says.**

3 11▷ **Listen to two conversations and write the names.**

1 _____

2 _____

4 **Work with a partner. Spell your first name, last name, and the name of your company to your partner. Write down what he / she says.**

> **Tip** | Saying phone numbers
>
> We usually say each number separately, except when two consecutive numbers are the same.
>
> *The code for Thailand is* **double oh double six** *(00 66).*
>
> In American English, we say *zero* and not *oh* for 0.

Business communication | Making and receiving telephone calls

1 12▷ **Listen to two telephone conversations and answer the questions.**

1 Which conversation is between
   a a consulting company and a sub-contractor? ___
   b a supplier and a customer? ___
2 What is the reason for each call?

2 12▷ **Match sentences 1–5 with responses a–e. Then listen to Conversation 1 again and check your answers.**

1 Is Mrs Ackers there, please? ___
2 Who's calling, please? ___
3 What can I do for you? ___
4 Can I call you back tomorrow? ___
5 Thanks for calling. ___

a This is Simon Ilago from AOS.
b I'm calling about a special price on our printers.
c Speaking.
d You're welcome. Goodbye.
e Sorry, but I'm out of the office tomorrow.

3 12▷ **Which sentences and responses in 2 are said by the caller and which by the receiver? Listen to Conversation 1 again and check your answers.**

4 **Work with a partner. Take turns to be the caller and the receiver. Have similar conversations using your own names.**

Call 1: You want to arrange a meeting to present your products.
Call 2: You want to ask about payment of an invoice.

5 12▷ **Work with a partner. Make five questions using the words in the table. Listen to Conversation 2 again and check your answers. What are the responses to each of the questions? Practise the questions and responses.**

Could	I you	speak leave have ask tell	Leo to call me back? me what it's about? your name, please? to Leo Keliher, please? a message?

>> For more exercises, go to **Practice File 2** on page 104.

6 **Work in groups of three. Have three phone conversations.**

Student A Call Student B. Ask to speak to Student C. You're an ex-colleague. You want to meet him / her for lunch or dinner tomorrow. You're only in town for one day.

Student B Student A calls you. You work with Student C. He / she is very busy and wants you to answer all phone calls. Ask who's calling and why, then call Student C and give him / her the message.

Student C Student B calls you. Listen to the message then call Student A. Decide together if you can meet tomorrow.

Key expressions

Asking to speak to someone
Could I speak to (*name*)?
Is (*name*) there, please?

Identifying the caller
Could I have your name, please?
Who's calling, please?
This is (*your name*).

Giving a reason for the call
I'm calling about …
I'm phoning to …

Saying the person is / isn't free
I'm sorry, but / I'm afraid she's not here today.
Can I take a message?

Leaving a message
Can / Could I leave a message?
Can / Could you ask him / her to call me back?

Finishing
I'll give him / her the message.
Thanks for your help / for calling.
Speak to you later / tomorrow.

ⓘ >> Interactive Workbook >> **Phrasebank**

ⓘ >> Interactive Workbook >> **Exercises and Tests**

Dealing with a public relations crisis

Background

Crisis? What crisis?

Sometimes a crisis in a company can be used as an opportunity for good public relations.

In 1982 seven people died after taking medicine produced by a big American pharmaceutical company. They had bought the contaminated medicine from different shops in the USA. It was discovered that somebody had put cyanide poison in the bottle.

The company's sales quickly fell to just 8% of the total market. The company knew that it had to deal with the situation quickly to protect its customers and its good name. Just six months later, it was once again the market leader, with 35% of sales in its market.

Discussion

1 Imagine that you are one of the directors of this company.
   What can you do
   1 to protect your customers?
   2 to develop your business again?
   3 to stop a crisis like this happening again?

2 Turn to File 02 on page 135 to see what really happened.

Task

You work for the local branch of an international cosmetics company. A hospital nearby has recently had several patients complaining of severe skin reactions to a new moisturizer you produce.

1 Work with a partner. Have two phone conversations. Student A, turn to File 03 on page 135. Student B, turn to File 36 on page 142.

2 Work in small groups.
   1 Discuss who else you need to tell about this problem, within your company and outside your company, and why.
   2 Decide what action you will take and why.

3 Share your ideas with the rest of the class.

Case study

3 | Visitors

Starting point

1 Do you visit other companies? If so, why? Who do you go with?

2 What sort of people visit the department you work in? Why?

3 Make a list of five departments you find in a company.

Working with words | Company structure

1 **Read the text and answer the questions.**
   1 What was the aim of the customer visit programme?
   2 How was it different from other programmes?
   3 Which departments participated in the visits?
   4 Was the programme a success? How?

The importance of customer contact

The American computer manufacturer Hewlett-Packard ran a very successful customer visit programme. The idea of the visits to HP customers was not to sell the company's products, but simply to listen and learn.

The visits were conducted by mixed teams who visited between ten and forty customers. These teams included a project engineer from the Research and Development Department, and a person from Marketing who played a part in putting the product on the market. In most cases, a sales rep who was responsible for each customer was also present.

In a questionnaire, 88% of staff involved in the programme said that customer satisfaction was better as a result of the visits. About 90% indicated that the visits gave them ideas for changing the products or services offered to customers.

This programme showed the value of customer contact for all employees in an organization. In so many companies, it is only those who work in Sales, Marketing, Customer Service, or Technical Support who have direct contact with customers.

2 **Which department in the text in 1 usually**

1 sells the products? _____

2 looks for new markets for new or existing products? _____

3 creates new products? _____

4 answers technical questions from customers? _____

5 answers all other questions from customers? _____

3 **Complete the sentences about other departments with words from the list.**

finds   buys   checks   ~~arranges~~   maintains   deals   organizes

1 The Logistics Department *arranges* the transport of products.

2 The Training Department _____ courses.

3 The Purchasing Department _____ from suppliers.

4 The Human Resources Department _____ new staff.

5 The IT Department _____ the computer system.

6 The Finance Department _____ with all the money.

7 The Quality Control Department _____ that the products have no defects.

4 **Work with a partner. Take turns to make sentences about different people who work in a company and to guess which department they work in.**

Example: **A** *She deals with all the money.*

B *She works in the Finance Department.*

5 13▷ **Three people are receiving visitors from other departments in their company. Listen to the three conversations and complete the table.**

Person	Which department does he / she work in?	Which department does his / her visitor work in?
1		
2		
3		

6 13▷ **Listen again and complete these sentences.**

1 I have a meeting today with Anna Neves, who's _____ _____ our software.

2 Our company is _____ _____ three business units.

3 He's the person in _____ _____ buying for the whole group.

4 I _____ _____ _____ a lot of training organizations.

5 I _____ _____ the HR Director.

>> For more exercises, go to **Practice file 3** on page 106.

7 **Work with a partner. Ask and answer questions about your own job.**

1 Which department do you work in?

2 What are you responsible for?

3 Who is in charge of your department?

4 Who do you report to?

5 Which department(s) do you have most contact with? Why?

6 Is your department divided into different sections or units? What are they?

8 **Work with a different partner. Take turns to describe your job and department. Then describe the other people and departments around you.**

(i) >> Interactive Workbook >> **Glossary**

Language at work | Asking questions

1 Work with a partner. Complete the questions. Then take turns to ask and answer them.

1 _____ _____ people does your company employ?
2 _____ did your company open in your town?
3 _____ department do you work in?
4 _____ often do visitors come to your company?
5 _____ are you working on at the moment?

2 Look at the word order for questions in the table. Then complete the table with the questions in **1**.

Question word or phrase	Auxiliary verb	Subject	Main verb	Rest of question
How often	*do*	*you*	*speak*	*English?*
How many people	*does*	*your company*	*employ?*	

3 14▷ An employee is showing a visitor round her company. Listen to extracts 1–4 and decide where they are or who they are meeting in each one.

1 Where: _____ 3 Where: _____
2 Who: _____ 4 Who: _____

4 Work with a partner. Put questions 1–8 in the right order.

1 this / often / use / How / does / office / he ?
2 from / does / he / come / Where ?
3 long / are / here / staying / How / you ?
4 see / you / here / while / want / do / to / you're / Who ?
5 open / did / it / When ?
6 do / receive / calls / a day / How / you / many ?
7 you / do / Which / visit / countries ?
8 about / much / you / market / know / the / How / Polish / do ?

5 14▷ Match questions 1–8 with responses a–f below. Then listen again and check your answers.

a One or two people in Sales and Marketing. ___
b In January. ___
c Sweden and Denmark mostly. ___
d Not very much. ___
e Just two days. ___
f New York. ___
g About one day a week. ___
h About 500. ___

▶▶ For more information and exercises, go to **Practice file 3** on page 107.

Tip | *which* and *what*

Which and *what* are very similar, but there is one main difference in meaning.
We use *which* when there is a limited choice of answers.
Which *city do you prefer – Rio or Buenos Aires?*
Which *department do you work in? The Sales Department.*
We use *what* when we are not thinking of a choice.
What *does your company produce?*

6 You have a new employee in your department. He / she has a lot of questions for you. Make complete questions using the prompts.

1 Person in charge of department?
2 Opening / closing hours?
3 Nearest toilets?
4 Lunch?

5 Photocopier?
6 Number of people?
7 Key or security pass?
8 Coffee or tea breaks?

7 Work with a partner. Take turns to ask and answer the questions in **6** about your departments.

Practically speaking | How to welcome visitors

1 15▷ You work for the Freebird Corporation in Lisbon. A customer is visiting you for the first time. Complete sentences 1–7 with phrases from the list. Then listen and check your answers.

Did you find …?   Where …?   Did you get …?   Welcome …
How long …?   Did you have …?   Would you like …?

1 _____ to Freebird.
2 _____ a good trip?
3 _____ your way here all right?
4 _____ are you staying?
5 _____ are you here for?
6 _____ something to drink before we start?
7 _____ the programme I sent you?

2 15▷ Listen again and write down the visitor's responses. Then practise the conversation with a partner.

3 16▷ We often ask follow-up questions to develop a conversation. Listen to a longer version of the conversation in **1**. Then complete follow-up questions 1–7.

1 Is this _____ in Lisbon?
2 What time _____ last night?
3 How did you _____ – by car?
4 Is it _____ for you?
5 Will you have time _____ around Lisbon while you're here?
6 How do you _____?
7 Would you like to _____ changes?

4 Work with a partner. Imagine someone is coming to visit you in your company. Have a conversation with them, using the questions in **1** and the follow-up questions in **3**.

ⓘ ❯❯ Interactive Workbook ❯❯ **Email**

Business communication | Presenting visual information

1 **Look at the information about Lenovo, the computer manufacturer.**

  1 Which slide is in the form of
     a a diagram?   **b** a graph?   **c** a pie chart?

  2 Which slide shows
     a rises and falls in market share?
     b the breakdown of sales by market?
     c some key figures in Lenovo's organizational structure?

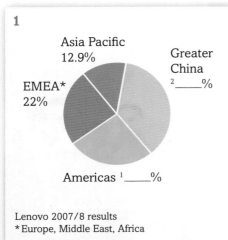

1

Asia Pacific
12.9%

EMEA*
22%

Greater
China
² ____%

Americas ¹ ____%

Lenovo 2007/8 results
*Europe, Middle East, Africa

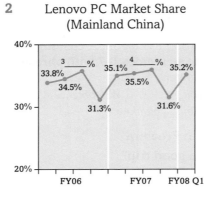

2   Lenovo PC Market Share
(Mainland China)

40%

  33.8% ³ ____% 35.1% ⁴ ____% 35.2%
    34.5%   35.5%

30%   31.3%   31.6%

20%   FY06   FY07   FY08 Q1

*FY2004/05 market share information reflects
combined shares of Lenovo and IBM PCD

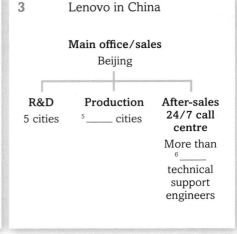

3   Lenovo in China

Main office/sales
Beijing

R&D   Production   After-sales
5 cities   ⁵ ____ cities   24/7 call
                 centre
                 More than
                 ⁶ ____
                 technical
                 support
                 engineers

2 **17▷ Listen to a presentation about Lenovo and complete the missing information on the slides.**

3 **17▷ Work with a partner. Which slide 1–3 does each sentence refer to? Listen and check your answers.**

  a *This pie chart gives you* the breakdown of Lenovo's sales. ___
  b *Note that* the company has operations in many different cities. ___
  c *This graph shows* the change in market share. ___
  d *This diagram summarizes* the company's main operations. ___
  e *The important thing here is* that Lenovo is still the market leader in China. ___
  f *As you can see*, 27.6% of sales are in the Americas. ___
  g But *notice that* China represents 37.5% of worldwide sales. ___

4 **Which phrases in *italics* in 3 are used to**
  1 describe briefly what is in each slide? ___, ___, ___
  2 say what is important in each slide? ___, ___, ___, ___

5 **Work with a partner. Choose two slides in 1. Cover the phrases in 3, and take turns to present a slide. Describe each slide briefly and say what is important about the information.**

  » For more exercises, go to **Practice file 3** on page 106.

6 **Work with a partner. Student A, turn to File 04 on page 135. Student B, turn to File 31 on page 141. Give a short presentation to your partner, using the slides. Say what is important or interesting about the information.**

Key expressions

Referring to visuals
This table / pie chart / graph / diagram gives you / shows / summarizes …
Let's look at this …
Have a look at this …

Checking
Can everybody see that OK?
Is that clear?

Focusing on important points
As you can see, …
Notice that …
Note that …
The important thing here is …

ⓘ **» Interactive Workbook »**
Phrasebank

ⓘ **» Interactive Workbook » Exercises and Tests**

The question game

Work with a partner. One of you is visiting the other's company. Take turns to be the visitor and the host. Have a conversation in each 'place' in the table below. The aim of the game is to ask more questions than your partner.

1 The host starts each conversation with the 'conversation opener'.

2 Use a question form in the 'Questions' column to continue the conversation.

3 Use the ideas in the 'Subjects' column to help you.

4 Tick (✓) the 'Points' column every time you use one of the question forms. You can use the same forms as often as you like, but try to use them all before the end of the game.

5 The winner is the person who has the most points.

RECEPTION   Host: *Nice to see you again.* **How** *are you? (1 point)*
Visitor: *I'm fine. Sorry I'm a little late.* **What** *time is it exactly?*

Place	Conversation opener	Questions	Subjects	Points (✓)
Reception	Nice to see you again.	*Is …?* *Are …?* *Do …?*	• Visitor's journey, hotel, etc. • Programme for visit	
Host's office or desk	This is where I work.	*Does …?* *Did …?* *Can …?*	• Host's job and department • Visitor's job and department	
Colleague's office or desk	My colleague isn't here today, but he / she …	*Where …?* *What …?* *Who …?*	• Colleague's job • Visitor's work colleagues	
Another department	Now we're in the (name) department.	*Why …?* *When …?* *How …?*	• What it does • Relations with host's department	
Meeting room	This slide shows the structure of our company.	*How often …?* *How many …?* *How much …?* *How long …?*	• Company structure and key people • Key people in visitor's company	
Restaurant	This is the best restaurant in town.	*Would you like …?*	• Town where company is located • Visitor's home town	
Total points*				

* Give yourself 1 point for each tick. Deduct 2 points for each question form you haven't used.

Activity

Unit 3 | Visitors

4 | New products

Learning objectives in this unit
- Talking about new products and the stages in their development
- Talking about the development of products using the past simple
- Showing interest
- Giving a report

Case study
- Re-launching an exhibition centre

Starting point

1 **What new products can you buy at the moment? Think about the following areas.**
   - electronic gadgets
   - food and drink
   - health and beauty

2 **How do companies create new products?**

3 **What makes a product successful?**

4 **Do you often try new products or do you usually keep to one brand?**

Working with words | The development process

1 18▷ **Listen to an interview about the development of a range of clothing, Fat Face, and answer the questions.**
   1 Where were the two friends working?
   2 Why did they start making T-shirts?
   3 Where did they print the T-shirts?
   4 Why did they call the company Fat Face?
   5 How do they describe their product?

2 18▷ **Complete the flow chart for the development of Fat Face with the words from the list. Then listen to the interview again and check your answers.**

   brand the product   design the product   have the original idea

1	→	2 do market research

4 do product trials	←	3

5	→	6 launch the product

3 Work with a partner. Discuss why each stage in **2** is important.

Example: You do product trials to find out if the public like the product.

4 Look at texts 1–4, which describe four new products. Match the texts to pictures a–d.

1 A **well-designed** piece of office furniture. Comes with very **user-friendly** assembly instructions.

2 A simple and **functional** item. Frequent travellers like it as it is **compact** and can fit easily into a washbag or overnight bag.

3 Travel in style with this brand new **stylish** and **attractive**, yet **practical**, item.

4 If you haven't already made the switch, do it now, if only because it's more **economical**.

5 Match 1–8 below to definitions a–h.

1 practical ___	**a** costs less to run
2 economical ___	**b** easy to use
3 attractive ___	**c** fashionable and good to look at
4 functional ___	**d** useful
5 stylish ___	**e** small
6 user-friendly ___	**f** useful with little decoration
7 well-designed ___	**g** beautiful
8 compact ___	**h** planned and made well

» For more exercises, go to **Practice file 4** on page 108.

6 Work with a partner. Take turns to describe different products you have or use, for example your mobile phone, car, coat, bag, or PC.

Example: My car wasn't cheap, but it is very economical because it doesn't use much petrol.

7 Work in a small group. Your company is launching a new product or service. Describe this product or service to your group, using the ideas below to help you.
- product or service brand
- product or service development
- description of the product or service

ⓘ **»** Interactive Workbook **»** Glossary

Tip | *cheap* or *economical*

Cheap means that something does not cost very much. *Economical* means spending less on something over a period of time.

Language at work | Past simple

1 Work with a partner. Look at pictures 1–4 and match the inventors with inventions a–d.

1 Tim Berners-Lee ___	**2** Sabeer Bhatia ___	**3** Otto Wichterle ___	**4** Martin Cooper ___

a 1961 Contact lenses **c** 1991 World Wide Web
b 1973 Mobile phones **d** 1996 Hotmail

2 19▷ Listen to the beginning of a radio programme about inventors and check your answers.

3 20▷ Listen to the second part of the radio programme and answer the questions.

1 What did Sabeer study in California?
2 Where did he get his first job?
3 Who did he meet there?
4 Why did Sabeer tell Jack to hang up his cell phone?
5 Why did they call the service 'Hotmail'?
6 How much did their first sponsor invest in their idea?
7 When did they launch Hotmail?
8 How much did Microsoft pay for Hotmail?

4 Look at these sentences about Sabeer Bhatia and match them to the rules about the past simple.

1 He arrived in the USA in 1988.
2 He didn't finish his doctorate.
3 He sold the company in 1997 for $400 million.
4 Why did he leave Microsoft?

Use the *past simple* to talk about finished actions in the past.

a The *past simple* form of regular verbs ends in *-ed*.
Example: _____

b The *past simple* form of irregular verbs does not end in *-ed*.
Example: _____

c The negative is formed by using *didn't* with the infinitive of the main verb.
Example: _____

d In questions we generally use *did* + subject + infinitive of the main verb.
Example: _____

Tip | pronunciation of regular past *-ed* endings

The *-ed* ending is only pronounced as an extra syllable when the final sound of the infinitive is /t/ or /d/.

need – needed
decide – decided
want – wanted
invite – invited

5 Complete the text about Tim Berners-Lee using the past simple form of the verbs in brackets.

The Man Behind The World Wide Web

Tim Berners-Lee [1]_____ _____ (be born) in London, England on 8 June 1955. He [2]_____ (study) physics at Oxford University, where he [3]_____ (build) his first computer. He [4]_____ (have) several jobs before he [5]_____ (become) an independent consultant. During this time he [6]_____ (spend) six months in Geneva, Switzerland, where he [7]_____ (write) his first program for storing information. He [8]_____ (call) the program 'Enquire', but he [9]_____ _____ (not publish) it. In 1990 he [10]_____ (start) work on the World Wide Web project, which first [11]_____ (appear) on the Internet in 1991.

In 1994 Tim [12]_____ _____ (set up) the World Wide Web Consortium at the Massachusetts Institute of Technology. Today he is the Director of this Consortium, which coordinates web development worldwide.

>> For more information and exercises, go to **Practice file 4** on page 109.

6 Work with a partner. Ask and answer questions about Martin Cooper. Student A, turn to File 06 on page 136. Student B, turn to File 37 on page 143.

7 Work with a partner. Take turns to write down an important date, place, and person in your life, preferably not connected. Ask and answer as many questions as possible about the words.

Example: **A** *Why is Spain important?*   **B** *I worked there.*
   A *How long did you work there?*   **B** *For a year.*

Practically speaking | How to show interest

1 21▷ Tick (✓) four phrases which we use to show interest in what another person is saying. Then listen and check your answers.

___ Oh.   ___ Oh really?
___ Did you?   ___ No, it wasn't.
___ Yes, I did.   ___ Thanks.
___ That's interesting!   ___ Was it?

2 21▷ Listen again and complete the extracts with a phrase from **1**.

1 **A** We went away for a change.   **B** _____
2 **A** We went to Monte Carlo.   **B** _____
3 **A** It was really exciting!   **B** _____
4 **A** The weather was fantastic.   **B** _____

3 Work with a partner. Practise the conversations in **2**.

4 Write down four things you did last weekend. Then work with a partner. Take turns to have a conversation about the weekend. Make the conversation last as long as possible by asking questions with *What?*, *Who?*, *Where?*, *When?*, *How?*, and *Why?*

Business communication | Giving a report

1 Work with a partner. Look at the picture of a Podpad. What do you think it's used for? Compare your ideas with the advert in File 07 on page 136.

2 22▷ Listen to a meeting of festival organizers. The speaker is giving a report on her research into the use of Podpads. Answer the questions.
1 What was the purpose of the research?
2 Why did they choose Podpads?
3 Who put the Podpads up and took them down?
4 How many Podpads did they order?
5 How did the researchers attract people to take part in the research?
6 How many times did they speak to the people in the Podpads?
7 What did the farmers think of the Podpad team?
8 Was the experiment a success or a failure?

3 22▷ Work with a partner. Match 1–9 with a–i to make sentences. Then listen again and check your answers.
1 The purpose of our research was ___
2 We wanted to find out ___
3 Why did we choose Podpads? ___
4 First, ___
5 Then, ___
6 We spoke to ___
7 Finally, ___
8 We asked them ___
9 We found that ___

a ... we visited the farmers who let us use their land.
b ... Because they are much stronger than tents.
c ... they were popular with both residents and farmers.
d ... which accommodation would keep people dry in bad weather.
e ... for their opinion of the company.
f ... to find the most comfortable accommodation for visitors to outdoor festivals.
g ... our Podpad residents after one night.
h ... we contacted Podpads.com and ordered 50 Podpads.
i ... we organized 50 people to sleep in them.

4 Work with a partner. Put phrases 1–9 from **3** in the correct category.

Aim of the research	Reason for doing something	Order of the process	Reporting

>> For more exercises, go to **Practice file 4** on page 108.

5 Work with a partner. Your company has asked you to research places where employees can have a short sleep in the middle of their working day. Give a report on your research at a meeting. Student A, turn to File 08 on page 136. Student B, turn to File 38 on page 143. Then decide which one is better.

ⓘ >> Interactive Workbook >> Email and >> Exercises and Tests

Key expressions

Stating aims
The purpose of this research was ...
We wanted to find out ...

Giving reasons
Why did we ...? Because ...

Explaining the order of the process
First, we ...
Then, we ...
Finally, we ...

Reporting
We spoke to ...
We asked ...
We found that ...

ⓘ >> Interactive Workbook >>
Phrasebank

Re-launching an exhibition centre

Background

> ## The Millennium Dome disaster
>
> The Millennium Dome was built in London to celebrate the beginning of the new millennium. The building housed a major exhibition which opened to the public on 1 January 2000. Many visitors were disappointed with the exhibition and access to the Dome by car was difficult. Consequently, the number of visitors was approximately half that expected and the project made a loss. Because of its unpopularity, when the Dome closed on 31 December 2000, there were no plans for its future and no sponsors to pay for its maintenance. As a result, it was reported that the empty building cost its owners £1 million every month.

Discussion

1 Why did the Millennium Dome project fail?

2 Why were no companies interested in investing in the Dome?

3 What could the site be used for?

4 Turn to File 09 on page 136 to read what happened.

Task

Your city hosted Expo last year, but since it closed, the site has been empty. The planning department of your local government wants the site to be re-developed as soon as possible. You work for a company which would like to do this.

1 Work in a small group and decide what you could do with the site. Think about:

- what it could be
- how you decided this
- what benefits it would bring
- how you did your research
- who you talked to

Turn to File 10 on page 137 for some possible ideas to help you.

2 Prepare a report to present to the planning department of your local government. Include your aims, the reasons for your choice, how you did your research, and who you talked to.

3 Work in a different group. You are in a meeting of the planning department. Take turns to give a report at this meeting on your company's choice. Then have a vote on the best choice.

4 Go back to your original group from your company and explain which one was chosen and why.

Case study

5 | Employment

Learning objectives in this unit
- Talking about job benefits and employment procedures
- Describing personal experiences using the present perfect
- Delegating work to others
- Discussing progress on projects

Case study
- Solving recruitment problems

Starting point

1 What benefits do employees have in companies, apart from their salary? Think about holidays, training, extra money, etc.

2 Which jobs or industries have the best benefits in your country?

3 Think of one benefit which you don't have, but would like.

Working with words | Job benefits and employment procedures

1 Read the text. Are these sentences true or false?
1 A majority of senior managers prefer health benefits to more money.
2 Most young employees would like a higher salary.
3 At DST International, all employees have gym memberships.
4 Most employees at Major Players are not interested in pension schemes.

Choosing your own benefits

What benefits are most popular with employees? A recent study shows that it depends on the age and position of the person in the company. For example, 63% of senior managers are more interested in private healthcare than a higher salary. However, a majority of employees under 35 would prefer more money to extra days of paid holiday.

More and more companies are operating flexible systems where staff choose their own benefits. At DST International, each full-time member of staff receives £800 a year, which they can spend on a number of things. These include private healthcare, childcare vouchers to help pay for their children's pre-school costs, or gym memberships for those who love sport.

Jack Gratton, the Managing Director of Major Players, says most people in his company are young, and they are not interested in pension schemes. Employees usually stay only for three years, so pensions are a waste of money. What his staff often prefer is mobile phones, gym memberships, and extra paid holiday.

2 Match 1–10 to a–j to give the names of ten job benefits. Some of these benefits are in the text in **1**.

1 maternity ___	6 company ___	**a** car	**f** hours
2 flexible ___	7 mobile ___	**b** healthcare	**g** bonus
3 paid ___	8 annual ___	**c** membership	**h** scheme
4 private ___	9 subsidized ___	**d** holiday	**i** childcare
5 gym ___	10 pension ___	**e** leave	**j** phone

3 23▷ Listen to three people describing their job benefits and check your answers to **2**.

4 23▷ Listen again. Which benefits are useful or not useful for Anna, Mark, and Valerie?

5 Work with a partner. Look at the benefits in **2** again. Which benefits are these people describing?

1 'I can get to work early and leave early too.'
2 'I use it for all my business calls.'
3 'I get more money if the company's results are good.'
4 'If I have a baby, I get six months off.'

6 Work with a partner. Take turns to describe and guess the other benefits in **2**.

7 Work with a partner. You are starting a new job in a new company. You can choose six of the benefits in **2**. Which do you want to have, and why?

8 Work with a partner. Look at the table below and decide if a candidate or an employer does the different things in the list.

GETTING A NEW JOB Who ...	candidate	employer
1 is shortlisted for interview?		
2 offers you the job?		
3 goes for an interview?		
4 updates their CV?		
5 asks for the names of referees?		
6 applies for the job?		
7 advertises the position?		
8 fills in an application form?		
9 looks through the applications?		

9 Work with a partner. Put the stages of getting a job in **8** in the right order.

> *Example: First, the employer advertises the position.*
> *Then the candidate …*

>> For more exercises, go to **Practice file 5** on page 110.

10 Work with a partner. Tell him / her about when you got your present job. Talk about

- how you heard about the job
- how you applied for it
- what interviews you had
- why you accepted the job.

ⓘ >> Interactive Workbook >> **Glossary**

Tip | *get*

The verb *get* has many different meanings.

*I **get** to work at eight in the morning.* (= arrive)

*He **gets** a bonus at the end of the year.* (= receives)

*Can you **get** him at the station this evening?* (= go and meet)

Language at work | Present perfect (1)

1 24▷ **Listen to two people discussing a new type of CV.**

1 How is it different from normal CVs?

2 Do you think it's a good idea?

2 24▷ **Listen again and <u>underline</u> the verb forms you hear.**

1 *Did you ever see / Have you ever seen* a video CV?

2 I *never saw / 've never seen* one.

3 I *read / have read* an article about them a few days ago.

4 Some companies *already started / have already started* offering video CV services.

5 Someone *emailed / has emailed* me a CV today.

6 I *didn't watch / haven't watched* it yet.

3 **Work with a partner. The past simple and the present perfect both describe past actions. Look at the sentences in 2. Decide if the verb forms are in the past simple or present perfect. Then complete the rules.**

1 Use the _____ to talk about past actions where the time includes the present.

2 Use the _____ when the time does not include the present.

3 The present perfect is formed with _____ / _____ + the past participle of the main verb.

4 With the present perfect, use the following time expressions: *ever*, _____, _____, _____.

4 **Look at the time expressions in sentences 1–7 and decide if they take the past simple or the present perfect. Then complete each sentence about yourself.**

1 This month I _____.

2 Yesterday I _____.

3 Last year I _____.

4 I _____ never _____.

5 When I was at school I _____.

6 Today I _____ already _____.

7 I _____ yet.

5 **Work with a partner. Take turns to say your sentences without the time expression and for your partner to guess what the time expression is.**

6 25▷ **Naomi Hasselin is applying for a job as project manager for a big non-profit organization with operations in Africa. Listen to this extract from her video CV. Where has Naomi worked?**

7 25▷ **Make the questions that the interviewer on the video asked, using the prompts to help you. Listen again and check your answers.**

1 when / start / non-profit sector? _____

2 ever / work for / big organization? _____

3 Africa / in the last year? _____

4 what / do there? _____

5 happy / results? _____

8 25▷ **What were Naomi's answers to the questions? Listen and check your answers.**

>> For more information and exercises, go to **Practice file 5** on page 111.

9 Work with a partner. Take turns to ask and answer questions about your experiences, using the prompts.

   Example: **A** *Have you ever interviewed someone for a job?*
   B *Yes, I have.*
   A *Who did you interview? What was the job? Did you enjoy it?*

- interview someone for a job
- go to an English-speaking country
- give someone a reference
- take maternity / paternity leave

10 Work with a partner. Look at questions 1–8 below. Decide which questions are not acceptable in a job interview and why. Are the other questions easy or difficult to answer?

1 Have you ever had any problems with your boss?
2 Why did you choose your present career?
3 Why did you leave your last job?
4 What does your partner do?
5 What have you enjoyed the most in your present job?
6 What have you learnt in your present job?
7 How old are you?
8 How have you changed in the last five years?

11 Work with a partner. Choose three questions each from **10** and take turns to ask and answer these questions.

Practically speaking | How to delegate work

1 26▷ Paula is asking her assistant Antonio for help with the preparation of a training course. Listen and complete the sentences.

1 I _____ _____ _____ make a list of participants.
2 _____ _____ all their mobile phone numbers.
3 I'd _____ _____ _____ phone the Sales Director.
4 _____ _____ tell him that the welcome party is at six thirty?
5 _____ _____ _____ _____ to go to the party too?

2 Which sentence is less direct? Why does Paula use it?

3 26▷ Listen and match responses a–e to questions 1–5 in **1**. What other information does Antonio give when the answer is negative?

a Yes, of course. Anything else? ___
b OK, I'll do that right now. ___
c I'm afraid I can't. ___
d No problem. ___
e I'm not sure I can do that. ___

4 Work with a partner. Choose Box A or Box B. Take turns to ask your partner to do the different tasks in the list and to respond. Say 'no' to at least one, giving a reason.

A	B
Go to the sandwich bar and get you something for lunch.	Go for lunch with one of your customers.
Write your end-of-month progress report for you this weekend.	Get you a coffee from the coffee machine.
Check an email you've written for spelling mistakes.	Phone the IT department and ask them to come and fix your computer.

Business communication | Discussing progress

1 27▷ Natasha Pieroni is the HR Manager of an engineering company. She's discussing the recruitment of engineers with Ben Coulson, the Project Manager. It's Friday 16 June. Listen and complete the notes in the report.

Task	Date
Ben and Natasha to shortlist candidates	Already done
Natasha to call candidates to arrange interviews	Early ¹_____
Ben to read all CVs	²_____
Interviews will take place	³_____
Ben to confirm availability for interviews	By ⁴_____
Natasha to prepare detailed job description	⁵_____
Ben to speak to MD about salaries	⁶_____

2 27▷ Listen again, then match 1–8 with a–h to make complete sentences.

1 Where are we ____
2 We've already ____
3 I emailed them to you ____
4 I've been very short of time ____
5 Time's ____
6 Leave it ____
7 Have you ____
8 Can you deal with ____

a … running out.
b … the salaries issue?
c … with me.
d … shortlisted twenty candidates.
e … finished the job description yet?
f … with recruitment?
g … this week.
h … last week.

3 Work with a partner. Which phrases in **2** have a similar meaning to the following?

a What progress have we / you made? ____ ____
b The work is / isn't finished. ____ ____ ____
c I'll do it. ____
d Can you do it? ____
e It's urgent. ____

4 Work with a partner. It's Monday 19 June. Natasha is asking Ben if he has done the different things. Have their conversation, using the notes below and the phrases in **2**.

Example: Where are we with the CVs? Have you read them?

> **Natasha** CVs – read them?
> **Ben** Read at weekend – all good candidates.
> **Natasha** Salaries issue – speak to MD?
> **Ben** Not yet – no time at meeting last Friday.
> **Natasha** This morning? Urgent!
> **Ben** OK. Interviews next week. Not arranged dates.
> **Natasha** No, need to know your availability.
> **Ben** Sorry – busy. Will confirm by midday. Prepared job description?
> **Natasha** Yes.

>> For more exercises, go to **Practice file 5** on page 110.

5 Work with a partner. Make a list of what you have and haven't done at work this month. Then take turns to ask your partner about progress on his / her list. If you haven't done something, then you can ask your partner to do it.

ⓘ >> Interactive Workbook >> **Email** and >> **Exercises and Tests**

Key expressions

Asking about progress
Where are we with …?
What about …?
Have you done … yet?

Describing progress
We've already done …
We haven't done … yet.
I did it last week.

Saying something is urgent
Time's running out.
We're very short of time.

Deciding who will do what
Leave it with me.
Can you deal with that?

ⓘ >> Interactive Workbook >>
Phrasebank

Solving recruitment problems

Background

Recruiting talent fast

Oxfam is an NGO (non-governmental organization) which deals with humanitarian crises abroad. As with all organizations, every part of the organization has different recruitment needs. Finance and IT have problems recruiting top-quality professionals because of the low pay. Marketing and Fundraising have to recruit quickly in response to an international crisis. Because it is an NGO, Oxfam has to spend as little money as possible on recruitment and at the same time make sure that it has a diverse workforce and equal opportunities. To help with these issues, Oxfam introduced Global Successor, a web-based e-recruitment solution.

Discussion

1 What kind of recruitment problems does Oxfam have?

2 In what ways is Oxfam different from companies?

3 How do you think e-recruitment helps Oxfam deal with its recruitment needs?

4 Turn to File 11 on page 137 to compare your answers to 3.

Task

You work for an international organization which employs 500 people. It has recently had problems recruiting and retaining staff.

1 Work with a partner. Read about some of the problems the organization had and what it has done in the last six months. Student A, turn to File 12 on page 137. Student B, turn to File 39 on page 143.

2 Take turns to discuss the problems and the progress made. Then decide on an action plan of what the organization needs to do next.

Case study

6 | Customer service

Starting point

1 What problems can you have when you contact a company?

2 Read the comments about poor customer service. Which of these experiences have you had? Which one is the most annoying?

'You have to wait so long to speak to someone.'

'They put you on hold and you can't turn off their awful music.'

'They ask you to repeat the information so many times and then nobody can help you.'

'They try and sell you other services.'

3 What is your idea of good customer service?

Working with words | Customer satisfaction

1 Read the six rules for good customer service in the text below. Does your company follow these rules? Do you have experience of them as a customer?

Six rules for good customer service

1 Answer your phone

The golden rule is 'never miss a phone call,' so someone should always be available to pick up the phone. Your company may have to set up a call centre to **meet the needs of customers**.

2 Keep your promises

Customers want a reliable service, so always do what you say you will do. **Keep to your delivery dates** and you'll **get repeat business** from your satisfied customers.

3 Listen to your customers

Conduct surveys periodically to find out what your customers think. Learn from their feedback and change your strategy if necessary.

4 Give complaints your full attention

Deal with complaints quickly and efficiently. If you have to give a refund, do it with a smile. Satisfied customers will recommend you to friends and get you more business.

5 Take the extra step

Offer a personalized service to your customers and they will feel more important. Deal with their requests on a personal basis and make sure they know what their options are at all times.

6 Give customers something extra

Encourage customer loyalty by giving your regular customers something extra. Your customers will be happy to get something they didn't expect.

2 Match these quotes from a company employee to the six rules in the text in **1**.

a We design every machine to meet the specific needs of customers. ___

b We negotiate special prices for our loyal customers. ___

c We give customers their money back if they are not completely satisfied. ___

d We send our customers questionnaires every two years to get their opinions. ___

e We employ 40 people to ensure we deliver on time. ___

f We have four receptionists taking calls at all times. ___

3 Match the phrases in **bold** in the text in **1** to definitions 1–7 below.

1 Try to make sure customers stay with your company. _____

2 Design a service suitable for each person. _____

3 Ask customers questions. _____

4 Provide the service people want. _____

5 Make sure you take the goods to the customer on time. _____

6 Solve problems. _____

7 Make a customer use you again. _____

4 Work with a partner. Complete the questions about your company / companies with a suitable verb. Then take turns to ask and answer the questions.

1 Does your company _____ the needs of its customers? Why? / Why not?

2 Does your company always _____ to its delivery dates? Why? / Why not?

3 How often does your company _____ surveys?

4 How does your company _____ with complaints?

5 How does your company _____ its customers a personalized service?

6 How does your company _____ customer loyalty?

5 28▷ Listen to three speakers talking about their experiences of bad customer service. What problems did they have?

1 _____

2 _____

3 _____

6 28▷ Complete the sentences with a word from the list. Then listen and check your answers.

dissatisfied   helpful   impossible   loyal   unreliable

1 They said it was _____ to give me a refund.

2 Actually, they weren't at all _____.

3 I'm not going to use that taxi company again because they're so _____.

4 We've been _____ to the same company for years.

5 We were _____ with the service this time.

7 Work with a partner. Take turns to explain and guess the words in **6**.

>> For more exercises, go to **Practice file 6** on page 112.

8 Work with a partner. Ask and talk about good or bad experiences you have had with customer service, using the prompts below to help you.

- what / buy?
- why / this company?
- rewards to regular customers?

- satisfied / dissatisfied?
- feel about experience?
- do repeat business?

ⓘ >> Interactive Workbook >> Glossary

Tip | Negative prefixes

Use the prefixes *dis-*, *un-*, and *im-* to make adjectives negative.

satisfied – dissatisfied
reliable – unreliable
possible – impossible

Language at work | Comparisons

1 Work with a partner and answer these questions.

1 Do you buy many things online? If not, why? If yes, have you had good customer service?

2 What is the quickest way of contacting an online retailer?

2 29▷ Listen to an extract from a radio programme about consumer affairs and compare your answers.

3 29▷ Listen again and <u>underline</u> the correct word in *italics*.

1 Online retailers are *less difficult / more difficult* to contact than before.

2 *The cheapest / the most expensive* way to contact an online retailer is by email.

3 The returns policy of most online retailers is *better / worse* now.

4 Customer service *is / isn't* as efficient as it should be.

4 Complete the rules about comparisons using the adjectives in 3.

1 The comparative form of one-syllable adjectives like *cheap* is *cheaper* and the superlative form is _____ _____.

2 The comparative form of three-syllable adjectives like *difficult* is _____ _____ and the superlative form is *the most difficult*. You can also use *less difficult* and *the least difficult*.

3 *Good* and *bad* have irregular comparative and superlative forms:

good, _____, the best

bad, _____, the worst

4 Use *as* + adjective + *as* to compare two things which are similar and *not* _____ + adjective + _____ to compare two things which are different.

5 30▷ Petr and Ludmila work for the Customer Service Department of an Internet provider company. Listen to Petr reporting the results of a recent survey to Ludmila and answer the questions.

1 Which age group and sex uses the Internet the most?

2 What are the two most popular activities?

3 Where do we usually log on?

4 Why don't we use the Internet more?

5 What do we buy the most of online?

6 30▷ Work with a partner. Complete the results with a comparative or superlative form of the adjective in brackets. Then listen again and check.

1 The age group with _____ (low) number of Internet users is the 65+ age group.

2 Sending and receiving emails isn't _____ (popular) as searching for information on goods or services.

3 Women are _____ (interested) than men in looking for health-related information.

4 It's _____ (common) for Internet users to access the Internet from work than from home.

5 _____ (important) reason why Internet users do not use the Internet more is that they don't have time.

6 Sales of travel, accommodation, and holidays aren't _____ (high) as sales of films, music, and DVDs.

▶▶ For more information and exercises, go to **Practice file 6** on page 113.

Tip | Two-syllable adjectives

Two-syllable adjectives ending in *-ful*, *-less*, *-ing*, *-ed*, *-ous* usually form their comparatives and superlatives with *more* and *the most*.

tiring – more tiring – the most tiring

careful – more careful – the most careful

A small number of two-syllable adjectives form their comparatives and superlatives with *-er* and *-est*.

quiet – quieter – the quietest

clever – cleverer – the cleverest

Two-syllable adjectives ending in *-y* form their comparatives and superlatives with *-ier* and *-iest*.

easy – easier – the easiest

7 Work with a partner. Make sentences about the best place to buy goods, using the ideas in the table.

> *Example:* *If you buy a plane ticket online, it is often cheaper, but the service is less personalized.*

goods	place	adjectives	things to think about
a laptop	online	fast / slow	choice
some flowers	in a supermarket	cheap / expensive	price
a CD	in a small shop	wide	quality
a desk		reliable	service
a book		fresh	delivery dates
a plane ticket		personalized	staff
a mobile		helpful	
a suit		good / bad	

Practically speaking | How to respond to complaints

1 31▷ Listen to three phone calls where people are making a complaint. Number the complaints in the order you hear them.

a ___ A supplier makes a mistake with an invoice.

b ___ A supplier doesn't deliver an order on time.

c ___ A supplier has sent the wrong product.

2 31▷ Listen again and match a response to a complaint in **1**.

1 ___ That is a problem.

2 ___ I see.

3 ___ Oh right.

3 31▷ Listen again and complete the apologies.

1 I'm _____ _____ about _____.

2 It's our _____. I'm _____ _____.

3 I do _____ _____ that.

4 Work with a partner. Look at situations 1–4. Take turns to complain and reply, using the apologies from **3** and the responses from **2**.

1 You returned a book to an online retailer, but you have not received a refund for it. Your order number is AX347219.

2 An IT technician repaired your computer yesterday, but it still doesn't work. The technician's name was Luc.

3 You ordered a taxi for 10.00. It is now 10.15 and it still hasn't arrived.

4 You ordered 50 desks, but received five. Your order number is OP32497.

Business communication | Asking for and giving opinions

1 32▷ **Listen to four managers of an international high street retailer talking in a meeting and answer the questions.**

1 What three complaints have customers made?

2 What two plans of action do the managers agree on?

2 32▷ **The verbs in the box are often used in phrases for *asking for* and *giving* opinions. Listen to the conversation again. Complete the box with any of these phrases you hear.**

think	agree	feel
1 *I think*	1 *I don't agree*	1 *I don't feel*
2	2	2
3	3	3
4	4	

3 **Which phrases in 2 are used to**

ask for an opinion?

1 _____

2 _____

3 _____

give an opinion?

1 _____

2 _____

3 _____

4 _____

agree?

1 _____

2 _____

disagree?

1 _____

2 _____

4 **Work with a partner. Ask for and give opinions on the following ideas, using the phrases in 3.**

1 Staff should always be polite to customers.

2 The best customers should get the best service.

3 The customer is always right.

4 Customer complaints are good for a company.

5 Customers don't always tell the truth in questionnaires.

6 Call centres are very popular with customers.

>> For more exercises, go to **Practice file 6** on page 112.

5 **Work with a partner or in small groups. You work for Pan-European Oil (PEO), which has petrol stations in your country / countries. PEO wants to improve customer service in its petrol stations. Have a meeting to discuss the proposals and decide which one is the best.**

- To introduce a new loyalty card: customers get one free litre of petrol for every 200 litres bought.
- To improve the quality of the food in petrol station cafés.
- To employ new staff to operate the petrol pumps for customers.
- To offer a half-price car wash when customers buy 40 litres of petrol.

Key expressions

Asking for an opinion
What do you think?
How do you feel about that?
Do you agree?

Giving an opinion
I think we should …
I don't think we should …
Personally, I feel we should …
I don't feel we should …

Agreeing
I agree with you.
I think you're right.

Disagreeing
I don't agree.
I don't agree at all.
I disagree.

ⓘ >> Interactive Workbook
>> **Phrasebank**

ⓘ >> Interactive Workbook >> **Email** and >> **Exercises and Tests**

Background

The WOW Awards

The WOW factor, or the ability to impress or surprise people, is something which Derek Williams believes is important in customer care. In fact, Derek is Mr WOW, whose mission in life is to inspire great customer service in the UK. He believes that price competition and product promotion are not as important as employees and existing customers. He says companies should make customers fall in love with them to achieve greater sales and profits. In 1998 he helped establish the National Customer Service Awards, which have an annual Oscar-style ceremony at a top London hotel.

Discussion

1 What do you think are the benefits to a company of winning a customer service award?

2 What categories of award do you think there could be?

3 Can you think of any companies you would or would not nominate?

4 Turn to File 14 on page 138 to find out about the different categories and one winning company.

Task

1 You are on the committee for the National Customer Service Awards. Turn to File 13 on page 137. Student A read about Company 1, Student B read about Company 2, Student C read about Company 3, Student D read about Company 4.

2 Have a meeting. Take turns to present your company's story. Then decide which company you think has given the best customer care and should be given the WOW Award.

Case study

7 | Travel

Learning objectives in this unit

- Talking about travel
- Asking for travel information using countable and uncountable nouns
- Reporting to a company reception
- Making small talk and developing a conversation

Activity

- The travel game

Starting point

1 Which form of transport do you usually use to
   - go to work?
   - travel on business?
   - go on holiday?

2 'The average business traveller takes seven trips per year.' How many trips do you take?

3 What do you like about travelling? What do you not like?

Working with words | Travel

1 Read the text and answer the questions.

1 How are Yotels different from other hotels?
2 When might passengers want to use a Yotel?
3 What facilities are there?
4 How do Yotels save passengers time?

Yotel: the ultimate experience in airport hotels

Yotel is a new chain of budget airport hotels where guests stay in small individual cabins. Situated in one of the **terminal** buildings at Gatwick Airport, the first Yotel in the UK offers passengers a place to catch up on their sleep if they have an early flight, a **delay**, or a long wait between **connections**. You can check in for a four-hour block and you don't have to make a **reservation**.

Check-in happens at a machine in Reception where guests pick up a **key card** to their cabin. **Facilities** include a techno wall containing a TV screen with a wide selection of films, radio, games, and the Internet. The 10m² premium cabins have a **double bed** which converts into a comfortable sofa and the 7m² standard cabins have a **single bed** instead. Both cabins have shower rooms, and **luggage** can be put under the bed. There is no need for a **safe**.

To **check out** guests use a credit card in the machines to pay their **bill**. While guests in other hotels have to take a **shuttle bus** to the airport, Yotel guests walk straight to the **check-in desk**, through the **departure lounge**, and waste no time in **boarding** their plane.

2 Work with a partner. Discuss the advantages of staying at a Yotel. Think about
- the location
- the facilities
- the time.

3 33▷ Listen and complete the three texts.

FLIGHT	DESTINATION	TIME	STATUS
BA7293	Singapore	14.45	¹d_____ until 16.30. Wait in ²d_____ .
UA0472	Boston	15.30	Now ³b_____ at ⁴G_____ J13.

> Guests are required to ⁵c_____ before 12 noon and return the ⁶k_____ to Reception. Please remember to remove all valuables from the ⁷s_____ before you pay your ⁸b_____ .

⁹f_____ EX3465 from London Stansted to Copenhagen
¹⁰o_____ ticket
Departs 13.00
¹¹l_____ at 15.45 ¹²t_____ 2

4 Work with a partner. Put the words in **bold** from the text in **1** and from **3** into these categories. Some words may fit in both categories.

hotels	airports / air travel

>> For more exercises, go to **Practice file 7** on page 114.

5 Work with a partner. Student A, turn to File 15 on page 138. Student B, turn to File 40 on page 143. Then have two conversations.

6 Work with a partner. Tell each other about your last business trip or holiday. Talk about
- the journey
- where you stayed
- anything that went wrong.

ⓘ >> Interactive Workbook >> **Glossary**

Tip | *travel, trip,* and *journey*

Use *travel* in a general sense to talk about visiting other places. It is a noun and a verb.
*Air **travel** is cheaper now than it has ever been.*
*I **travel** abroad for work once or twice a month.*

Use *trip* to talk about the whole visit to a place we go to.
*She's gone on a business **trip** to Paris.*

Use *journey* to talk about the act of travelling from one place to another.
*The **journey** to my parents' house takes five hours.*

Language at work | Countable and uncountable nouns

1 Work with a partner. Read the Frequently Asked Questions (FAQs) sent to an airport. Which of the questions can you or your partner answer about your nearest airport?

1 Can I get to the airport on public transport? If not, how much does a taxi cost?

2 How much time will I need to travel between terminals? Is there a shuttle bus?

3 I need to get ready for a meeting. How many shower rooms are there?

4 I need to get some money. Where are the cash machines?

5 I don't need my suitcase. Are there any lockers where I can leave my luggage?

6 My mobile phone isn't working. Can I rent one to use on my trip?

2 34▷ Listen to a representative from Tokyo Narita International Airport giving information about the airport. Which question in **1** <u>doesn't</u> he answer?

3 34▷ Listen again and answer the FAQs in **1** about Narita International Airport.

4 Nouns in English can be countable, for example *job(s)* or uncountable, for example *work*. Complete the rules with the words *countable* or *uncountable*.

1 _____ nouns have a plural form (e.g. *bank – banks*).

2 _____ nouns have no plural form (e.g. *information – information*).

3 Use *How many?* with _____ nouns, and *How much?* with _____ nouns.

4 Use *Is there?* with singular _____ nouns and _____ nouns, and *Are there?* with plural _____ nouns.

5 Look again at the FAQs in **1**. <u>Underline</u> all the countable nouns and ⓒircle the uncountable nouns.

6 Work with a partner. Are the words in the list countable (*C*) or uncountable (*U*)? Choose six and put each one into a sentence.

ticket _C_   taxi ___   night ___   bank ___   research ___
equipment ___   minute ___   product ___   hour ___   business trip ___
travel ___   job ___   work ___   news ___   information ___

7 Complete these questions with *How much …?*, *How many …?*, *Is there …?*, *Are there …?* Then work with a partner and ask and answer the questions.

1 _____ a bus stop near your office?
2 _____ time do you spend packing for a holiday?
3 _____ business trips do you make in a year?
4 _____ many employees from overseas in your company?
5 _____ work do you have at the moment?
6 _____ a good restaurant near your office?

>> For more information and exercises, go to **Practice file 7** on page 115.

8 Work with a partner. Take turns to ask and answer some travel information questions. Student A, turn to File 16 on page 138. Student B, turn to File 41 on page 143.

Practically speaking | How to report to a company Reception

1 35▷ Listen to a conversation between a client and a company receptionist. Is the client polite? How could he be more polite?

2 35▷ Listen to a second conversation and order the information the client gives the first time she speaks.
a the name of her company ___   c the name of the person she is meeting ___
b the time of the appointment ___   d her own full name ___

3 35▷ Complete these sentences from Conversation 2 with words or phrases from the list. Is the customer (C) or the receptionist (R) speaking? Listen again and check your answers.

security pass   an appointment   a seat   sign in   I'm from

1 _C_   My name's Helen Edwards and _____ Citibank.
2 ___   I have _____ with Susana Kechel at 11 o'clock.
3 ___   Would you like to take _____ while you're waiting?
4 ___   Do I need to _____?
5 ___   Here's your _____.

4 Work with a partner. Take turns to be a customer checking in at a company Reception and a company receptionist. First use your own names and then the names and companies below.
1 Judith Kerr / Aviva / Lewis Ferrero / 12.30
2 Lenny Granger / Samsung / Ruth Chan / 2.15
3 Yann Jaffrey / Nokia / Ned Hussein / 9.45
4 Pino Ten / UPS / Carmen Winters / 10.30

Business communication | Making small talk and developing a conversation

1 Work with a partner. Look at the topics below. Which ones is it normal to talk about in your country when you meet someone from abroad for the first time?

> work   the journey   money   the visitor's country
> family   politics   interests   holidays

2 36▷ Listen to Dan Ford meeting Jozef Dropinski at the airport. Which topics from **1** do they talk about?

3 36▷ Complete the questions from the conversation in **2** with *do*, *did*, or *are*. Then listen and check your answers.

1 _____ you have a good flight?

2 _____ you often travel abroad on business?

3 _____ you see the Alhambra?

4 What _____ you think of it?

5 _____ you interested in architecture?

6 When _____ you usually take your holiday?

4 Complete the table with the questions in **3**.

Asking about a journey	Asking about experiences
How was your journey?	Is this your first time in Tokyo?
_____	Have you been here before?
Was the flight delayed?	_____

Asking about habits	Asking about opinions / interests
Do you ever go skiing?	_____
_____	What kind of music do you like?
_____	_____

>> For more exercises, go to **Practice file 7** on page 114.

5 Work with a partner. Choose three of the topics in **1** and make four questions about each topic.

6 Work with a different partner. Take turns to ask and answer your questions.

7 Work with a partner. You are visiting each other's countries. Take turns to make small talk and develop a conversation, using the ideas below.

- the hotel
- the journey
- their interests
- food
- their families
- holidays

(i) >> Interactive Workbook >> **Email** and >> **Exercises and Tests**

Key expressions

Asking about a journey
How was your journey?
Did you have a good trip?
Was the flight delayed?

Asking about experiences
Is this your first time in Tokyo?
Have you been here before?
Did you see the match last night?

Asking about habits
Do you ever go sailing?
Do you often go abroad on business?
When do you usually take your holiday?

Asking about opinions
What did you think of it?
What kind of food do you like?
Are you interested in tennis?

(i) >> Interactive Workbook >> **Phrasebank**

The travel game

Work with a partner. You are both travelling to Chris Stein's office in Prague. Student A takes one route and Student B takes another. Use a counter and throw a coin. If the coin lands on heads, move forward one space and role-play the conversation with your partner on that space. If the coin lands on tails, stay where you are and pass the coin to your partner. The winner is the first person to reach Chris's office.

Buy a plane ticket to Prague at the ticket office.	Take a taxi to the airport. Make small talk with the taxi driver.	A ◄ YOUR OFFICE ► B	Call a hotel and make a reservation for two nights.	Buy a ticket for the Airport Express train.
Ask where you can change money.				Ask what time the next train leaves.
Buy a drink and something to eat at the airport.				Check in for your flight at the airport.
Your plane is late boarding. Ask the reason for the delay.				Ask how to get to Gate B22.
Make small talk with the person sitting next to you on the plane.				Order a drink and something to eat on the plane.
Ask at Tourist Information for the phone number of a hotel in the Old Town.				Ask at the Information desk in Prague where the taxis are.
Call a hotel from the airport and book a room for the night.				Take a taxi to your hotel.
Ask which bus goes to the Old Town and how much a ticket costs.				Check into your hotel and ask what time breakfast is.
Check into your hotel and order a taxi to take you to the New Town.	Check into the company Reception.	CHRIS STEIN'S OFFICE	Make small talk with Chris Stein when he picks you up.	Ask the hotel for a wake-up call and a newspaper the next morning.

Activity

8 | Orders

Learning objectives in this unit

- Talking about orders and deliveries
- Talking about the future using the present continuous, *going to*, and *will*
- Making arrangements
- Making and responding to suggestions

Case study

- Choosing a delivery company

Starting point

1 What goods and services are often bought online? Why?

2 What do you buy online?

3 Is there anything you would not buy online? If so, why not?

Working with words | Orders and deliveries

1 **Read the text and answer the questions.**

1 In what ways are Amazon.com and UPS similar?
2 What do customers expect from Amazon.com?
3 In what ways does UPS help Amazon meet these expectations?
4 How does this relationship help Amazon.com?

The Amazon.com and UPS relationship

Two market-leading companies which were founded in the same city in the USA, Seattle, one almost a hundred years before the other, signed an important business deal in 1995. UPS, founded in 1907, is now the largest express delivery company in the world and Amazon, founded in 1995, has become the world's most popular online retailer.

On Amazon.com, customers can **purchase goods** 24 hours a day, seven days a week after they have **checked that they are in stock**. Once the customer **places an order**, Amazon is expected to **deliver the goods** quickly and offer customers choice, competitive prices, and excellent customer service at the same time. UPS helps Amazon meet all of these needs.

Firstly, UPS allows Amazon to **process the customer's order** faster. With UPS Online Tools on its website, Amazon can **quote its customers prices** for a wide choice of delivery options. Secondly, customers can **track their shipment,** using the UPS order tracking system. Finally, customers can use UPS's excellent Returns on the Web services if there is a problem with the product on delivery.

These tools are not only popular with customers, who can **make an enquiry** about the status of their order online, but they also help Amazon cut costs. Nearly all customer contact is made via the website, including billing, as customers **pay the invoice** online before UPS **makes the delivery**.

2 Match 1–10 below from the text to definitions a–j.

1 to purchase _____   **a** a question
2 in stock _____   **b** things you buy or sell
3 goods _____   **c** transporting products to a customer
4 to process _____   **d** a request for something to be sent
5 an order _____   **e** to say how much something will cost
6 to quote _____   **f** to deal with, e.g. an order
7 a shipment _____   **g** to buy
8 an enquiry _____   **h** goods which are being transported
9 an invoice _____   **i** a document you must pay
10 a delivery _____   **j** ready to sell

3 Work with a partner. Complete 1–10 with a suitable verb, using the phrases in **bold** in the text to help you. Then take turns to put the phrases into a sentence.

1 _____ a price   6 _____ an order
2 _____ an invoice   7 _____ a shipment
3 _____ an order   8 _____ a delivery
4 _____ a product is in stock   9 _____ an enquiry
5 _____ goods   10 _____ the goods

4 37▷ Work with a partner. Put the process of ordering in the right order. Then listen and compare your answers with a manager from an online retail company.

a ___ **The customer** tracks the progress of the order online.

b _1_ **The customer** makes an enquiry about the supplier's products and the price.

c ___ **The customer** pays the invoice.

d ___ **The customer** places an order with the supplier by phone, fax, or email.

e ___ **The supplier** provides information and quotes a price for the product or service.

f ___ **The supplier** delivers the goods to the customer.

g ___ **The supplier** confirms the order with the customer.

h ___ **The supplier** checks that the product is in stock.

i ___ **The supplier** gives the customer a date for delivery of the goods.

j ___ **The supplier** begins to process the order.

▶▶ For more exercises, go to **Practice file 8** on page 116.

5 Work with a partner. What was the last thing you ordered by phone, fax, or the Internet? Take turns to explain what happened, using the words and phrases from the unit.

ⓘ ▶▶ Interactive Workbook ▶▶ Glossary

Tip | *invoice* and *bill*
In British English we use *invoice* in more formal English and *bill* in informal English. In a restaurant we use *bill*. In American English a restaurant *bill* is called a *check*, and a banknote is a *bill*.

Language at work | *will / going to* / present continuous

1 **38▷ Listen to a customer phoning a supplier about a delivery and complete the information on the message pad below.**

> Client: _____ Consulting
>
> Order number: _____
>
> Original delivery date: _____
>
> New delivery date: _____
>
> Action: change delivery date to _____

2 **Read these sentences from the phone conversation and complete the rules about future verb forms.**

　a We're going to deliver the cards next Thursday morning.
　b We're attending the company conference in Toronto on 5th March.
　c As soon as I've spoken to him, I'll call you back.

　1 Use _____ to make a decision at the moment of speaking.
　　Example: _____
　2 Use _____ to talk about a plan that's already decided.
　　Example: _____
　3 Use _____ for an arrangement with a fixed time or place.
　　(You can often use *going to* here instead.)
　　Example: _____

3 **Match sentences 1–6 to responses a–f. Then put the verbs in brackets in a–f into the correct form.**

　1 Do you have any plans for the weekend? ___
　2 I'm afraid I can't answer your question. ___
　3 Have you decided what to do about the new sales post? ___
　4 Can you stay a bit later tomorrow night? ___
　5 I can't come to the meeting in the morning. ___
　6 Have you thought about how to get to your new job? ___

　a OK. I _____ (change) it to the afternoon.
　b No, sorry. I _____ (meet) some friends for
　　a drink.
　c Yes, I have. I _____ (buy) a car.
　d Yes, it's my birthday and I _____ (have) a
　　party. Do you want to come?
　e Don't worry. I _____ (ask) someone else.
　f We _____ (advertise) in the national
　　newspapers.

4 Work with a partner. Take turns to ask the questions and to respond, using the prompts in *italics* with *going to*, present continuous, or *will*.

1 A Shall we go for coffee?
  B Sorry. *I / meet* the manager at 11.

2 A Can you bring me to work tomorrow?
  B OK. *I / pick* you up at 8 o'clock.

3 A What's going to happen about your job?
  B *I / look* for a new one.

4 A Can we talk about this next week?
  B Yes. *I / give* you a call.

5 A Are you happy where you live?
  B No. *I / look* for a new flat.

6 A Can we have lunch together?
  B Sorry. *I / go* to the gym.

7 A What are you doing tonight?
  B *I / play* tennis with a friend.

8 A Have you thought about your holiday yet?
  B Yes. *We / book* a cruise.

9 A Can I have a glass of water?
  B Yes. *I / go* and get you one.

>> For more information and exercises, go to **Practice file 8** on page 117.

5 Work with a partner. Ask and answer the questions in **4** with your own ideas.

Practically speaking | How to make arrangements

1 Work with a partner. Look at the phrases from a conversation in **A** below. Is the conversation formal or informal?

A	B
1 I'd like to meet you.	_____ _____ _____ for lunch next week?
2 When are you available?	When _____ _____ _____?
3 Does ... suit you?	_____ Tuesday OK _____ _____?
4 I'm afraid I'm not available on Tuesday.	Sorry, I can't _____ _____ on Tuesday.
5 Shall we say ...?	_____ _____ Thursday at 12.30 instead?
6 That suits me.	_____ good.

2 39▷ Listen to Fenola Young using the language from **1** to talk to a supplier on the phone. Why and when are they meeting?

3 40▷ Listen to Fenola now using more informal language to talk to a colleague, Sven. Why and when are they meeting?

4 40▷ Listen again and complete column **B** in **1** with the equivalent informal phrases. Check your answers with the audio script on page 153.

5 Work with a partner and role-play the following situations.
1 A supplier calling a new customer to arrange a presentation.
2 A colleague calling another colleague to arrange a tennis match.

Business communication | Making and responding to suggestions

1 Work with a partner. Talk about your company logo. Do you like it?

2 41▷ Listen to a meeting between four colleagues who are discussing changing the logo of their company. What decisions do they make about
1 the company name on the logo?
2 the designer of the logo?

3 41▷ Listen again and match suggestions 1–6 with responses a–f.

1 Why don't we …? ___	**a** I'm not sure about that.
2 Maybe we should … ___	**b** OK. Let's …
3 We could … ___	**c** Fine.
4 How / what about …? ___	**d** I don't think that will work.
5 I suggest … ___	**e** That's a great idea!
6 Shall we …? ___	**f** Yes, I think we should …

4 Look at the responses in **3**. Which responses are used to accept a suggestion and which responses are used to reject a suggestion?

5 Work with a partner. Look at situations 1–6 and take turns to make a suggestion and respond, using the ideas in the box.

> *Example:* **A** *Shall we have lunch in that new Italian restaurant?*
> **B** *Yes, that's a great idea. I fancy a pizza.*

Situation	Suggestion
1 You want to have lunch with a colleague.	The new Italian restaurant.
2 You are launching a new product.	An email to all customers.
3 A friend is unhappy with her salary.	Ask for a pay rise.
4 You need a new supplier.	Search on the Internet.
5 A colleague looks unwell and tired.	Leave early.
6 There are communication problems in your office.	A weekly meeting.

>> For more exercises, go to **Practice file 8** on page 116.

6 Work with a partner or in small groups. Your company is going to open a canteen and would like your suggestions. Have a meeting to discuss what you would like, using the prompts below to help you. Present your ideas to the class.
- location
- hours – all day starting with breakfast?
- cost – average price of a meal?
- types of food

ⓘ >> Interactive Workbook >> **Email** and >> **Exercises and Tests**

Key expressions

Making suggestions
Why don't we (do) …?
Maybe we should (do) …
We could (do) …
How / what about (doing) …?
Shall we (do) …?
I suggest we (do) …

Accepting suggestions
Yes, I think we should (do) …
Fine.
OK. Let's (do) …
That's a great idea.

Rejecting suggestions
I'm not sure about that.
I don't think that will work.

ⓘ >> Interactive Workbook
>> Phrasebank

Choosing a delivery company

Background

Company sets up online retail service

Dixons is a leading electrical retailer and part of the DSG International Group, which owns stores across much of Europe, including Electro World. Dixons once had a store in most towns and cities across the UK and Ireland. In response to the crisis in the retail industry, the company is now concentrating on its online service. It has seen its Internet sales grow 50% each year during the last four years, and it now gets over one million visitors per month. The company's CEO has stated that the company intends to become 'the most successful electrical retailer on the web'.

Discussion

1 Why are companies like Dixons setting up an online retailing service?

2 What do you think would make a good online retail service?

3 What does an online retailer look for in a delivery company?

Task

1 42▷ Listen to a logistics expert talking about what online retailers should consider when choosing a delivery company. Listen to the interview and number the following characteristics in the order you hear them. Were your answers to 3 similar?

speed of delivery ___ *tracking system* ___ *delivery options* ___
first time delivery rate ___ *price* ___

2 You work for a company which wants to set up an online service. You need to find a suitable delivery company. Work in groups of three. Student A, turn to File 17 on page 138 for information on Interglobal Ltd., Student B, turn to File 42 on page 144 for information on Stable & Sons, and Student C, turn to File 54 on page 146 for information on Nova Solutions. Look at your information and decide on the main advantages and disadvantages of the company.

3 Have a meeting to present the information about your company. Decide which company you think is best.

Case study

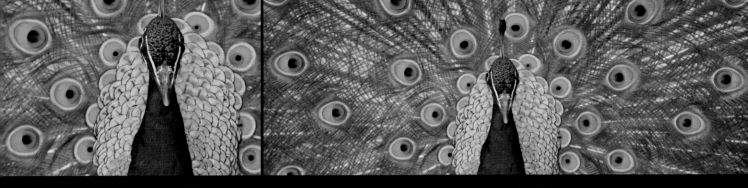

9 | Selling

Starting point

1 'Everyone is in sales. It doesn't matter what area you work in, you have clients and you need to sell.' Do you agree?

2 Which of these do you agree with?
'There is too much advertising on TV and the Internet.'
'Advertising is necessary in a free world.'
'There should be strict controls on what is advertised, and to who.'

Working with words | Sales and advertising

1 **Read the text about Carrefour, the French supermarket group. Are these sentences true or false?**

1 Carrefour is increasingly successful in China.
2 All of the Carrefour stores in China sell the same products.
3 Chinese consumers have always drunk wine with their food.
4 Chinese consumers can buy Carrefour products and pay later.
5 Internet shopping is now possible at Carrefour.

A global retailer

Carrefour is the second largest retail company in the world and was the first to open a hypermarket in China. It **entered the Chinese market** in 1995. It now has annual sales in the country of more than €2 billion and is opening an increasing number of stores to **improve its market share** (currently 5%).

Carrefour has **attracted customers** by adapting to and copying local customs. For example, Chinese consumers traditionally bought live fish at markets, so Carrefour introduced live fish at stores near the sea. However, in stores hundreds of miles from the sea, live fish would not be practical. Frozen fish was introduced instead and this **boosted sales** of fish by 30–40%.

Carrefour has tried to stay ahead of the customer by not introducing products and ideas that are so new and radical that they don't sell, but not being too late either. One way Carrefour has done this is by introducing Chinese consumers to the idea of drinking wine with a meal by selling a few wines which go well with fish and seafood. It has also **expanded its range of services**, introducing loyalty cards as a way to **offer discounts**, and providing consumer credit. In 2006 it **launched an advertising campaign** for online shopping. All of these have helped **promote the Carrefour name**, both in China and around the world.

2 Match verbs 1–8 to a–h to make phrases. Then look at the text to check your answers.

1 to improve ___   a ... sales
2 to enter ___   b ... new customers
3 to attract ___   c ... a discount
4 to launch ___   d ... a new market
5 to expand ___   e ... the company's name
6 to offer ___   f ... an advertising campaign
7 to promote ___   g ... your range of products or services
8 to boost ___   h ... market share

3 Which verbs 1–8 in **2** mean to
a make someone like something? ___   d increase? ___, ___, ___
b start selling in? ___   e start an activity? ___
c give publicity to? ___

4 Which words or phrases a–h in **2** mean
1 a series of advertisements using different media? ___
2 the number of items sold? ___
3 a lower price? ___
4 your sales in comparison with your competitors? ___

5 Work with a partner. Complete the questions with verbs from **2**. Then ask and answer the questions.
1 When did Carrefour _____ the Chinese market?
2 How did it _____ sales of fish in China?
3 In what other way did it _____ more customers?
4 How has it _____ its services?
5 What did it _____ in 2006?

6 Match pictures 1–3 to three of the forms of advertising from the list.

press ads   online adverts   outdoor advertising
direct mailing   word-of-mouth   TV advertisements

7 Work with a partner. *Word-of-mouth advertising* is often described as the best form of advertising. Why do you think this is? When is it not true?

>> For more exercises, go to **Practice file 9** on page 118.

8 Work with a partner and answer the questions.
1 What can the companies below do to
   a attract new customers?
   b advertise their products or services?
   • clothes shops   • mobile phone companies   • computer manufacturers
2 What does your company do to attract new customers? How does it advertise?

ⓘ >> Interactive Workbook >> **Glossary**

Tip | *ad, advert, advertisement, advertising*

Advertisement is a countable noun. We see an advertisement for a product in the newspaper, on TV, etc. The short forms of the word are *an advert* or *an ad*.

Advertising is an uncountable noun. It's the general word to describe the action of promoting companies, products, or services.
*There's a lot of **advertising** on TV.*
*He works in **advertising**.*

Language at work | Modal verbs

1 Read the text and answer the questions.

1 How is São Paulo different from before?

2 What do you think of the mayor's idea?

São Paulo – the city that said 'no' to advertising

The residents of São Paulo in Brazil **don't have to** look at advertising in the street any more. Companies **can't** advertise outdoors any longer. That means an end to the city's 8,000 billboards.

The law was introduced by the Mayor of São Paulo, Gilberto Kassab, in January 2007. He said that the city authorities **need to** fight pollution, and that the 'visual pollution' of outdoor advertising is one of São Paulo's biggest problems.

Advertisers who don't respect the new law **have to** pay a fine. In the first nine months the city collected $8 million from companies who continued to advertise. Shops **can** continue to put ads in their windows, but they **aren't allowed to** use more than 15% of their window space to promote their products and services.

2 Look at the text in 1 again and put the verbs in bold in the table below.

It's necessary		
It's not necessary	*don't have to*	
It's possible / permitted		
It's not possible / permitted		

3 Complete the table in 2 with *are allowed to* **and** *don't need to*.

4 43▷ Listen to four people talking about advertising. Which speaker thinks

a some advertising laws aren't good? ___

b online advertising is important? ___

c outdoor advertising isn't attractive? ___

d advertising laws are necessary? ___

5 43▷ Complete the sentences with verbs from 2. Then work with a partner and discuss your answers. Then listen and compare your answers.

1 Companies _____ advertise to sell their products.

2 You _____ have big billboards everywhere.

3 You _____ have laws on advertising.

4 You _____ stop companies advertising products which are bad for you.

5 In my country, you _____ advertise cigarettes.

6 You _____ advertise beer and alcohol on TV, but you _____ do it before 8.00 p.m.

7 When we use the Internet, we usually _____ pay to get the information we need.

8 Many website owners make their profits from advertising, so we _____ use their websites for free.

9 There are a lot of ads online, but you _____ look at them.

6 Work with a partner. Look at these sales and advertising messages. Say what they mean, using the verbs in **2**.

Example: You can buy now, but you don't have to pay before next year.

1
**Buy now
Pay next year**

2
CARD PAYMENTS
ONLY

3
Reply before 31 October
to benefit from this
once-in-a-lifetime chance.

4
NB This ticket is non-refundable. Click here for cancellation insurance.

5
ALL MAJOR
CREDIT CARDS
ACCEPTED

6
NO ADVERTISING
PLEASE!

>> For more information and exercises, go to **Practice file 9** on page 119.

7 Work with a partner. Ask and answer questions about advertising laws in your country, using the language from the list and the prompts below.

Can you …?   Are you allowed to …?   Do you have to …?
Do you need to …?   I'm not sure, but I think …

- compare products with your competitors
- advertise credit cards and loans
- promote products directly to children
- have a health warning on certain foods
- advertise alcoholic drinks
- advertise slimming products

Practically speaking | How to interrupt and avoid interruption

1 44▷ Listen to two people talking about relocation and answer the questions.
   1 What exactly are they talking about?   2 Do they agree or not?

2 44▷ Listen again and number these phrases in the order you hear them.
   1 Can I just say something here? ___   4 Can I just finish? ___
   2 Please let me finish. ___   5 Sorry, but … ___
   3 Sorry, go ahead. ___

3 Which phrases in **2** are used when you want to
   1 interrupt someone who is speaking?
   2 continue speaking?
   3 tell the other person to continue speaking?

4 Work with a partner. Choose a subject from below and prepare a few ideas about it on your own. Then take turns to talk about it and interrupt each other.
- supermarkets
- producing in low-cost countries
- advertising to children

Business communication | Controlling the discussion in meetings

1 45▷ Three managers of Fitstart, a sports-shoe manufacturer, are discussing a new sales campaign in Central Europe. Listen and complete the notes.

ADVERTISING:
- Money spent last year: _____
- Budget this year: _____
- Extra money to be used for: _____
_____

SALES:

This year + _____ %
- Next two years: _____ %
- Key markets: the Czech Republic,
_____ , _____

2 45▷ The sentences in B are the follow-up sentences to A. Match 1–6 with a–f and then listen and check your answers.

A	B
1 We're here today to talk about Central Europe. ___	a Can we sum up what we've agreed?
2 Sorry, I didn't catch that. ___	b Could you be more specific?
3 We're getting off the subject. ___	c What was that you said?
4 OK, I think we've covered advertising. ___	d Can we move on to the next point?
5 Sorry, I'm not with you. ___	e Can we come back to that later?
6 I think that's everything. ___	f We need to discuss our new marketing campaign.

3 Work with a partner. Put the phrases from **2** into these categories.
1 introduce the subject ___
2 say you didn't hear something ___
3 say you didn't understand something ___
4 keep to the right subject ___
5 change to a new subject ___
6 close the meeting ___

4 Work with a partner. You are in a meeting. Take turns to say the sentences and to think of different responses, using the phrases in **2**.
Example: *Sorry, I didn't catch that. What do you want to discuss?*
1 We need to discuss sales figures.
2 We need a few more people in the department.
3 Can we talk about the Christmas party now?
4 The figures were 17.9% for May, 19.3% for June, and 18.8% for July.
5 Does anybody have anything else to say on advertising?
6 It's 12.30 now. Any other business?

>> For more exercises, go to **Practice file 9** on page 118.

5 Work in small groups. You work for a small regional chain of six supermarkets. You want to boost sales. Have a meeting to discuss how you are going to do this, using the ideas below.
- expand all stores   • introduce new products   • have an advertising campaign

ⓘ >> Interactive Workbook >> Email and >> Exercises and Tests

---

Key expressions

Introducing the subject
We're here today to talk about …
We need to discuss …

Saying you didn't hear
Sorry, I didn't catch that.
What was that you said?

Saying you didn't understand
Sorry, I'm not with you.
Could you be more specific?

Keeping to the right subject
We're getting off the subject.
Can we come back to that later?

Changing the subject
I think we've covered (this point).
Can we move on to (the next point)?

Closing the meeting
I think that's everything.
Can we sum up what we've agreed?

ⓘ >> Interactive Workbook
>> Phrasebank

Background

Companies target young people

Young people aged 14–24 spend between 21 and 31 hours online each week. The majority of them communicate with friends every time they go online. The average young person has 78 contacts in his or her 'digital community' (mobile phone, instant messaging, etc.). Interestingly, TV is one of the most common subjects of online conversations and watching TV is still the most popular pastime for young people.

  These are statistics from the largest-ever global study on the youth market, undertaken by MTV and Nickelodeon. It is, therefore, no surprise that companies are having now to use all available new media to try and reach youth audiences.

  To promote two new brands of sports shoe, Adidas created a dynamic online soccer game: 13 million games were played in the six-week campaign. Levi's advertised on Hotmail during the 9.00–12.00 a.m. and 6.00–9.00 p.m. time slots, when its target audience were usually writing emails. In addition, before the launch of the 'Chicken Little' movie, users of MSN Instant Messenger could download dancing chickens to send to their friends.

Discussion

1 **Why are some companies advertising their products online?**

2 **Do the results of the study surprise you?**

3 **Which other forms of advertising can companies use to target young people?**

Task

In six weeks' time your bank is launching a new credit card for a target audience aged 16–21: the 'Cool Cash Card', or the '3C'. You have to decide how you are going to promote the card in the six weeks preceding the launch.

1 Work in small groups. Student A, turn to File 18 on page 139. Student B, turn to File 43 on page 144, Student C, turn to File 55 on page 146.

2 Have a meeting to discuss the best ways to promote the '3C'. Your total promotional budget is €500,000.
   1 Choose the best ideas within your budget.
   2 Decide the best time to launch each promotion or advertisement.

Unit 9 | Selling

Case study

10 | New ideas

Learning objectives in this unit

- Talking about new green initiatives
- Talking about innovative practices using the passive
- Asking for clarification
- Giving a formal presentation

Case study

- Making a company carbon neutral

Starting point

1 Has your company introduced any new green ideas recently? If so, what?

2 'We all need to do more about the environment.' Do you agree?

3 What is the best green policy you have heard of? Why?

Working with words | Green initiatives

1 Read the text about GreenCitizen and find out what service it offers businesses.

GreenCitizen: the solution to electronic waste

The **disposal** of old computers has always been a problem for companies. Now with the introduction of fines in many countries for companies that do not respect the environment, the problem is even greater. One company in the USA, GreenCitizen, has come up with a new **initiative** to deal with the equipment in an **affordable** and responsible way.

GreenCitizen provides a **convenient** service for businesses by picking up the machines from the workplace and taking them away for **recycling**. GreenCitizen uses only registered recycling companies, which process the components so that they can be used again. Soon it hopes to create a system which tracks all the units it deals with.

GreenCitizen's **original** service is **good value for money** for companies who need to update their computer systems and at the same time maintain an **environmentally friendly** image.

2 Work with a partner and answer the questions.

1 Why do companies have to take care when they dispose of their old equipment?

2 In what ways is GreenCitizen a responsible recycler?

3 What are the advantages to a company of using GreenCitizen?

3 Work with a partner. Match a word or phrase in **bold** from the text to a quote from a customer.

1 'The cost of the service was easily within our budget.'
2 'It was so easy and quick.'
3 'It's a new and interesting service.'
4 'We got an excellent service for relatively little money.'
5 'The process enables people to re-use old components.'
6 'It helps to protect the planet from damage.'
7 '… getting rid of the items we no longer need.'
8 'This new plan is an excellent idea.'

4 Work with a partner. Take turns to explain and guess the words and phrases in **bold** from the text.

5 46▷ Listen to four people talking about green initiatives in their companies. Match the speakers 1–4 to pictures a–d.

a ___

b ___

c ___

d ___

6 46▷ Listen again and complete the table.

Speaker	Green initiative	Advantages
1		1
		2
2		1
		2
3		1
		2
4		1
		2

7 Match adjectives 1–4 from the listening in **6** to meanings a–d. Which initiatives were the adjectives describing?

1 It's unusual. ___   a It works.
2 It's useful. ___   b People like it.
3 It's popular. ___   c It's different.
4 It's effective. ___   d It's good and helpful.

▶▶ For more exercises, go to **Practice file 10** on page 120.

8 Work with a partner. Discuss the initiatives in **5**. What do you think of them?

9 Work with a partner and answer the questions.
1 What does your company do to help the environment?
2 What other measures could your company take?
3 What do you do at home to help the environment? What more could you do?

ⓘ ▶▶ Interactive Workbook ▶▶ Glossary

Tip | green
We can use the word *green* to describe things that help protect the environment.
  *My company hasn't got a very clear **green** policy.*
  *Sales of **green** products have increased in recent years.*

Language at work | The passive

1 **Read the text about the 'Give 1 Get 1' (G1G1) initiative and answer the questions.**

1 What problem did the OLPC have?
2 What makes the XO laptop suitable for underdeveloped countries?
3 How did the G1G1 initiative help the OLPC?

Give a Laptop and Get One

An affordable $100 laptop for poor countries seemed a good idea until the cost of producing each computer rose to $188. The big question then became how to pay for the distribution of the laptops.

The XO laptop is aimed at children in underdeveloped countries. It uses very little power and it can be charged by solar panels. The screen is designed to be used outside in the sun and there are no moveable parts. The computers are produced by Quanta Computer in Taiwan.

How did the One Laptop Per Child (OLPC) organization solve the problem of price? They came up with the 'Give 1 Get 1' (G1G1) initiative. The laptops were sold in the USA at a price of $399 for two for a period of two weeks. One was given to the customer and the other was sent to a child in Afghanistan, Cambodia, Haiti, or Rwanda. OLPC are currently studying sales figures to judge the success of the initiative.

2 **Complete these sentences from the text with the correct passive verb.**

1 The XO laptop _____ at children in underdeveloped countries.
2 The computers _____ by Quanta Computer in Taiwan.
3 The laptops _____ in the USA at a price of $399 for two.
4 One _____ to the customer.

3 **Complete the rules about the passive using the sentences in 2 to help.**

1 Use the passive when it is not important to say *who* has done something. We are more interested in *what* has happened to the subject.
2 Form the passive with the verb _____ and the past participle of another verb.
3 For the present passive use _____ or *are* + the past participle.
   Example: *is aimed* and *are produced*
4 For the past passive use *was* or _____ + the past participle.
   Example: *was given* and *were sold*

>> For more information and exercises, go to **Practice file 10** on page 121.

Tip | *by*

When we say *who* has done something in a passive sentence, we use the preposition *by*.
   *The machines are made **by** Quanta.*
   *The XO laptop was developed **by** Nicholas Negroponte.*

4 47▷ Listen to Tony Chan, who works for an advertising agency, and Blanca Reynoso, who works for a small pharmaceutical company, discussing what is outsourced in their companies. Tick (✓) the services which are outsourced for each company.

	Advertising agency		Pharmaceutical company	
	Outsourced?	Reason	Outsourced?	Reason
Cleaning (clean)				
Maintenance (do)				
IT (provide)				
Human Resources (employ)				
Training (carry out)				
Food + catering (cook)				

5 47▷ Listen again for the reasons why the services are or are not outsourced and complete the table.

6 Work with a partner. Student A, talk about outsourcing in the advertising agency. Student B, talk about outsourcing in the pharmaceutical company. Use the passive form of the verbs in brackets in the table.

> *Example:* *The advertising agency is cleaned by a private cleaning service because …*

7 Work with a partner and answer the questions.
1 What services are outsourced in your company? Why?
2 What other services do you think could be outsourced?

Practically speaking | How to ask for clarification

1 48▷ Listen to a conversation between an office manager, Guido Tito, and a head of department, Teresa Bordoni, about cutting carbon emissions. Underline the correct alternative.
1 Guido is referring to *Teresa's department / the whole company.*
2 The company has to cut its carbon emissions by the end of *this year / next year.*
3 Guido wants to tell people they *can / can't* open the windows.
4 Teresa *agrees / disagrees* that they should turn the heating off for part of the day.

2 48▷ Listen again and complete 1–4 asking for and giving clarification.
1 _____ in my department, or in the whole company?
2 _____ by the end of this year?
3 _____ we should tell people they can't open the windows?
4 _____ part of the day?

3 Work with a partner. Ask for clarification using an expression from 2.
1 the 21st / 31st October?
2 all our customers / just our VIP customers?
3 we should cancel all our orders with that supplier?
4 15 / 50?
5 the staff on the first floor / all the staff?

Business communication | Giving a formal presentation

1 Work with a partner. Discuss the advantages for companies who have green policies.

2 49▷ Carbon Reductions is a company which works with other companies to help reduce carbon emissions. Listen to one of their representatives, Christoffer Jonsson, giving a talk. Complete his notes. How many of the advantages did you talk about in **1**?

> ADVANTAGES OF ADOPTING GREEN POLICIES
>
> 1 Increase company _____
> 2 Attract more _____.
> 3 Improve reputation as an _____.
> 4 Be prepared for new _____.

3 49▷ Work with a partner. Match 1–8 to a–h to make complete sentences from the listening. Then listen again and check your answers.

1 I'm here today to tell ___
2 I'll talk about ___
3 First of all, we're going to ___
4 Let's move on to ___
5 My next point is ___
6 As I said before, ___
7 That brings me ___
8 Thanks very much ___

a … about your reputation as an employer.
b … for listening.
c … you'll make bigger profits if you start saving energy.
d … to the end of my talk.
e … the new regulations later.
f … you about the advantages of going green.
g … the question of your company image.
h … look at the benefits of a clear green policy.

4 Put phrases 1–8 from **3** into these categories. Then work with a partner to remember the phrases in each category.

1 Starting the talk ___, ___
2 Moving on to another subject ___, ___
3 Referring backwards and forwards ___, ___
4 Finishing the talk ___, ___

5 Work with a partner. You work in the Accounts Department of your company. Your company has decided to switch to 100% ebilling. Take turns to present this idea to your department, using the notes below and the phrases in **3**.

> **Subject**
> • switching completely to ebilling
>
> **Advantages**
> • customers can view bill at any time of day or night
> • faster and cheaper than post
> • helps environment – saves on paper + plastic bags for collecting waste paper
>
> **Disadvantages**
> • some customers may not have access to Internet
> • some customers are worried about security
>
> **Conclusion**

>> For more exercises, go to **Practice file 10** on page 120.

6 Work with a partner. Give a formal presentation to your partner. Student A, turn to File 19 on page 139. Student B, turn to File 44 on page 144.

>> For more exercises, go to **Practice file 10** on page 120.

Student A, turn to File 19 on page 139. Student B, turn to File 44 on page 144.

Key expressions

Starting a talk
I'm here today to tell you about …
First of all, we're going to …

Moving on to another subject
Let's move on to …
My next point is about …

Referring backwards and forwards
As I said before, …
I'll talk about that later.

Finishing the talk
That brings me to the end of my talk.
Thanks very much for listening.

ⓘ >> Interactive Workbook >>
Phrasebank

ⓘ >> Interactive Workbook >> **Email** and >> **Exercises and Tests**

Reducing a company's carbon footprint

Now that people are more aware of global warming, businesses need to show what they are doing to reduce their impact on the environment. The following are examples of measures companies have taken.

Commerzbank
Commerzbank, Germany's second largest bank, commissioned a building for its head office in Frankfurt which included winter gardens in its design. The gardens allow natural light to enter all of the offices in the building, making it a much more pleasant and ecological place to work in.

Swiss Re
Swiss Re, the world's largest reinsurance company, introduced the 'COyou2 reduce and gain' scheme to refund its employees half of the money they invest in green measures like hybrid cars, solar power installation, or the use of public transport, up to a maximum of 5,000 Swiss francs.

Chess
Chess, a telecom service company, set up a 'green team' to organize 'green days' which focus on a particular environmental theme. On that day, employees have to make a special effort to take measures to help the planet in the area suggested by the theme. If they take part, they receive a little reward. In addition, to save paper, a new website encourages customers to order on the Internet, and all billing is now done online.

carbon footprint = the measure of the impact a company's activities have on the environment.

Discussion

1 Do you agree that people are responsible for global warming?

2 Which human activities are thought to be the main causes of greenhouse gases?

3 What can businesses and employees do to reduce their carbon footprint?

Task

1 Your company would like to improve its 'green' image and reduce its carbon footprint. It has appointed three 'green teams' to come up with suggestions. Each green team has a different 'green' issue. Group A, turn to File 20 on page 139. Group B, turn to File 45 on page 144. Group C, turn to File 56 on page 146. Read the information and discuss in your group what your company can do. Make notes on what you decide.

2 Prepare a presentation about your issue, using your notes. Then work in a different pair or group and give your presentation.

3 Discuss all the ideas in your group and decide which ones would work best in your company.

Case study

11 | Entertaining

Learning objectives in this unit

- Talking about corporate entertainment
- Talking about future possibilities using the first conditional
- Talking about food and drink
- Making and responding to invitations and offers

Case study

- Organizing a successful corporate event

Starting point

1 'Corporate entertainment is only about making money.' Do you agree?

2 What sort of entertainment do companies offer?

Working with words | Corporate entertainment

1 Read the text and find seven examples of corporate events.

Corporate entertainment

Why is it impossible to get tickets for most major sports and cultural events? Because so many of the tickets are bought by firms to entertain their clients and other VIPs. It is called corporate entertainment, but why do companies do it?

Corporate entertainment is a marketing tool. Companies use it to improve relationships with their customers, suppliers, or staff. 'I work for a law firm,' says Virginia Allen. 'Every year, I invite my best clients to a concert sponsored by the firm. I hope to reinforce their positive feeling towards us.' So the main **purpose** of corporate entertainment is to make customers feel good. Invite them to a special **event** and you will ensure their loyalty for the coming year.

The **venue** for corporate events varies from country to country. In the USA **guests** might play golf with a professional player. In France they could go on a wine-tasting cruise. In Japan they might watch some sumo wrestling. Other events depend on the **budget** of the **host company**, but possibilities include parachute jumping, paintballing, or a night at the opera. The list is endless.

2 Work with a partner and answer these questions.
1 Which events is it often difficult to get tickets for? Why?
2 Why do companies spend money on corporate entertainment?
3 What should a host company consider first when it plans an event?

3 Complete the table with the words in **bold** from the text.

Information	Details
	HSBC bank
	Leading VIPs from banking world
	To reinforce relationship with clients
	Wimbledon Lawn Tennis Club
	Wimbledon Men's Singles Final
	£90,000

4 50▷ Listen to two people talking about corporate events they have attended. Complete the table.

	1	2
Host company		
Guests		
Purpose		
Venue		
Events		

5 50▷ Match verbs 1–6 to nouns a–f. Then listen again and check your answers.

1 hold ___	a clients
2 reinforce ___	b an invitation
3 arrange ___	c a venue
4 entertain ___	d a relationship
5 book ___	e a trip
6 accept ___	f an event

6 Work with a partner. Which phrase in **5** has a similar meaning to

a make a connection stronger?   d organize a journey to a place and back?

b say yes to a request?   e find a place?

c look after guests?   f organize something special for your clients?

7 Work with a partner. Take turns to explain and guess the phrases in **5**.

> *Example:* **A** *When you organize something special for your clients.*
>
> **B** *Hold an event.*

>> For more exercises, go to **Practice file 11** on page 122.

8 Work in small groups. You work for a corporate entertainment company. Plan a corporate event for your company or one of your companies, using the ideas below.

- budget
- venue
- food and drink
- guests
- activities
- entertainment
- time
- accommodation
- transport

9 Work with a partner. Have you ever been to a corporate event? Tell your partner about it. If not, what would your ideal event be?

ⓘ >> Interactive Workbook >> Glossary

Tip | *customer* and *client*

A *customer* buys a product from a company.

The shop gives loyalty cards to its regular customers.

A *client* receives a service from a company or professional person.

My lawyer has many important clients.

Language at work | First conditional

1 Work with a partner. Decide what you need to consider when choosing a restaurant to entertain a guest.

2 51▷ Listen to Luigi, Francesca, and Jacquie discussing where to take some visitors for dinner and complete the table.

Restaurant	Benito's	La Galette
Type of food	Continental	¹_____
Price range	€35–40 per head	²€_____
Entertainment	Singer every night	³_____
Opening times	⁴_____–11.30 p.m.	7.30–10.30 p.m.

3 51▷ <u>Underline</u> the correct answer from the words in *italics*. Then listen and check your answers.

1 If it *will be / 's* nice, we*'ll be able / are able* to sit outside.
2 If we *choose / 'll choose* La Galette, it *costs / 'll cost* us about €300.
3 But if we *go / 'll go* to La Galette on Thursday, there *is / 'll be* live jazz.
4 But it *won't be / isn't* full if we *get / 'll get* there for just after seven.

4 Look at the sentences in **3**. Then complete the rules about the first conditional.

1 Use the first conditional when something will probably happen in the

_____.

2 Form the first conditional with
If + _____, *will / won't +*_____
Example: If we go to La Galette, it will be an expensive evening.

3 When you change the order of the sentence, don't use the

_____.

Example: It will be an expensive evening if we go to La Galette.

5 Work with a partner. Look at the situations below. Take turns to ask questions and respond using the first conditional.

Example: A What will your customers think if you cut your prices?
   B I think they'll be very happy.

Situation	Question	Response
1 You cut your prices.	What / customers think?	Be happy.
2 Your flight to Paris is cancelled.	How / get there?	Rent a car.
3 Your company closes a department.	How / staff react?	Be very worried.
4 Your company changes location.	What / benefits be?	Be easier to park.
5 You change your job.	What / happen?	Earn more money.

▶▶ For more information and exercises, go to **Practice file 11** on page 123.

6 Work with a partner. Ask and answer questions using the prompts.

> *Example: A What will your boss do if your company makes a loss this year?*
> *B I'm not sure, but he'll probably ask us to work overtime.*

1 boss – company makes a loss this year
2 you – don't get a pay rise soon
3 your company – makes a large profit next year
4 you / at the weekend – sunny

Practically speaking | How to talk about food and drink

1 52▷ Listen to two colleagues discussing what to eat. Tick (✓) their choices on the waiter's notepad.

STARTERS	MAIN COURSES	WINES
Parma ham	Spaghetti carbonara	Red
Mixed salad	Seafood pizza	Rosé
Tomato soup	Vegetable lasagne	White

2 52▷ Listen again and match questions 1–3 to responses a–c.

1 What do you recommend? ___   **a** I think I'll have the lasagne.
2 What are the pizzas like? ___   **b** You must try the Parma ham.
3 What are you having? ___   **c** They're not bad, but I recommend the pasta.

3 52▷ Work with a partner. <u>Underline</u> the stress in the phrases in **2**. Then listen and check your answers. Take turns to practise the questions and responses.

4 Work with a partner. Have a similar conversation using the menu below.

THE LEMON TREE

STARTERS
Garlic mushrooms
Seafood salad
Chicken soup

MAIN COURSES
Steak
Salmon
Cheese and onion pie

WINES
Red
Rosé
White

Tip | *the*
We use the word *the* in food expressions when we are talking about specific food, for example, food on the menu.
***The** cheese is delicious.*
*What's **the** salmon like?*

Business communication | Invitations and offers

1 53▷ **Listen to four conversations and match each one with a place a–d.**
   a outside a hotel ___
   b by a hot drinks machine ___
   c in a company Reception ___
   d in a manager's office ___

2 53▷ **Complete invitations and offers 1–4 and responses a–d from the conversations. Then match each invitation or offer to a response. Listen again and check your answers.**
   1 _____ join us?
   2 _____ get you a glass of water?
   3 _____ a coffee?
   4 _____ book a ticket for you?

   a Yes, please. That's very _____ of you.
   b No, thanks. I'd _____ have tea.
   c Yes, please. That would be _____.
   d Thanks for the _____, but …

3 **Put the phrases in 2 into these categories.**
   a Inviting ___
   b Offering ___, ___, ___
   c Accepting ___, ___
   d Declining ___, ___

4 **Work with a partner. Look at these situations and take turns to make and respond to invitations and offers, using the phrases in 2.**
   1 Your visitor is looking tired.
   2 Your visitor doesn't have enough copies of a document she needs for her talk.
   3 It's the opening night of *Madame Butterfly*. You know your visitor loves opera.
   4 The meeting is over and your visitor's hotel is on the other side of town.
   5 It's lunchtime and your visitor hasn't eaten since breakfast at 8.00.
   6 Your visitor wants to set up a PowerPoint presentation, but they need help.
   7 There's a Picasso exhibition at the art gallery and your visitor has a free afternoon.

   》》 For more exercises, go to **Practice file** 11 on page 122.

5 **Work with a partner. You are going to visit each other's companies. Think of six ideas to look after and entertain your partner. Then take turns to be the host and invite and offer, and to be the visitor and accept or decline.**

   ⓘ **》》** Interactive Workbook **》》 Email** and **》》 Exercises and Tests**

Key expressions

Inviting
Would you like to …?

Offering
Would you like …?
Would you like me to …?
Shall I …?

Accepting
Yes, please. That's very kind of you.
Yes, please. That would be nice.

Declining
Thanks for the invitation, but …
No, thanks. I'd rather (do) …

ⓘ **》》** Interactive Workbook
   》》 Phrasebank

Organizing a successful corporate event

Background

A hospitality disaster

When SFO, a leading bank, organized an event to entertain clients at a UEFA Champions League football match last year, things did not go as well as expected. First of all, the corporate hospitality company didn't offer guests coffee and biscuits when they arrived, and there were no free newspapers. Secondly, SFO was extremely dissatisfied with the meal arrangements, complaining that the starters were too small, the pasta was cold, and the dessert arrived too late. On top of this, SFO found the service very slow and was unhappy that guests were not provided with cigars or cigarettes. Finally, the free beer that SFO had arranged to be served throughout the match was warm and ran out early.

SFO paid €900 for each of the 71 clients and 28 bankers who attended, but says that the event has caused the company a considerable financial loss. SFO is currently suing the corporate hospitality company for nearly €135,000.

Discussion

1 Why was the SFO corporate event not a success?

2 How could SFO have avoided these mistakes?

3 What other problems can cause a corporate event to fail?

Task

You are on the committee to arrange SFO's next corporate event.

1 Work in small groups. Group A turn to File 21 on page 139, Group B turn to File 46 on page 144, Group C turn to File 29 on page 141, and Group D turn to File 58 on page 146.

2 Discuss the possible problems that could occur during your event and how you could avoid them.

3 Work in a different group. Have a meeting. Present your event including your ideas for dealing with possible problems. Then decide which event would be best for SFO's next corporate event.

Case study

12 | Performance

Starting point

1 How can you measure the performance of a company? Put these in order from the most important (*1*) to the least important (*5*).

_____ how much money the company makes

_____ how green the company is

_____ who it employs

_____ how it treats its staff

_____ how safe it is to work there

2 How can you measure the performance of

a a government?

b an employee?

Working with words | Evaluating performance

1 Work with a partner. Read statements 1–5 and discuss whether you think they are true or false. Then read the text and check your answers.

1 Everybody loves a company that makes money.

2 It's not enough for a company to have good sales results.

3 Companies have to show that they look after their employees.

4 Employees would work harder and for a lower salary if they were with a socially responsible company.

5 Only a small minority of employees think they work for a socially responsible company.

Company performance in a socially responsible world

Every investor loves a company when it **achieves its sales targets, manages its costs,** and **perform**s **well** on the stock market and, therefore, makes money.

However, a company nowadays also needs to think about its **reputation** with the public and its own staff. In other words, it has to be **socially responsible.** For example, it is expected to improve its **environmental performance.** In addition, it is often judged these days on the **diversity of its workforce**: the number of women, people from ethnic minorities, and disabled people in all positions, including senior management. This has become an important factor in recruitment. Finally, a company needs to have a good **safety record**, both in terms of its workers and the products it produces.

In a recent survey, 40% of workers said they would work longer hours and 48% would work for less pay with a socially responsible company. Interestingly, 46% of employees believed they already work for a socially responsible company. Without doubt, profits are no longer the only way to measure a company's success. Employees and customers expect a lot more.

2 Complete the sentences with words and phrases in **bold** from the text in **1**.

1 If a company is open to both sexes and all races, it believes in the

_____ .

2 A company which protects people and nature is _____ .

3 If your company has good results, its shares usually _____ .

4 If people like or respect the company, it has a good _____ .

5 If the company doesn't spend too much, it _____ its

_____ .

6 If there aren't many accidents, the company has a good _____ .

7 If the company sells what it plans, it _____ its

_____ .

8 If a company doesn't pollute too much, it has a good _____ .

3 Work with a partner. Which of the performance factors in **2** are important
in your place of work, and why?

4 54▷ Listen to five people talking about their employers. Which aspects of
the company's performance is each person evaluating?

1 _____

2 _____

3 _____

4 _____

5 _____

5 54▷ Complete the sentences with these adjectives. Then listen again and
check your answers.

poor   excellent   satisfactory   encouraging   disappointing

1 It's very _____ – I really thought I had a big future here.

2 Last year was _____, because the number of serious injuries went down
dramatically.

3 We've had a really _____ year, much better than we expected.

4 It's been a very _____ performance – I don't like to tell people who I
work for.

5 I suppose I could say we've had a _____ year.

6 Which adjective in **5** means

1 good enough?   4 very good?

2 positive for the future?   5 bad?

3 not as good as we wanted?

>> For more exercises, go to **Practice file 12** on page 124.

7 Choose three of the following topics and evaluate their performance in the
last year. Then work with a partner and explain your answers.

> *Example: My company's performance has been disappointing. We lost an
> important customer in June.*

- your company
- your department
- your government
- your country's economy
- the stock market
- a sports personality or sports team that you like

ⓘ >> Interactive Workbook >> **Glossary**

Tip | *disappointed /
encouraged* or
*disappointing /
encouraging*

A thing is *disappointing* or
encouraging, but a person is
disappointed or *encouraged*.
  The company's performance
  is *disappointing*.
  The employees are
  disappointed by the
  company's performance.
  The results were *encouraging*.
  The CEO was *encouraged* by
  the results.

Language at work | Present perfect (2) with *for* and *since*

1 55▷ Listen to Lionel Chang and Raul Aguilar talking at a sales conference. Where do they work? When did they arrive there?

2 55▷ Look at these sentences from the conversation. Listen again and <u>underline</u> the correct answer from the words in *italics*. Which verbs are in the past simple, and which are in the present perfect?

1 We *opened* / *have opened* our first sales office in 2004.
2 We *had* / *have had* disappointing results for the first two years.
3 Since 2006, our market share *went* / *has gone* up to nearly 5%.
4 I *was* / *'ve been* in Dubai for three years now.
5 My wife and children *moved* / *have moved* here last year.

3 Complete the rules about the past simple and present perfect, using the sentences in **2** to help.

1 Use the _____ when an action starts and finishes in the past.
   Example: _____
2 Use the _____ when an action starts in the past, but includes the present.
   Example: _____
3 Use _____ with the present perfect and past simple to describe the length of time of the action.
   Example: _____
4 Use _____ with the present perfect to describe the start of the action.
   Example: _____

4 Work with a partner. Make sentences in the present perfect and past simple using the prompts in the table.

Lionel's company	have	a sales office in Dubai	
Its market share	live	in Dubai	for …
Raul	start	working in Dubai	
Raul's family	work	going up	since …
	arrive	more encouraging results	in …

5 Read about the history of Dubai's economy and answer the questions.
1 What is Dubai trying to do?   2 Has it been successful? How do you know?

DUBAI DIVERSIFIES

1970s	Dubai earns 64% of its GDP from oil.
Early 1990s	Government realizes that oil revenues are not enough for the economy. It begins to invest in services: tourism, trade, transportation, and financial services. The aim is to build the first non-oil economy in the Gulf region.
2000–2005	The economy grows by an average of 13.4% a year.
2005	Dubai achieves GDP target of $30 bn, five years earlier than expected.
2007	Government launches 'Dubai Strategic Plan'. New GDP target is $108 bn by 2015 with more and more investment in services.
Today	Only 3% of GDP comes from oil.

GDP (Gross Domestic Product) – the total value of all goods and services produced in a country

Tip | *How long?* and *When?*

Use *How long?* with the present perfect and the past simple tenses.
Use *When?* with the past simple tense, but not the present perfect tense.

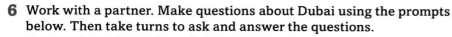

6 Work with a partner. Make questions about Dubai using the prompts below. Then take turns to ask and answer the questions.

> *Example:* **A** *When did the government decide to build a non-oil economy?*
> **B** *In the early 1990s.*

1 When / government / decide / build / non-oil economy?
2 How long / Dubai / invest / services?
3 When / the economy / begin / grow very quickly?
4 How long / it grow / 13.4% a year?
5 How long / GDP / be / over $30 billion?
6 How long / 'Dubai Strategic Plan' / be / in operation?

>> For more information and exercises, go to **Practice file 12** on page 125.

7 Work with a partner. What do you have in common? Take turns to ask and answer questions with *How long?* and *When?* using the ideas below.

- work for your present company
- work for your last company
- do your present job
- need English for your job
- know your English teacher
- live in your last house / flat
- learn English at school

Practically speaking | How to say numbers

1 56▷ Work with a partner. How do you say these numbers? Listen and check your answers. When do we use a full stop or a comma? When do we say 'nought' and 'oh'?

> 1.39%   0.033   102   7,467   906,570

2 57▷ Listen to the stock market report for 21 May. Which markets are in the report? Has each market gone up or down?

3 57▷ Listen again and complete the table.

| 21 May 5.55 p.m. GMT | | World Stock Markets Summary | |
Index	Value	Change	%
Nikkei	13,688.28	+ 377.91	+ _____%
FTSE 100	5,932.20	+ _____	+ 0.65%
DAX	6,904.85	+ 5.17	+ _____%
Dow Jones	12,357.41	- _____	- 0.56%
Nasdaq	_____	- 10.19	- 0.44%

4 Work with a partner. What were the stock market values for 21 May?

> *Example:* *The Nikkei was 13,688.28. It was up 377.91.*

5 It is often easier to use an approximation when we are saying numbers. Look at these approximations and match them with a figure in the report.

1 nearly 380 __*377.91*__
2 roughly 6,000 _____
3 just under 70 _____
4 just over 5 _____
5 around 40 _____

6 Work with a partner. Say these numbers, using the approximations in **5**.

> 17.8% $899   7,068   49%   €141.05
>
> *Example:* *Nearly 18%*

Tip | *nearly, around, and roughly*
Nearly means slightly less or just under.
About and *roughly* can mean slightly more or slightly less.
In written English we often use *approximately* to mean *about* or *roughly*.

Business communication | Describing trends

1 58▷ A consultant is presenting the graph below about car production in four countries. Listen and label the graph with the names of the countries from the list.

Japan   USA   Germany   China

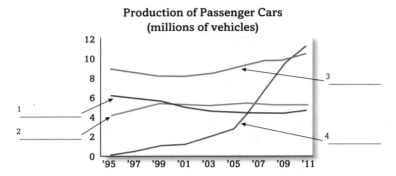

Production of Passenger Cars
(millions of vehicles)

2 Look at the verbs in the table. Decide if they describe an upward movement [↑], a downward movement [↓], or no change [↔]?

	↑, ↓, or ↔?		↑, ↓, or ↔?
rise		grow	
decrease		fall	
remain stable		decline	
drop		increase	

3 Work with a partner. Take turns to ask and answer questions about the graph in **1**, using the verbs in **2**.

> *Example:* **A** *Did production rise in China at the end of the nineties?*
> **B** *Yes, it did.*
> **A** *Has production increased in the USA since 1997?*
> **B** *No, it hasn't. It's declined.*

4 58▷ Look at these sentences from the audio. Decide which country they are describing, using the graph in **1**. Then listen and check your answers.

1 Car production grew **from** five **to** five point five million at the end of the nineties.
2 Since 1999, it has remained stable **at** just under six million vehicles per year.
3 In fact, new car production has fallen **by** two million since 1997.

5 Look at how *from*, *to*, *at*, and *by* are used in **4**. Then complete the description of a company's sales below, using each word once.

Our sales went up _____ 500 units, _____ 2,500 in October _____ 3,000 in November. They stayed _____ 3,000 units in December.

>> For more exercises, go to **Practice file 12** on page 124.

6 Work with a partner. Compare the sales of two car producers. Student A, turn to File 22 on page 139. Student B, turn to File 47 on page 144.

7 Find or draw a graph describing the recent performance of your company or department, or your country (inflation, unemployment, etc.). Then present it to your partner.

(i) >> Interactive Workbook >> **Email** and >> **Exercises and Tests**

The performance game

1 Work in groups. You are starting a new company which manufactures plastic tables and benches from recycled plastic. Your furniture looks like wood, but is stronger and lasts longer. It's also more expensive. Your main customers will be local councils, who will buy your products for parks, schools, and other public areas.

Your objective is to achieve the highest level of performance. This means excellent sales and profits, but also a good reputation for socially responsible action.

Discuss the questions below and agree on the best answer. After each question, go to the number of your choice in File 24 on page 140.

Where are you going to locate your factory?

a In an old industrial town with high unemployment? **Go to 6**

b In a pleasant middle-class town with a reputation for 'green' policies? **Go to 16**

Sales have been very disappointing in Year 1, and you need to reduce your salary costs. What will you do?

a Ask your production workers to go part-time? **Go to 13**

b Lay off five male production workers because they earn more than the women? **Go to 18**

In Year 3, your business has grown so quickly that your factory is now too small. What will you do?

a Extend your existing factory – this will give you 20% more capacity? **Go to 5**

b Outsource part of your production to a low-cost country? **Go to 11**

What will your recruitment policy be?

a Equal numbers of men and women? **Go to 3**

b Just advertise and take the best? **Go to 10**

Your results in Year 2 are more encouraging, but the price of recycled plastic is rising dramatically. What will you do?

a Increase the prices of your products? **Go to 8**

b Use cheaper recycled plastic from Asia? **Go to 15**

You want to promote your image to the public as a socially responsible company. What will you do?

a Include new pages on your website about your employment and environmental policies? **Go to 4**

b Visit schools in towns which have bought your products to teach children about recycling? **Go to 9**

What will be your key advertising message to promote your products?

a Helps to preserve the environment? **Go to 7**

b High quality and durable? **Go to 2**

Two people are injured when a bench collapses. You discover that this is due to a defect in the screws you bought from a supplier in Year 1. What will you do?

a Replace all the 200 benches you sold in Year 1 with new ones? **Go to 14**

b Replace any damaged benches which are returned? **Go to 17**

It's Year 5, and you have two offers to buy shares in your company. Who will you sell them to?

a A company which manufactures and recycles plastic packaging? **Go to 1**

b A multinational oil company which wants to improve its image by investing in environmentally friendly companies? **Go to 12**

---

2 How did you score?

21–27 points
You have combined successful sales policies with a great sense of social responsibility. This will help you to achieve even better growth in the next few years.

11–20 points
You've made some good and bad decisions. To optimize your performance in the future, you should look back and learn from your mistakes.

0–10 points
Your sales performance has been disappointing and your public image is very poor. It's probably time to make some changes in your management team!

Activity

13 | Future trends

Learning objectives in this unit
- Talking about global issues
- Making predictions
- Responding to ideas
- Predicting future trends in the workplace

Case study
- Modernizing a company

Starting point

1 What global issues are in the news at the moment?

2 Which issues are you most worried about? Why? Are there any you are not worried about?

3 Which ones affect your company, your working life, and you personally?

Working with words | Global issues

1 Read the text and find out when the global oil crisis is predicted to start.

Countdown to crisis

Oil is running out and the race is on to find an alternative source of energy. Over the last 40 years oil has been used worldwide to give us food, warmth, chemicals, medicine, clothing and, most of all, mobility. But now Jeroen van der Veer, CEO of the oil multinational Royal Dutch Shell, has named the year that our needs will exceed the supply of oil. He predicts **global demand** for oil will rise dramatically in the next few years due to **population growth** and the rapid **economic development** of countries, such as China and India. He forecasts that, because of this, the **world supply** of oil will no longer be able to meet that demand as early as 2015.

Despite the urgency of this problem and the millions invested in **renewable energy** using sources, such as wind, waves, and sunlight, world governments are far from finding a solution. This means that if we don't take the **oil shortage** seriously, the **energy crisis** will happen sooner than we think.

2 Work with a partner and answer these questions.
1 What is oil used for, apart from cars?
2 What reasons does Jeroen van der Veer give for the rise in the demand for oil?
3 What measures are governments taking to prevent the energy crisis?

3 Match the phrases in **bold** in the text to definitions 1–7 below.

1 energy whose source will always exist _____
2 the need for something in the world _____
3 an improvement in financial conditions _____
4 a time when energy will cause problems _____
5 an increase in the number of people _____
6 a situation where there is not enough oil _____
7 the amount available in the world _____

4 Work with a partner. Take turns to say the first word of the phrases in **3** and for your partner to say the second word.

    Example: A *global*
                 B *demand*

5 59▷ Listen to Judy Collins, an economic analyst, discussing the effects of the oil crisis on the economy. Number the effects she mentions in the order you hear them.

a Meetings will be by video conference. ___
b Fewer people will own cars. ___
c More employees will work from home. ___
d Oil prices will rise. ___
e Consumer goods will become more expensive. ___

6 59▷ Listen again and complete each sentence with a verb.

1 Economists _____ that a 5% reduction will cause the price of oil to rise.
2 All plastic goods will become more expensive as the oil starts to _____ .
3 Experts _____ that only a few people will be able to run cars in the future.
4 Recent advances in technology will _____ working conditions for many employees.
5 The situation will _____ until a substitute for oil is found.

7 Work with a partner. Replace the words and phrases in **bold** with a verb from **6**. Then take turns to ask and answer the questions.

1 How much do you **think** a mobile phone will cost in ten years' time?
2 Do you think your working conditions will **get worse** because of the oil crisis?
3 What do you do at work when the ink for your printer **comes to an end**?
4 How could your company **make** its image **better**?
5 What do you **predict** your company will be like in 2015?

  ➤➤ For more exercises, go to **Practice file 13** on page 126.

8 Choose the three global issues from the list that concern you most. Write a sentence about each issue. Then work with a partner and compare your sentences.

    poverty   *the energy crisis*   *population growth*
    climate change   *sex equality*   *racism*

9 Work with a partner. Look at your list of issues in **8**. What action could you take? What action would you like governments to take?

  ⓘ ➤➤ Interactive Workbook ➤➤ **Glossary**

Language at work | Future predictions

1 Work with a partner. Discuss what trends you think there will be in the workplace in the future. Then read the text and compare your answers.

Adapting to future trends in the workplace

Companies who adapt to changing trends in the workplace are more likely to survive than those who resist a change. So what trends should companies be looking at and how can they adapt?

Business pressures

Competition between businesses will be much stronger in the future and the winner will be the first to get its products onto the market. Managers may have to consider restructuring their companies.

Age of employees

In the future employees might not retire at the age of 65 because of a possible pensions crisis. Employers will have to adapt the workplace to meet the needs of an older workforce.

Work–life balance

Employees will expect more flexibility from their companies so that they can spend more time with their families. Managers will have to design new timetables in order to keep their staff.

Technological changes

Advances in technology will mean that employees won't need their own desk any more. In the future, employers will need to redesign work areas so they can be used for meetings and leisure activities.

2 Choose the correct answer from the words in *italics*. Then read the text again and check your answers.
1. Managers *may / may not* have to consider restructuring their companies.
2. In the future employees *might / might not* retire at the age of 65.
3. Employees *will / won't* expect more flexibility from their companies.
4. Employees *will / won't* need their own desk any more.

3 Complete the rules about making future predictions.
1. Use _____ + infinitive when we are sure something will happen.
   Example: _____
2. Use _____ or _____ + infinitive when we think that perhaps something will happen.
   Example: _____
3. Use _____ or _____ + infinitive when we think that perhaps something will not happen.
   Example: _____
4. Use _____ + infinitive when we are sure something will not happen.
   Example: _____

4 60▷ Listen to a representative from the Work Association give a talk on the typical workplace in the year 2020. Tick (✓) the correct column in the table.

In 2020 …	will	may / might	may / might not	won't
The working population / be older	✓			
There / be many management positions				
Colleagues / see each other often				
Most people / work from home				
There / be a lot of offices in office buildings				
Office buildings / contain a gym				
Employees / stay with the same company				
Employers / offer better conditions				
Employees / take career breaks				

5 Work with a partner. Compare your answers by making sentences about the typical workplace in 2020, using *will*, *may*, *might*, and *won't*.

>> For more information and exercises, go to **Practice file 13** on page 127.

6 Work with a partner. Make predictions about your jobs using the ideas below. Which of your ideas were similar?
- hours
- salary
- technology
- benefits
- office
- pensions

Practically speaking | How to respond to ideas

1 Work with a partner. Put the responses in order from the most positive (1) to the most negative (5).
   a That's a good idea. ____
   b I'm not happy about that at all. ____
   c That might work. ____
   d I think that's a great idea. ____
   e I'm not sure about that. ____

2 61▷ Listen to manager Luis de Sousa discussing how to reduce staff turnover with his colleague Gina Ronaldo. Match the responses in **1** to suggestions 1–5 below.
   1 have a team-building weekend ____
   2 hold a weekly department meeting ____
   3 offer specialized courses ____
   4 give everyone a pay rise ____
   5 introduce a bonus system for employees who stay ____

3 Work with a partner. Your company is having problems with staff turnover. Look at these ideas and take turns to make a suggestion and to respond.
- improve the office environment
- recruit the right staff
- offer flexitime
- stop all overtime

Business communication | Predicting

1 **Work with a partner and answer the questions.**
1 What is teleworking?
2 What are the advantages and disadvantages of teleworking?

2 **62▷ Listen to three people asking their manager about their company's new teleworking scheme. Compare your list of advantages from 1 with the ideas the manager mentions.**

3 **62▷ Listen again and put sentences a–h in the order you hear them.**
a ___ **I hope** employees **will** feel more motivated.
b ___ **Hopefully**, productivity **won't** decrease because of the new scheme.
c ___ The new scheme **will definitely** save the company a lot of money.
d ___ **Do you think** people **will** do more work from home?
e ___ **It probably won't** be easy for some people to start with.
f ___ So **is** our office building **likely to** close?
g ___ Just how much **are** we **likely to** save?
h ___ The office **is unlikely to** close completely.

4 **Complete the table with the words in bold from the sentences in 3.**

Asking for predictions	Making predictions	Expressing hope
1 Are … likely to …?	1 … will definitely …	1
2	2	2
3	3	

5 **Work with a partner. You are taking part in the teleworking scheme in 2. Take turns to talk about the changes in your life, using the language in 4 and these ideas.**
- get bored?
- miss your colleagues?
- get up early?
- work more?
- have more free time?
- save money?
- enjoy working at home?
- go out more?

>> For more exercises, go to **Practice file 13** on page 126.

6 **Work with a partner. You have received an instruction from the Head Office of your company to stop all business trips abroad and make use of videoconferencing instead. Have a meeting to predict the effects of this measure on your company, using the ideas below.**
- reduce costs?
- buy new equipment?
- where to put equipment?
- technical problems?
- clients have video equipment?
- clients like idea?

ⓘ >> Interactive Workbook >> **Email** and >> **Exercises and Tests**

Key expressions

Asking for predictions
Is … likely to …?
Are … likely to …?
Do you think … will …?

Making predictions
… will probably / definitely …
… probably / definitely won't …
… is likely / unlikely to …

Expressing hope
I hope … will / won't …
Hopefully, … will / won't …

ⓘ >> Interactive Workbook
>> **Phrasebank**

Modernizing a company

Background

BMW transforms its Cowley plant

When BMW took over the Rover site at Cowley, Oxford, the plant's low productivity was a major concern. The outdated factory machinery meant that the manufacturing process was extremely expensive. Many of the car parts were imported from abroad, which was both impractical and expensive. The workforce at Cowley had spent many years fighting to keep their jobs, and so relations with management were poor. Finally, one of Rover's main brands, the Mini, could no longer meet the needs of the customer regarding safety, noise, and environmental concerns. For the Cowley car plant to continue production, radical change was necessary.

Discussion

1 What problems did BMW face when it took over the Cowley car plant?

2 What changes do you think BMW made to transform Cowley into a successful plant?

3 Turn to File 25 on page 140 to compare your answers with the changes BMW actually made.

Task

Textiles Inc. used to be a successful textile manufacturer, but it is now losing out to competitors.

1 Work with a partner. Turn to File 26 on page 140 to find out more about the problems at Textiles Inc. You are consultants for a company which has been employed to try and solve these problems. Discuss the problems and decide what the company needs to do to become successful again.

2 Work with another pair and have a meeting to present your possible solutions.

3 Choose the six best ideas to present to the management of Textiles Inc.

Case study

14 | Time

Learning objectives in this unit

- Talking about managing time
- Speculating and discussing consequences using conditional sentences
- Talking about time
- Negotiating conditions

Case study

- Negotiating new schedules

Starting point

1 'There is never enough time in the day.' Do you agree with this?

2 Are these sentences always, sometimes, or never true for you?

'I organize my working time well.'

'I have a lot of interruptions at work.'

'When I have important work to do, I finish it on time.'

3 How do you feel about people who are always late or early?

Working with words | Managing time

1 **Look at questions 1–3 and answer them. Then work with a partner and discuss your answers.**

1 What percentage of workers read email while speaking on the phone?
   a a third   **b** more than half   **c** more than three quarters

2 'Multitasking' means doing more than one job at the same time, e.g. writing an email and answering the phone. Does it allow you to work more quickly?
   a Yes   **b** No   **c** Sometimes

3 What's the worst thing about people who multitask?
   a They don't really listen.   **b** They make lots of mistakes.
   c They think they're the best.

2 **Read the text and compare your answers.**

Multitasking: time-waster or time-saver?

On the other end of the phone, you hear the sound of fingers on a keyboard. During a Monday department meeting, a colleague has his head down, **planning his schedule** for the week. At home, your husband or wife is answering emails while helping the children with their homework.

We have all learnt to multitask because we feel we don't **have enough time** to get everything done. 45% of workers feel they are asked to work on too many tasks at once, according to a study by the Families and Work Institute. Another survey by ComPsych, a provider of employee assistance programmes, reports that 54% of workers **spend time** reading email while on the phone and 11% make to-do lists during meetings.

We all have to **meet deadlines**, but is multitasking really the solution for finishing everything **on time**? Not really, if you believe the scientists. We think we **save time** by doing two tasks at once, but studies show that the brain is less efficient when performing similar tasks, such as reading and listening. And each time we switch to another task, we have to **allow time** for our brains to adapt to the new situation.

Perhaps the worst thing about people who multitask is the feeling that they are only giving you half an ear. So next time you ask a caller to repeat something because you are reading your emails and not listening to him or her, just remember one thing: you're **wasting time**, both yours and the caller's.

3 Work with a partner. Look at these sentences about managing time. Choose the correct answer from the words in *italics*, using the words and phrases in bold in the text to help you.

1 If you *waste / save* time on something, you don't use your time well.
2 Before you *plan / meet* your schedule, you need to know the deadline.
3 When preparing a presentation, you should *allow / spend* time to practise it.
4 If there's *on / enough* time to do everything, you'll meet your *deadline / task*.

4 Make similar sentences with these expressions.

1 save time
2 spend time
3 on time

5 Work with a partner. Give advice on how to run a successful meeting, using the vocabulary in **3**.

6 Read this advice on how to run a successful meeting and complete the sentences with a suitable word or phrase. How do these ideas compare with yours in **5**?

1 _____ your meeting in advance, so you know exactly what subjects you want to cover.
2 Don't wait until the meeting starts to tell participants the agenda. _____ time by sending it to them in advance.
3 Start your meeting _____.
4 _____ time getting everybody's opinions on the different subjects.
5 For each subject, decide who will take the necessary action and what the _____ is.
6 Don't _____ time talking about subjects that aren't on the agenda. But _____ a few minutes at the end to discuss these points briefly.
7 If you don't have _____ to discuss all the important subjects, agree on a date for a new meeting.

» For more exercises, go to **Practice file 14** on page 128.

7 Work with a partner. Discuss what problems you have with time management, using the ideas below to help you. What could you do to solve the problems?

• meeting deadlines
• getting to work on time
• planning your schedule for each day
• multitasking
• being interrupted by the phone or email

ⓘ » Interactive Workbook » **Glossary**

Unit 14 | Time

Tip | *enough*

We use *enough* before nouns, but after adjectives.
We don't have **enough** *time.*
The meeting wasn't long **enough**.

Language at work | Second conditional

1 63▷ **Silvia has just returned to Argentina after working on a project in New York for three months. Listen and answer the questions.**

  1 Did she enjoy her time in the USA?
  2 Would she like to work there?

2 63▷ **Listen again and <u>underline</u> the words in *italics* you hear.**

  1 *I'll / I'd* go crazy if I *lived / live* in the USA.
  2 What *would / will* you do if they *offer / offered* you a job there?
  3 If it *is / was* only for a year or two, I *would / might* say 'yes'.
  4 If they *want / wanted* me for longer, I *wouldn't / won't* accept it.

3 **Look at these two conditional sentences and complete the rules.**

  If they gave me a promotion, I wouldn't leave. (second conditional)
  If they give me a promotion, I won't leave. (first conditional)

  1 The _____ is used to talk about something which is probable and its result (they will probably give her a promotion).
  2 The _____ is used to talk about something which is less probable and its result (they probably won't give her a promotion).
  3 We form the second conditional with *If* + _____, *would* + _____.

4 **Look at the sentences in 2 again. What do we use instead of *would* when we are unsure of the result?**

5 **Complete the questions in the second conditional with the correct form of the verbs in brackets.**

  1 If _____ (you / have) the chance to work in another country, which country _____ (you / choose)?
  2 How _____ (you / feel) if _____ (your boss / ask) you to work at weekends?
  3 If _____ (you / can) study full-time for a year, what subject _____ (interest) you most?
  4 If _____ (there / be) an extra hour in your working day, how _____ (you / spend) it?
  5 _____ (you / be) happier if _____ (mobile phones / not exist)?
  6 If you _____ (not / have) a clock or watch to see the time at work, _____ (it / be) a problem for you?

6 **Work with a partner. Ask and answer the questions in 5.**

  Example: *A If you had the chance to work in another country, which country would you choose?*
      B I don't know, but I might choose China. What about you?
      A I think I'd go to Vietnam.

  ≫ For more information and exercises, go to **Practice file 14** on page 129.

7 **Read the text. Then work with a partner and answer the questions.**

1 Do you think people in your country live on 'event time' or 'clock time'?

2 Would you like to live in a country with a different time culture to yours?

The idea of time

The social psychologist Robert Levine, who has spent years studying people's ideas about time, says that cultures can be divided into those which live on 'event time', where events are allowed to dictate people's schedules, and those which live on 'clock time', where people's schedules dictate events. People who live on 'clock time' are more punctual than those who do not, and their countries tend to be more successful economically – if perhaps less fun at night – than those which live on 'event time'.

8 **Work with a partner. Do you live on 'event time' or 'clock time'? Student A, turn to File 27 on page 141. Student B, turn to File 48 on page 145. Then turn to File 57 on page 146 for the answers.**

Practically speaking | How to use time expressions

1 **64▷ Listen to two conversations about deadlines. In each conversation, what do they have to do?**

2 **64▷ Listen again and match 1–7 to a–g.**

1 by ___	**a** away
2 within ___	**b** as possible
3 before ___	**c** have time
4 as soon ___	**d** Monday
5 right ___	**e** the end of next week
6 on ___	**f** a week
7 when you ___	**g** Friday

3 **Look again at the phrases in 2. Which two phrases do not give a specific deadline? Today is Wednesday. Put the other phrases in the right order, from the most to the least urgent.**

4 **Work with a partner. Take turns to ask for the things in 1–6, using the words in brackets.**

Example: Can you give me an answer within two days?

1 Today is 13th April. You want an answer by 15th April. (within)

2 It's 9.00 a.m. You want to receive the report today. (by)

3 You want confirmation of the meeting before Friday evening. (end)

4 It's 3rd December. You want the budget figures within four weeks. (before)

5 It's Friday. You want to see the new product now! (right)

6 Today is Tuesday. You want to have a meeting the day after tomorrow. (on)

Business communication | Negotiating conditions

1 65▷ **Hans-Peter Berg works for a machine tool manufacturer. He receives a phone call from one of his foreign suppliers, Luca Peretti. Listen and complete the information.**

Problem: _____

First solution: _____

Disadvantage of first solution: _____

Second solution: _____

Who will pay? _____

2 65▷ **Match 1–10 with a–j to make complete sentences from the listening. Then listen again and check your answers.**

1 We have a problem ___	**a** … be possible.
2 Basically, ___	**b** … pay the extra cost?
3 Would it be OK ___	**c** … with delivery.
4 Yes, that would ___	**d** … we've got a lorry drivers' strike.
5 What if ___	**e** … get the parts to the factory on time.
6 Could you ___	**f** … be acceptable.
7 I think we ___	**g** … we transported them by train to the border?
8 That would allow us to ___	**h** … send a lorry to pick them up?
9 Would you agree to ___	**i** … if we sent them by train?
10 Sorry, that wouldn't ___	**j** … could do that.

3 **Which phrases in 2 are used to**

1 introduce the problem? ___, ___
2 propose solutions? ___, ___
3 describe the consequences of a solution? ___
4 ask if someone can do something for you? ___, ___
5 agree to a solution? ___, ___
6 reject a solution? ___

Key expressions

Describing the problem
There's / We have a problem with …
Basically, …

Negotiating conditions
What if we did X?
Would you agree to do Y?
Could you do Y?
Would it be OK if …?

Responding
Yes, that would be possible.
I think we could do that.
Sorry, that wouldn't be acceptable.

Describing advantages
That would allow us / you to …

ⓘ ⟫ Interactive Workbook
⟫ **Phrasebank**

---

4 **Work with a partner. Student A is a supplier of computer processors. Student B is a computer manufacturer. Have a phone conversation, using the notes below.**

A Describe problem: processor ordered (Version 2.1) not in stock. Propose solution: send version 2.2.

B Accept solution. Ask if **A** can send it by end of this week.

A Reject proposal. Give reason: final tests on Version 2.2. No stock until next week.

B Propose solution: delivery by Friday of next week if same price as Version 2.1 ($30).

A Reject proposal. Propose unit price of $40 for Version 2.2 (normally $50).

B Accept or reject proposal.

⟫ For more exercises, go to **Practice file 14** on page 128.

5 **Work with a partner. Have a phone conversation to negotiate new conditions for an order which has been placed. Student A, turn to File 28 on page 141. Student B, turn to File 49 on page 145.**

ⓘ ⟫ Interactive Workbook ⟫ **Email** and ⟫ **Exercises and Tests**

Negotiating new schedules

Background

The world's tallest (unfinished) building

The Ryugyong Hotel in North Korea has 105 floors, making it the largest building in the country and one of the tallest in the world. However, more than 20 years after construction began, it was still unfinished.

Started in 1987, the Ryugyong's 3,000 rooms and seven revolving restaurants were scheduled to open in June 1989 for the World Festival of Youth and Students, but problems with building methods and materials delayed it.

Building work stopped in 1992. In recent years, the North Korean government has tried to invite foreign investment of US$300 million to improve and finish the hotel. However, the final cost could be more if it has to be rebuilt due to structural problems.

Discussion

1 Why is the hotel still not finished today?

2 Why is it so difficult to meet deadlines in the construction industry?

3 Why are projects like these often much more expensive than planned?

Task

Phoenix Office Design constructs and designs office buildings. Phoenix constructs the outside of the building, but subcontracts all the interior work to Metropolis Construction. Today is Monday 24 September. Phoenix is having problems with the building of the roof and the site needs to be closed for at least a month before work can start again.

1 Look at the Gantt chart showing the project schedule for today.

PHOENIX OFFICE DESIGN	Client: Odensa. Delivery deadline: 31 December											
*Phoenix #Metropolis												
	July		August		September		October		November		December	
External walls*												
Roof*												
Internal walls#												
Plumbing#												
Electricity#												
Floors#												
Decoration#												

2 Work with a partner. Use the Gantt chart above to plan a new construction schedule. Turn to File 30 on page 141 for more information.

3 Work with a different partner. Student A, turn to File 23 on page 139. Student B, turn to File 50 on page 145. Then negotiate the conditions of the new schedule, including the extra costs.

Case study

15 | Training

Starting point

1 What skills do you need for your present job? Did your company offer you any special training?

2 What new skills would you like to learn for your professional and / or personal development?

Working with words | Personal development and training

1 Read the text. Would you like a business coach?

The benefits of business coaching

In recent years business coaching has grown, with companies such as Unilever and KPMG taking part. It can cost up to £3,000 a day. However, the results are so impressive that some companies want all their executives to enrol to **improve** their **performance**.

What do business coaches do? Basically, they let you talk about the problems you are having in your professional life and help you **set** new **goals**. They then meet or speak with you regularly to see if you are **achieving** those **goals**. For example, they can find ways for you to get better sales results, to **motivate** your team to work better, or to **improve** your **promotion prospects** in your company. Coaches do not actually make decisions for you, but **give** you **feedback** on your ideas. They can also help you identify what training you might

need to **develop** your **skills**.

The coaching experience can be an ideal opportunity to **take a step back** and evaluate your lifestyle. The result is often a better work–life balance. Jeremy Lang, former Chief Executive of Chilprufe, the underwear manufacturer, said, 'I am working 50% more *on* my business and 50% less *in* my business. I am 100% happier.'

2 Read the text again and answer the questions.

1 What's the maximum you might pay for a day's coaching?

2 What are some companies asking their top managers to do?

3 Do business coaches usually

   a help you organize your working time better?

   b listen to your problems?

   c make written recommendations on what action to take?

   d help you get better results?

   e recommend jobs for you in other companies?

4 What does Jeremy Lang mean when he says 'I am working 50% more *on* my business and 50% less *in* my business'?

3 Match words and phrases in **bold** in the text to meanings 1–8 below.

1 think about your life in a calm way _____
2 give somebody the desire to do something _____
3 learn how to do things better _____
4 do your job better _____
5 decide on your objectives _____
6 reaching your objectives _____
7 increase the possibilities of a better job in your company _____
8 tell someone what you think of their performance _____

4 Complete these sentences with a form of the words and phrases from **3**. Then work with a partner. Take turns to ask and answer the questions.

1 What things _____ you to do your job well?
2 When was your last annual appraisal? Did you _____ any _____ for this year? What are you doing to try and _____ them?
3 How often does your boss _____ you _____ on your performance?
4 Do you think training is the best way to _____ your _____ _____? What other ways are there to move up in the company?
5 When is the best time to _____ a _____ _____ from your job?
6 What new _____ would you like to _____ in your professional life?
7 Have you done any training courses recently to _____ your _____ at work? How have these courses helped you?

5 Match a company training course from the list to 1–5 below.

Project management   Managing stress   Motivating employees
Communication skills   Time management

PERSONAL DEVELOPMENT AT WORK

Five training courses to help you achieve your personal and professional goals:

1 _____ to achieve a work–life balance and take a step back.
2 _____ to be a better listener and run effective meetings.
3 _____ to speed read and deal with emails.
4 _____ to give better feedback and set clear goals.
5 _____ to plan work schedules and learn to delegate.

>> For more exercises, go to **Practice file 15** on page 130.

6 66▷ Listen to Scott Wesley, a sales director, speaking with different colleagues. Match conversations 1–3 to situations a–c.

a At the coffee machine ____
b At an annual appraisal ____
c At a meeting ____

7 66▷ Work with a partner. Listen again and answer the questions.

1 Why aren't Scott's colleagues happy with what he says?
2 What courses in **5** would you recommend for him?

8 Which of the courses in **5** would be useful for you? Why?

9 Work with a partner. Take turns to describe what skills you need and to recommend a course.

ⓘ >> Interactive Workbook >> Glossary

Language at work | Modal verbs for giving advice

1 Read the advice on how to conduct an appraisal with an employee. Ignore the gaps in the sentences for now. Do you agree or disagree with the different points? Then work with a partner and compare your answers.

> **Annual appraisals**
>
> **Advice for managers**
>
> **1** You _____ use your own office for the interview.
>
> **2** You _____ do most of the talking.
>
> **3** You _____ start with one or two questions about the employee's personal life.
>
> **4** You _____ give negative feedback first.
>
> **5** You _____ discuss if the employee achieved last year's goals.
>
> **6** You _____ offer solutions when goals haven't been achieved.

2 67▷ Listen to a Human Resources manager giving a presentation to department managers on annual appraisals. Compare her advice with your opinions in **1**.

3 67▷ Listen again. Complete the advice in **1** with the modal verbs which the HR manager uses. Choose from this list.

   must   mustn't   should   shouldn't   could

4 Complete the sentences with a modal verb from **3**.
   1 If it's really important to do something, you _____ do it.
   2 If it's a good idea to do it, you _____ do it.
   3 If it's possible, you _____ do it.
   4 If it's not a good idea, you _____ do it.
   5 If it's a very bad idea, you _____ do it.

5 Look at the advice for improving your promotion prospects. Are the points
   a important?   **b** a good idea?   **c** possible?
   d not a good idea?   **e** a very bad idea?

   1 Work longer hours than your colleagues. ___
   2 Apply for every management position advertised in the company. ___
   3 Tell colleagues which jobs you are applying for. ___
   4 Get to know your boss personally. ___
   5 Tell your boss you are thinking of leaving. ___
   6 Help work colleagues with their problems as much as possible. ___
   7 Ask for training courses at least once a year. ___
   8 Always send copies of your work to your boss. ___
   9 Speak loudly on the phone so your boss can hear your conversations. ___

6 Work with a partner. Discuss your answers, using a modal verb from **3**.
   Example: You shouldn't work longer hours than your colleagues because …

Tip| *have to* and *must*

Have to describes things that our employers, the government, etc. ask us to do.
   I **have to** work 39 hours a week.
   We **have to** pay tax three times a year.
Must describes things that are urgent or personally important for us.
   You **must** pay our tax bill this week.
   I **must** try to work harder.

7 Work with a partner. Read about Marek and Klaudia. Decide what problems they have at work and what advice you could give them.

> **Marek Podolski:** 45-year-old project manager for a software company. Works 60–70 hours a week and is very stressed. Has too many projects to manage at the same time, all with impossible deadlines. His team refuse to do extra hours and his boss refuses to recruit another team member. His wife complains that she and the children never see him.

> **Klaudia Wojcik:** 28-year-old sales rep for an insurance company. In the job for five years. Excellent sales results. CEO promised her quick promotion when she arrived, but her boss says she's too young to be a manager. Applied three months ago for the position of Sales Manager, but didn't get the job. Her boss was on the interview panel, but the CEO wasn't.

➤➤ For more information and exercises, go to **Practice file 15** on page 131.

8 68▷ Listen to two experts talking about the problems in **7** and compare their ideas with yours.

9 Work with a partner. Take turns to explain the problems below and to give advice.
- improve your personal performance
- develop your skills
- get the most from your annual appraisal
- get a better work–life balance to have more free time

Practically speaking | How to say thank you and respond

1 What would you say in these situations?
- **a** An ex-colleague invited you to a restaurant and has just paid the bill.
- **b** It's your annual appraisal with your boss. The meeting has been useful.
- **c** A colleague has spent two hours showing you a computer program.
- **d** A supplier you work with has just sent you a birthday message.

2 69▷ Listen to four conversations. Match each one to a situation in **1**.

3 69▷ Listen again to the conversations and complete the sentences in A. Then match the two parts of the responses in B.

A	B	
It was very nice of you to _____.	You're	at all.
Thanks _____.	No	welcome.
Thanks for _____.	That's	problem.
Thank you for _____.	Not	OK.

4 Which of the sentences and responses in **3** are more informal?

5 Work with a partner. Say thank you and respond in the situations in **1**.

6 Work with a partner. Have similar conversations for these situations.
1 Someone has helped you carry a heavy box to your office.
2 You've spent the weekend on your boss's yacht.
3 A colleague has helped you write a report.

> **Tip | nice**
> *Nice* has many different meanings in English.
>   *It was **nice** of you to invite me.* (nice = kind)
>   *Did you have a **nice** time in Beijing?* (nice = enjoyable)
>   *My colleagues are very **nice**.* (nice = friendly)
>   *That brochure looks **nice**.* (nice = attractive)

Business communication | Showing understanding and suggesting solutions

1 Work with a partner. Answer the questions.
1 Why do people sometimes have to work late?
2 Do you ever work late? If so, how often and why?

2 70▷ Marisa is talking to her colleague Glen. Listen and answer the questions.
1 Why does Marisa's boss Tom want her to work late today?
2 Why can't she do it?
3 Why can't she work late tomorrow?
4 Why is it taking her so long to finish her work?
5 Why doesn't the company want to give her training?
6 When does her work have to be finished?
7 What does Tom say about deadlines?

3 70▷ Listen again and number these phrases in the order you hear them.
1 Right. ____
2 It's not easy for you. ____
3 I'm sure there's a solution. ____
4 Don't worry. ____
5 I see. ____
6 I understand totally. ____
7 I know how you feel. ____
8 It's not your fault.

4 Work with a partner. You are both having some problems at work at the moment. Take turns to explain your problems and show understanding. Student A, turn to File 34 on page 142. Student B, turn to File 51 on page 145.

5 71▷ Work with a partner. Discuss what you think Marisa should do. Then listen to Glen talking about Marisa's problem.
1 What solutions does he suggest?
2 Which idea does Marisa accept?

6 71▷ Listen again and complete the suggestions and responses.

Suggestions	Responses
1 _____ go to your son's school …	a No, I _____
2 _____ coming in at the weekend?	b That _____
3 _____ tell Tom that you can work on Saturday?	c Yes, _____

>> For more exercises, go to **Practice file 15** on page 130.

7 Work with a partner. Take turns to explain some problems, suggest solutions, and respond. Student A, turn to File 32 on page 142. Student B, turn to File 05 on page 135.

ⓘ >> Interactive Workbook >> **Email** and >> **Exercises and Tests**

Key expressions

Showing that you are listening
I see.
Right.

Expressing sympathy
I understand totally.
I know how you feel.
It's not easy for you.

Reassuring
I'm sure there's a solution.
It's not your fault.
Don't worry.

Suggesting possible solutions
Perhaps you could do …
Have you thought of doing …?
Why don't you do …?

Responding to suggestions
Yes, (that's a) good idea.
That might be possible.
No, I can't do that.

ⓘ >> Interactive Workbook
>> **Phrasebank**

Introducing personal development programmes

Background

Helping employees to succeed and grow

LSI Corporation, a leading provider of innovative silicon, systems, and software technologies, believes that personal development benefits both employees and the company. It knows that lack of skills and low morale can reduce performance, quality of work, and efficiency. For this reason, it offers a wide range of programmes which give staff the opportunity to

- have quick access to the technical information they need, with an online database of mentors who can be contacted to give help and advice on specific subjects
- continue or complete their higher education with assisted programmes at accredited universities
- identify and develop the skills necessary to improve their job prospects in the company with online tools to create a personal job and skills analysis
- be recognized for exceptionally good performance with special award programmes.

Discussion

1 How can a lack of skills cause problems for a company?

2 What do you think of the programmes that LSI has?

3 Do you have any personal development programmes in your company?

Task

You work for Lektra, an international firm of engineering consultants. The HR Department is concerned that many employees are dissatisfied with their personal development in the company.

1 72▷ Listen to some of the employees' comments. What aspects of personal development does the company need to work on?

2 Work with a partner or in small groups. Discuss what programmes and ideas could be introduced to improve personal development in the company.

3 Present your ideas to the rest of the class. Choose the three best ideas to suggest to management.

Case study

16 | Your career

Learning objectives in this unit

- Talking about ambitions and careers
- Revising grammar and tenses
- Saying goodbye
- Giving a personal presentation

Activity

- Ambition!

Starting point

1 What are the most popular careers in your country?

2 Which careers have the longest training?

3 Are there too many graduates in any one career area?

4 'A change is as good as a rest.' Do you agree with this idea?

Working with words | Careers

1 Read the text and find out which jobs Greg Mortensen does or has done.

How to move a mountain – the story of Greg Mortensen

It's been over fifteen years since Greg Mortensen attempted to climb K2, the world's second highest mountain. At the time, Greg was working as a trauma nurse in the USA, but his adventure in the Himalayas set him on a new **career path**.

During the climb, 50-year-old Greg became ill and lost the rest of his group. He walked to a local village and while recovering there, he realized that the children in the village did not have a proper school. He **made the decision** to return to the USA and **concentrate on** raising money so that a school could be built in the village. When he got home, his life **changed direction** dramatically. He **gave up** his house, lived in the back of his car, and wrote hundreds of letters to celebrities asking for money. However, at first he had little success.

Greg's luck changed when a student in his mother's class in a school in Wisconsin found out that one penny

would buy a pencil for a child in South Asia. Together the class collected more than 62,000 pennies. Next, a Seattle IT specialist saw an article about Greg's experience on K2 and sent him a cheque for $12,000.

Since then Greg has **spent** six months of every year in the area, building over 60 schools. In 2006 he **completed** a best-selling book, *Three Cups of Tea*, about his adventures.

2 Read the text again. Then work with a partner and answer these questions.

1 When and where did Greg Mortensen's life change?
2 What were his fundraising methods?
3 How does Greg spend his time now?

3 Match the words or phrases in **bold** in the text in **1** to these definitions.

1 stopped having or doing _____
2 finished _____
3 a planned series of jobs or professions _____
4 took a different way _____
5 decided (to do something) _____
6 give all your attention to something _____
7 passed (time) _____

4 Work with a partner. Look at the quotations from people talking about their careers. Take turns to use a word or phrase in brackets in the correct form to report what each person said.

> *Example:* **A** *I chose to go to Oxford and not Cambridge University.*
> **B** *He **made the decision** to go to Oxford and not Cambridge.*

1 'I chose to go to Oxford and not Cambridge University.' (make the decision)
2 'I finished my studies in 1989.' (complete)
3 'I trained in an architect's studio for two years.' (spend)
4 'I'm going to study medicine, go abroad for some work experience, do my exams, and qualify as a family doctor.' (career path)
5 'I left my job in the city and moved to the country.' (give up)
6 'I was studying maths, but I hated it, so I tried drama and became an actor instead.' (change direction)
7 'All I want to do is paint.' (concentrate on)

5 73▷ Listen to four people talking about career changes they have made. Which speakers are happy with the change?

6 73▷ Listen again and complete the sentences with one word each.

1 Dealing with the public is one of Speaker 1's _____.
2 Time management is her greatest _____.
3 Speaker 2 joined the army at 16 because he had no _____ plan.
4 Speaker 3 studied human resources because she wanted a _____.
5 To hold an exhibition of his own pictures was Speaker 4's _____.

7 Match the words and phrases from **6** to meanings 1–5.

1 A new and difficult thing that needs effort. _____
2 A fault in your character. _____
3 The good qualities that you have. _____
4 The direction you want to go in your working life. _____
5 Something that you really want to do. _____

>> For more exercises, go to **Practice file 16** on page 132.

8 Work with a partner. Take turns to talk about your career path, using the ideas below to help you. What do you have in common?

- your strengths and weaknesses
- your career plan
- challenges in your work
- your ambitions

ⓘ >> Interactive Workbook >> **Glossary**

Tip | *qualification, degree,* and *diploma*

A *qualification* is an exam you have passed or a course you have completed.

> *Jack left school with no formal **qualifications**.*

A *degree* is the qualification you receive when you have successfully completed a course at university.

> *My brother is doing a chemistry **degree**.*

A *diploma* is a shorter and more practical course, often at a college.

> *Chloe's studying for a **diploma** in hotel management.*

Language at work | Revision of grammar and tenses

1 Read the text. Why do many people decide to change their career path?

Career changes that make a difference

An American university has recently carried out a survey into why people decide to change direction in their career. The results show that 61% of the people interviewed would prefer to do something more useful with their lives. Most of them think that they would have more job satisfaction if they could give something back to the community.

A typical example of this is Jeff Short, whose original aim when he set up his own company was to make money. However, after 18 years running the company, he realized that something was missing in his life. After his company was sold, he joined a teaching programme online and now gives classes in industrial technology at his local high school.

Nowadays there is an increasing number of educational programmes that give people the opportunity to make a difference. Many of them are part-time so that you only have to give up your current job once you become qualified. 'If you go back to studying, you'll find a job that makes you happy,' says the head of one of the programmes. 'Those people who have doubts about their current job should get in touch immediately with their local university to find out what's on offer,' she recommends.

2 Read the text again and find one example of 1–7 below.

1 the comparative form of an adjective ___*more useful*___
2 an uncountable noun _____
3 a modal verb used to talk about obligation

   _____
4 the past passive form of a verb _____
5 a first conditional sentence _____
6 a second conditional sentence _____
7 a modal verb used to give advice _____

3 74▷ Listen to part of a business documentary about successful people who give some of their money to good causes and answer the questions.

1 What does Ulises de la Cruz do?
2 Where does he come from?
3 What has he spent his money on?

4 74▷ **Work with a partner. Look at the information about Ulises de la Cruz and choose the correct verb form in *italics*. Then listen again and check your answers.**

1 Several times a week he*'s sending / sends* money back to his hometown.
2 Ulises *grew up / 's grown up* in a very poor village in the Chota valley.
3 Since then he *set up / 's set up* a medical centre.
4 At the moment he *builds / 's building* a sports and community centre.
5 He*'ll open / 's opening* it at the end of the season if it's finished.
6 Next he*'s going to build / 's building* 40 new homes for the villagers.

>> For more information and exercises, go to **Practice file 16** on page 133.

5 Student A, turn to File 33 on page 142. Student B, turn to File 52 on page 145. Take turns to read out a sentence. Your partner must decide if it is right or wrong. If the sentence is wrong, your partner must correct it. Give your partner one point for every correct answer.

6 Work with a partner. Imagine a friend of yours is looking for a job and there is a vacancy in your partner's company which would be perfect for your friend. Tell your partner about your friend and recommend him / her for the job, using the ideas below to help you.

- how you know him / her
- your friend's current job and why he / she wants to leave
- his / her education and qualifications
- his / her previous jobs
- his / her strengths and weaknesses
- his / her ambitions
- his / her plans for the future

Practically speaking | How to say goodbye

1 75▷ **Work with a partner. Match ways of saying goodbye 1–4 to responses a–d. Then listen and check your answers.**

1 Bye then. See you on Monday. ___
2 It was nice meeting you. ___
3 Bye, Sue, I'm off. ___
4 Goodbye. Have a good trip. ___

a Bye, Brian. See you tomorrow.
b Bye. Have a good weekend.
c Thanks and goodbye, Dylan.
d And you too. See you next time.

2 75▷ **Listen again and decide if the conversations are formal or more informal.**

3 Work with a partner. Practise saying goodbye to each other in the following situations.

1 To your Managing Director at the airport.
2 To your office on a Friday evening.
3 To someone you have met for the first time after a conference.
4 To the colleague who sits next to you.

Business communication | Giving a personal presentation

1 76▷ **Listen to two people, Thorsten Richter and Amy Chang, giving a presentation about themselves at the beginning of their talk at a company conference. Who gives the most information about themselves?**

2 76▷ **Listen again. Which speaker says the following?**
1 Last year I was promoted to this position. _1_
2 I studied economics and business. ___
3 Recently I have worked on several successful cases. ___
4 In my previous role I ran the Creative Department in Bonn. ___
5 Up to now I've managed to find solutions for all the companies I have worked with. ___
6 Over the last year I've met with all the country managers. ___
7 In my current role as consultant to your company, I'm looking to improve your sales figures. ___
8 At the moment we're working together with a consultant. ___
9 Over the next year I'll spend two weeks in each department. ___
10 In the future we may have to target a different market. ___

3 **Complete the table with the time phrases in 2.**

Talking about the past	Talking about recent experiences	Talking about the present	Talking about the future
Last year	___	___	___
___	___	___	___
___	___		

4 **Work with a partner. You have been asked to introduce a speaker at a conference. Student A, turn to File 35 on page 142. Student B, turn to File 53 on page 146. Take turns to give your presentation.**

>> For more exercises, go to **Practice file 16** on page 132.

5 **Give a presentation about yourself to a partner. Include:**
- your education
- your previous employment
- your recent experiences
- your present role
- your plans for your future.

(i) >> Interactive Workbook >> **Email** and >> **Exercises and Tests**

Ambition!

1 Work with a partner. You need two coins and two copies of the *Student's Book*. Use the board in one book to play the game. The object of the game is to reach the final square first and become the M.D.

2 Start on the FIRST DAY square. Student A, toss your coin. If it lands on heads, move one square. If it lands on tails, move two squares. Follow the instructions written on the square you have landed on.

3 Student B, toss your coin, and so on.

4 Refer to the second *Student's Book*, if necessary, to remind yourselves of the language you need to use.

IT'S THE **FIRST DAY** OF YOUR NEW JOB!	Introduce yourself to a partner and tell them something about yourself. **1**	Ask politely what your colleague's phone number is. **2**	Call a client to confirm a delivery. He / she isn't in the office. **3**	Spell your first name, surname, and the name of your company. **4**
Discuss your progress on the new company catalogue. Chosen photos ✓ Written text ½ Sent to printers ✗ **9**	Delegate three jobs to your partner. **8**	You are off sick. MISS A TURN **7**	Welcome a visitor to your company. **6**	Your laptop is stolen. MISS A TURN **5**
You are SACKED for losing a client. GO BACK TO START **10**	Check in at a company Reception. **11**	Make a lunch arrangement with your partner for next week. **12**	Suggest how to deal with the number of days off taken by staff in your department. Respond to your partner's suggestions. **13**	Give a short formal presentation about your company. **14**
Explain the trends and changes in one area of your company to your partner. Choose from: size; employees; sales; markets. **19**	Tell your partner 1 the number of employees in your company 2 the percentage of women 3 the population of your country. **18**	Invite your partner to go to the theatre with you this weekend. **17**	You are having a business lunch. Recommend some food to a partner. **16**	You are SACKED for missing a meeting. GO BACK TO START **15**
Your company is going to outsource the IT Department. Make predictions about what will happen. **20**	You go on holiday. MISS A TURN **21**	Thank your partner for showing you around their company and say goodbye. **22**	You are at an interview for the post of Managing Director. Give a presentation about yourself. **23**	WELL DONE! YOU'VE BECOME M. D.

Activity

Working with words

1 Match 1–6 to a–f.

1 Our annual sales are _d_
2 We're based ___
3 We make ___
4 We sell ___
5 We specialize ___
6 We provide ___

a ... phone services.
b ... in many different countries.
c ... in phones for children under twelve.
d ... €300 million.
e ... mobile phones.
f ... in the north of Italy.

2 Choose the correct word in *italics* to complete the text.

My company ¹*produces / products* specialized software for the film industry. Our ²*head / based* office is near San Francisco, but we also ³*specialize / operate* in Europe and the Far East where we have two ⁴*services / subsidiaries*. There are 450 ⁵*employs / employees* in the company. We ⁶*sell / sales* our ⁷*produce / goods* to companies like Dreamworks which ⁸*provide / make* animated movies. Our technology is very new, so we don't have many ⁹*competitors / companies*.

3 Complete the sentences using a suitable word from **2** in the correct form.

1 We have annual __sales__ of $25 million.
2 Not many _____ in the world have more than 100,000 employees.
3 Totalgaz is one of the _____ of Total Group.
4 We only sell these _____ in Europe and North America.
5 Where exactly is your company _____?
6 H&M _____ in good-quality clothes at low prices.
7 A lot of pizza restaurants _____ home delivery services.
8 The TATA Group _____ on all six continents.
9 We offer a wide range of consulting _____.
10 What exactly does your company _____?

Business communication

1 Rachel Steadman meets Gideon Lack at an international car show. Complete the conversation below with sentences a–j.

a Nice to meet you too,
b Can I introduce you to her?
c And what do you do?
d What's your name again?
e What about you?
f This is Rachel.
g So why are you at an international car show?
h Can I introduce myself?
i Nice to meet you.
j What does the company do?

Rachel Excuse me. Can I sit here?
Gideon Yes, of course.
Rachel Thanks very much. ¹_h_ I'm Rachel Steadman.
Gideon ²___ I'm Gideon Lack.
Rachel ³___ Gideon. Where are you from?
Gideon I'm from Switzerland originally. But I live in the Czech Republic now. ⁴___? Where are you based?
Rachel In Toronto.
Gideon And who do you work for?
Rachel Bos. Perhaps you don't know it.
Gideon No, I don't. ⁵___
Rachel It's an advertising agency. I'm here with Honda. It's one of our clients. ⁶___
Gideon I'm a teacher of Greek literature.
Rachel That's unusual. ⁷___
Gideon I'm here with my wife. She works for BMW. Ah, there she is now. ⁸___
Rachel Yes, of course. That would be nice.
Gideon Sorry, ⁹___
Rachel Rachel. Rachel Steadman.
Gideon Ursula. ¹⁰___ She works for an advertising agency in Canada.

Language at work | Present simple

Present simple

Form

Positive: Add *-s* or *-es* after the verb with *he / she / it*.

I / you / we / they **specialize** in Latin American music.

He / She / It **specializes** in high-tech products.

Negative: Use the auxiliary *do / does* + *not* + verb.

It **doesn't produce** software.

We **don't produce** mobile phones.

Questions

1 Use *do* and *does*, but don't change the form of the main verb (no *-s*).

Does it **have** a subsidiary in China?

Do you **have** many competitors?

2 With question words (*who, what, where, how*, etc.), use *do* and *does* after the question word.

Where **do you work?**

What **does he do?**

3 To give a short answer to questions in the present simple, use the subject + *does / do* or *doesn't / don't*.

Do you work for a multinational company?
Yes, **I do.** / No, **I don't.**

Does your company operate in South America?
Yes, **it does.** / No, **it doesn't.**

Exceptions

1 The verb *be* is irregular.

I **am**

You / We / They **are**

He / She / It **is**

2 In questions with *be*, do not use *do* and *does*.

Is he Spanish?

Where **are** the subsidiaries?

3 In negative sentences with *be*, add *not* or *n't*.

I'm not from China.

They **aren't** in the company today.

Use

1 To talk about facts or things which are generally true.

The company **provides** insurance services.

2 To talk about regular actions.

We **have** sales meetings every month.

3 Do not use the present simple to talk about actions in progress at this moment. Use the present continuous for this (see page 105).

1 Complete the sentences with a verb from the list.

start   starts   work   works   is   are
specialize   specializes   have   ~~has~~

1 The company ___*has*___ three subsidiaries in the Far East.

2 She _____ in Manchester today.

3 We _____ in the advertising of children's toys.

4 The meeting always _____ at 2.30 p.m.

5 She _____ for an engineering company.

6 They usually _____ work at about 7.00 a.m.

7 I _____ one office in Paris and another in Buenos Aires.

8 He's a lawyer. He _____ in company law.

9 Most of our competitors _____ in Europe.

10 I _____ in sales.

2 Choose the correct words or phrases in *italics*, then match the questions to answers 1–10 in **1**.

a What *do / ~~does~~* you specialize in? _*3*_

b Who *do / does* your wife work for? ___

c *Have you / Do you have* an office in Paris? ___

d Where *be / is* she? ___

e What *do / does* you do? ___

f Who *do be / are* your competitors? ___

g Where *has / does* the company have subsidiaries? ___

h When do they *start / starts* work? ___

i What time *do / does* the meeting start? ___

j What *is / does* he do? ___

3 Complete the missing words. The last letter of each word is given.

1 A __*I*__s your Head Office in London?

   B No, our company __*isn*__'t British. It's American.

2 I'm sorry, but we _____'t have a sales office in the Middle East.

3 What sort of products _____s your company sell?

4 A He _____'t work in Munich any more.

   B Really. So why _____s he have a flat there?

5 They _____'t in the company today. They're on a business trip.

6 I _____'t know how many employees they have.

Working with words

1 Match the jobs or organizations in the list to the people talking in 1–7.

a customer	a supplier	a subcontractor
a consultant	~~a colleague~~	an employment agency
a training organization		

1 If you want to leave early, I can finish that for you.
a colleague

2 There are three new management courses starting next month. _____

3 We now have those chairs you ordered. I'll send them today. _____

4 I have two more CVs which look interesting for that sales job. _____

5 I'm afraid we can't accept any more work from you this month. _____

6 I'm interested in your products. Can you send me some more information? _____

7 I'll email you a report on Monday, and then we can talk about it. _____

2 Match 1–5 to a–e to make complete sentences.

1 My job involves _d_
2 I deal ____
3 My job consists ____
4 I'm involved ____
5 I'm taking ____

a ... of taking orders from customers.
b ... in training new staff.
c ... part in an interesting new project.
d ~~... working very long hours.~~
e ... with a lot of customer problems.

3 Choose the correct word in *italics*.

1 He's ~~involves~~ / *involved* in two or three big research projects.
2 I want to *deal* / *take part* with my email before I leave.
3 Her job *consists* / *involves* travelling all round the world.
4 He can't *involve* / *take part* in this morning's meeting – he's too busy.
5 His work *consists* / *involves* of finding new customers in Eastern Europe.

Business communication

1 Seth Guterson wants to speak to Yolanda Cascarino, but she isn't there. Complete his phone conversation with the receptionist using the words in the list.

| help | ~~speak~~ | calling | afraid | give |
| take | back | Does | ask | This |

Seth Could I ¹ _speak_ to Yolanda Cascarino, please?
Receptionist Who's ² _____, please?
Seth ³ _____ is Seth Guterson.
Receptionist I'm ⁴ _____ Yolanda's in a meeting at the moment. Can I ⁵ _____ a message?
Seth Yes, sure. Can you ⁶ _____ her to call me ⁷ _____?
Receptionist OK. So that's Seth Guterson. ⁸ _____ she have your number?
Seth Yes, she does.
Receptionist OK, Seth. I'll ⁹ _____ her the message.
Seth Thanks for your ¹⁰ _____. Goodbye.

2 A few hours later, Seth is still waiting for Yolanda to call. He phones her again. Put the words in *italics* in the correct order to complete the conversation.

Seth *please / Yolanda / there / Is*
¹ _Is Yolanda there, please_ ?

Yolanda *Seth / is / speaking / that / Yes,*
² _____?

Seth Yes, it is. Hi, Yolanda.
Yolanda Hi, Seth.

customer / about / you / Japanese / phoning / Are / that
³ _____?

Seth Yes, I am. I have his contact details.

I'm / I'm / to / that / sending / calling / them / you / tell / now ⁴ _____.

Yolanda Great, Seth.

calling / very / Thanks / for / much
⁵ _____.

Seth You're welcome.

or / tomorrow / you / later / to / maybe / Speak
⁶ _____.

Language at work | Present continuous

Present continuous

Form

Positive: Use *am / is / are + -ing* form.

*He's **preparing** his presentation.*

Negative: Use *am / is / are + not + -ing* form.

*They're **not working** today.*

Questions

1 To make questions with the present continuous, put *am / is / are* before the subject.

Are you staying in this hotel?

Where is she working?

2 To give a short answer to *yes / no* questions in the present continuous, use the subject + *am / is / are*.

Are you working on this now?

Yes, I am. / No, I'm not.

Use

1 To describe actions in progress at the moment of speaking.

Hi. I'm calling you from my car.

2 To describe actions in progress around the present time, but not always at the moment of speaking.

He's doing a very interesting course this month.

3 To describe current trends.

The company is doing well in South-East Asia.

Language tip

Use the present simple to talk about regular or repeated actions (see page 103).

Do say: *She **calls** me once or twice a month.*

Don't say: *She's calling me twice a month.*

---

1 Complete the sentences with the present continuous form of the verbs in brackets.

1 (we / develop) *We are developing* a new range of products for South America.

2 (he / stay) _____ at the Intercontinental Hotel?

3 (you / not / listen) _____
_____ to me. What did I say?

4 (I / leave) _____
now. See you tomorrow.

5 Why (those German engineers / visit) _____
_____ the company?

2 Match questions 1–6 with answers a–f.

1 What is she doing? _c_

2 What does she do? ____

3 Are you working this week? ____

4 Do you work at weekends? ____

5 Why do you leave the office so late? ____

6 Why are you leaving the office so late? ____

a She's a teacher.

b Yes, but only four days.

c A Master's in Business Studies.

d My boss always asks to see me at about 7.00 p.m.

e We had a very long meeting.

f No, never.

3 Read this email and choose the correct form of the verb in *italics*.

Hello,

I ¹*write / am writing* to ask if you ²*have / are having* a sales office or sales rep in Argentina. I ³*work / am working* for a small computer producer here and we ⁴*look / are looking* for a new supplier of sound cards. We usually ⁵*buy / are buying* from a supplier in the USA, but their products ⁶*become / are becoming* too expensive for us.

We have over 30 shops in Argentina and we ⁷*open / are opening* another five this year.

We also regularly ⁸*get / are getting* business by mail order via our website.

We ⁹*try / are trying* to find a new supplier before the end of this month, so please contact me as soon as possible.

Best regards
Elena Suarez

Working with words

1 The people in sentences 1–10 all have problems. Match problems 1–10 to the departments a–j that they call for help.

1 5% of the products we made today were defective. _d_

2 My phone doesn't work. ___

3 I need a new assistant in my department. ___

4 I want to do a course to improve my English. ___

5 I don't know if we have enough cash in the bank to pay this supplier. ___

6 I want customers to know about this new product. ___

7 I want to buy some new furniture for my office. ___

8 A customer has just called to say he isn't happy. ___

9 I want to know if we can transport an order to a customer before Friday. ___

10 I need a new program which works more quickly. ___

a Customer Services

b Logistics

c Technical Support

d ~~Quality Control~~

e Training

f Finance

g Human Resources

h Marketing

i IT

j Purchasing

2 Choose the correct answer from the phrases in *italics*.

1 The company *is divided into* / ~~*divides into*~~ / ~~*is divide between*~~ three business units.

2 She's *charged of* / *in charge of* / *charge for* the Logistics Department.

3 The Sales Manager *is reported to* / *reports to* / *reports at* the Sales and Marketing Director.

4 The IT Manager is responsible *for* / *of* / *to* developing new software solutions.

5 We have a lot of contact *to* / *on* / *with* the Finance Department.

Business communication

1 Look at the three diagrams. Which diagram

1 is a pie chart? _b_

2 is a graph? ___

3 is a table? ___

4 shows rises in sales? ___

5 shows rises and falls in sales? ___

6 shows the breakdown of sales by region? ___

7 doesn't give any figures ? ___

a　　　　　Export sales

b　　　　　Export sales

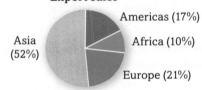

Asia (52%)　Americas (17%)　Africa (10%)　Europe (21%)

c　　Total sales by quarter

Q1	$24.5 m
Q2	$22.3 m
Q3	$25.1 m
Q4	$28.2 m

2 Put the words in *italics* in the right order to complete the sentences from a presentation.

1 Here's a diagram of our company structure. *that / clear / Is*   _Is that clear_   ?

2 Here are our sales figures. *OK / see / everybody / that / Can* _____?

3 *see / you / As / can* _____ _____, we had a good year.

4 *thing / The / here / is / important* _____ _____ the number of new customers.

5 *at / look / Have / table / a / this* _____ _____. It shows our sales figures for the first quarter of the year.

6 *breakdown / of / table / the / This / shows / sales* _____ _____. Can you see that?

Language at work | Asking questions

Questions

Form

1 The normal order of words in a question is:
question word or phrase + auxiliary + subject + verb.
Where do you work?
How many days is he staying?

2 The order of words is the same even when the subject consists of several words.
*What time are **the CEO and the Production Manager** arriving?*

3 In questions with a *yes / no* answer, the order of words is:
auxiliary + subject + verb.
Does he work in production?
Are you opening a new office?

4 The auxiliary and verb form are different for each tense:
Present simple: *do / does* + verb
*Where **does he live**?*

Present continuous: *am / is / are* + *-ing*
*Why **are** you **calling**?*

Past simple: *did* + verb
*What time **did you arrive**?*

For more information on the past simple, see page 109.

Exceptions

1 When the verb *be* is the main verb, there is no auxiliary. The order of words in a question is:
question word(s) + verb + subject.
When is the meeting?
Where was he yesterday?

2 When the question word (or words) is the subject of the sentence, there is no auxiliary. The order of words is:
question word(s) + verb.
Who works here?
How many people are coming?

1 Choose the correct question from a or b.

1 a Where does your boss work?
  b ~~Where works your boss?~~
2 a What do you make products here?
  b What products do you make here?
3 a Why is changing your logo?
  b Why is your logo changing?
4 a Do you have a canteen here?
  b Have you a canteen here?
5 a How often the company does launch new products?
  b How often does the company launch new products?
6 a Who does the Sales Manager report to?
  b Who the Sales Manager reports to?
7 a Does the company opening any new factories?
  b Is the company opening any new factories?
8 a How long ago did you move here?
  b How long you did move here ago?
9 a When do your offices are open?
  b When are your offices open?
10 a How many people are work in this department?
   b How many people work in this department?

2 A manager of Wrigley's, famous for its chewing gum, is answering questions about the company. Look at his answers and decide what questions the journalist asked. Use the words in *italics* to help you and add any other words you need.

1 *your / Where / sell / products / you*
  Q _Where do you sell your products_ ?
  A In more than 150 countries.
2 *the company / When / start*
  Q _____?
  A In 1891.
3 *its head office / have / Where / it*
  Q _____?
  A In Chicago.
4 *people / employ / many / the company / How*
  Q _____?
  A About 15,000.
5 *chewing gum / much / Americans / How / eat*
  Q _____?
  A About 180 servings of gum per year.

Working with words

1 Complete the text by finishing the words.

Masai Barefoot Technology

The Swiss engineer, Karl Muller, had the ¹ _original idea_ for MBTs when he noticed that walking in Korea with no shoes helped his back pain. Back in Switzerland he started experimenting with shoes that copied barefoot walking. He did some ²m_____ r_____. After ten years, he completed the ³d_____ of his first shoe, the Schritt Masai (Masai Step), but he did many more ⁴p_____ t_____ before it went on the market. When he was satisfied he ⁵b_____ the p_____ with the name of an East African tribe, the Masai, who are well known for running barefoot through the bush. He ⁶l_____ the shoes in 2000 and sold 20,000 pairs that year. Since then, Karl Muller has sold over a million pairs of MBTs in 20 different countries in the world.

2 Complete the clues to the crossword. Then use your answers to complete the crossword.

Clues across

4 Our carpooling system is much cheaper for the staff. It's more _economical_.

6 Our new car is much easier to park. It's very _____ for driving in the centre.

7 The new reception area looks more modern. It's quite _____.

8 They took a long time planning the new model. It's very _____.

Clues down

1 The new office furniture is exactly what we needed. It's very _____.

2 The operating system on my computer is easy to use. It's very _____.

3 Jack's new PDA fits in his pocket. It's quite _____.

5 I really like our new uniforms. They're really _____.

Business communication

1 A catering company has done some research into buying a new marquee. Put the sentences in the report about the research in the right order.

a __1__ The purpose of our research was to find a new marquee to replace our old ones. We wanted

b ____ Finally, we interviewed the customer and our employees. We asked

c ____ our technicians what they thought of the marquee. We found

d ____ that the T-system was easier to pack and transport than our old ones.

e ____ to the Sales Director who agreed to let us have one on trial.

f ____ Why did we choose the T-system Marquee? Because of its spacious design.

g ____ Then, we took the marquee to our next venue and put it up.

h ____ First, we contacted Bond Fabrications which produces marquees. We spoke

i ____ to find out how easy the marquee would be to transport.

2 A restaurant has done some research into buying new uniforms for its staff. Complete the report about the research using the phrases below.

Finally	We found that	We wanted
Then	Why do we need	We spoke to
First	~~The purpose~~	We asked customers and staff

I'm here to report on our research into companies that make staff uniforms.

¹ _The purpose_ of our research was to find a company that creates original designs at a reasonable price.
² _____ to find the best company to design our next set of uniforms.
³ _____ new uniforms? Because customers have complained about the appearance of our serving staff. ⁴_____, we made a list of all the possible companies we could find.
⁵ _____, we chose the top three companies. ⁶_____ the Sales Department of each of the companies and asked them to send us a sample design.
⁷_____, three members of staff wore the samples in the restaurant for a week.
⁸_____ for their opinion of the uniforms. ⁹_____ the most popular uniform with customers was the one designed by Business Style because of its bright colours and modern design. The staff also preferred this uniform because it was comfortable and easy to wash.

Language at work | Past simple

Past simple

Form

Positive: Add -ed to the infinitive of regular verbs.

We started work at 7.00 yesterday.

Add -d to the infinitive or **regular verbs** ending in -e.

She lived in Switzerland.

Change the -y to -i and add -ed to **regular verbs** ending in consonant + -y.

He tried to find a new job.

Double the final consonant of short **regular verbs** ending in vowel + consonant.

I stopped the car.

Many verbs are irregular. Irregular verb forms do not end in -ed.

For **irregular verb forms** see page 134.

Negative: Put *didn't* before the infinitive of both regular and irregular verbs.

I didn't want to be late for the meeting.

They didn't see the manager.

Questions

1 Put *did* before the subject and the infinitive of both regular and irregular verbs.

When did they arrive?

Where did you go?

2 To give a short answer to *yes / no* questions in the past simple, use the subject + *did / didn't*.

Did he email you yesterday? Yes, he did. / No, he didn't.

Use

Use the past simple to describe a finished action in the past.

They sent the parcel on Monday, but it didn't arrive until Friday.

Words and phrases we often use with the past simple are:
yesterday, last week, last year, in 2005, five years ago.

Language tip

The verb *be* does not use the auxiliary verb *did* to form the negative or questions.

The manager wasn't in the office yesterday.

Were the products well-designed?

---

1 Complete the text with the past simple form of the verbs in brackets.

Last week I ¹ _was_ (be) very busy. On Monday morning our biggest customer ² _____ (visit) our factory. I ³ _____ (meet) her at the airport at 7.00 in the morning and ⁴ _____ (take) her to the plant. In the afternoon we ⁵ _____ (have) a meeting which ⁶ _____ (not finish) late, and she ⁷ _____ (want) to see a show afterwards. On Tuesday I ⁸ _____ (fly) to Berlin for a conference. In the afternoon I ⁹ _____ (make) a presentation which ¹⁰ _____ (not go) very well. The next day I ¹¹ _____ (go) to Stuttgart to meet a supplier. On Thursday we ¹² _____ (interview) candidates for the new sales jobs, but we ¹³ _____ (not find) anybody suitable. In the evening I ¹⁴ _____ (play) squash in the company tournament, but, unfortunately, I ¹⁵ _____ (not win). On Friday I ¹⁶ _____ (reply) to all my emails and ¹⁷ _____ (write) a proposal for an Austrian company. In the afternoon I ¹⁸ _____ (attend) a planning meeting which ¹⁹ _____ (end) very late in the evening. I ²⁰ _____ (not get) home until midnight!

2 Complete the questions.

1 What _time did they arrive_____ ?
They arrived at 9 o'clock.

2 Where _____ ?
We had lunch in the staff canteen.

3 Who _____ at the conference?
I saw our colleagues from the Buenos Aires office.

4 Why _____ the meeting?
The manager left the meeting because he had an urgent phone call.

5 Which hotel _____ at?
They stayed at the Hilton.

6 When _____ the company?
She joined the company last year.

7 How long _____ with the visitors?
I spent all day with them.

8 How many emails _____ ?
We sent about a hundred.

Working with words

1 Name these company benefits by matching a word from A to a word from B.

A	B
maternity	membership
flexible	childcare
~~paid~~	scheme
private	phone
gym	hours
company	~~holiday~~
mobile	leave
pension	car
annual	healthcare
subsidized	bonus

1 I get five weeks a year. ____*paid holiday*____

2 I don't pay any medical bills. _____

3 I use it during the week for work, but I can also use it at the weekend for family trips. _____

4 I don't think about it now, but it will be very useful when I'm 65. _____

5 My daughter hasn't started school, so it's great to have help with this. _____

6 It's a new club, so all the equipment is really up-to-date. _____

7 We get an extra two days' pay if our results are 5% higher than the last year. _____

8 I do all my hours from Monday to Thursday. Then I have Friday free. _____

9 It's a really important benefit for women who want a family. _____

10 I can even watch TV on the new one they've given me! _____

2 Complete the text from a company's jobs website with a suitable word.

How do I ¹ _apply_ for the job?

Go to the 'Documents' page (click here) and print a copy of the ²_____ form. ³_____ in the form, and attach an updated version of your ⁴_____. This should include a description of your work experience, educational qualifications, and the names of three ⁵_____, together with their contact details. Send both documents to the address at the top of this page.

What happens next?

If you are shortlisted for this ⁶_____, we will contact you by phone before 31 March to arrange an ⁷_____. Unsuccessful ⁸_____ will be informed by letter, also by 31 March.

Business communication

1 Choose the correct response.

1 Where are we with the Lufthansa contract?
   a ~~We're in Munich.~~
   b They haven't signed yet.
   c ~~Yes, we are there.~~

2 I can't contact the IT Manager – his line's always busy.
   a I'm very busy at the moment.
   b Can you call him?
   c OK, leave it with me.

3 Have you prepared the job description yet?
   a I did it last week.
   b I can deal with that.
   c You're very short of time.

4 Can you deal with that customer in Lagos for me?
   a Have you done it?
   b I'll leave it with you.
   c I've already spoken to him.

5 It's Friday, and we haven't even finished the first part of the presentation.
   a Yes, time's running out.
   b We've already done it.
   c Where are we?

2 Stella Wu and Antonio Brocci are discussing the introduction of a new flexitime system in their company. Complete these sentences from their conversation with the words in the list.

short	already	about
Where	out	with
Leave	~~hasn't~~	yet

1 The clock-in machine ___*hasn't*___ arrived yet.

2 Can you deal _____ that issue?

3 _____ it with me.

4 I've been very _____ of time this week.

5 _____ are we with the new flexitime system?

6 I've _____ talked to the Human Resources Manager.

7 Time's running _____.

8 What _____ the clock-in system?

9 Have you talked to the staff _____?

Language at work | Present perfect (1)

Present perfect

Form

Positive: *have / has* + past participle form.

> I **have (I've) finished** my work.

> He **has (He's) written** three letters today.

Negative: *have / has* + *not* + past participle.

> They **haven't done** the work this week.

> The post **hasn't arrived** yet.

Questions

1 Put *have / has* before the subject.

> **Have you** seen the new Production Manager?

> Where **has she** been today?

2 To give a short answer to *yes / no* questions in the present perfect, use the subject + *has / have* or *hasn't / haven't*.

> Have you seen that report yet?

> Yes, **I have**. / No, **I haven't**.

> Has the HR Manager seen the CVs?

> Yes, **she has**. / No, **she hasn't**.

Use

1 To talk about past actions where the time includes the present.

> I've **made** three presentations today / this week / this month.

2 To describe progress in a list of things to do, we use *already* and *(not) … yet?*

> Have you visited that customer **yet**?

> No, I haven't had time **(yet)**. But I've **already** made an appointment with him.

3 To ask someone about general experiences in his / her life, we use *ever*.

> Have you **ever** seen the Taj Mahal?

> No, never.

4 Use the present perfect to talk about actions which started in the past and are continuing now. For more information, see page 125.

> I've **worked** here for three years (and I still work here now).

5 For past actions where the time doesn't include the present, use the past simple.

> I **haven't seen** him **today**, but I **saw** him **yesterday**.

Language tip

For regular verbs, the past participle form is **always** the same as the past simple: verb + *-(e)d*
For irregular verbs, the past participle and past simple forms are **sometimes** the same. For a list of irregular verbs, see page 134.

---

1 **A customer service manager is talking about the situation in his department. Complete the text with the present perfect form of the verbs in brackets.**

This month ¹ _hasn't been_____ (be) a very good one for me. Three more members of my team ²_____ (tell) me that they are leaving the company. Two of them ³_____ (not / find) another job yet, but they say that the pressure of work ⁴_____ (become) too much for them. It's true that there ⁵_____ (be) a big increase in their work this year because two other customer service assistants ⁶_____ (already / leave) the department and we ⁷_____ (not / recruit) anybody to replace them. I ⁸_____ (ask) my boss several times if we can employ some new people for the team, but each time he ⁹_____ (say) that we need to reduce our salary costs. But I know we ¹⁰_____ (lose) some business because we ¹¹_____ (not / have) enough people to deal with customer calls.

The situation can't continue like this. I ¹²_____ (not / made) a final decision on this yet, but I'm thinking of leaving the company myself.

2 **Choose the correct answer from the words in *italics* to complete questions 1–8. Then match them with responses a–h.**

1 *Did you read / ~~Have you read~~* that article about e-recruitment last week?

2 *Did you see / Have you seen* the new Dali exhibition yet?

3 *Have you ever / Did you yet* applied for a job online?

4 *Have you had / Did you have* any work experience when you joined this company?

5 *Has / Have* she made many calls today?

6 *Have / Did* all the candidates come for interview yesterday?

7 *Have you received / Did you receive* a bonus in the last six months?

8 *Have you learnt / Did you learn* a lot in your last job?

a No, never. ____

b No, I haven't. Our results haven't been very good. ____

c Just one or two this morning. ____

d Yes, I did. I did several jobs when I was a student. ____

e No, I didn't. I didn't have much responsibility, so it was very boring. ____

f Yes, it was very well-written. _1_

g Just one person wasn't there. ____

h No, I haven't had time. ____

Working with words

1 Match the verbs 1–6 to nouns a–f.

1 conduct _e_   a a personalized service
2 encourage ___   b repeat business
3 offer ___   c customer loyalty
4 deal with ___   d complaints
5 get ___   e ~~surveys~~
6 meet ___   f the needs of customers

2 Complete the text about the Customer Service Department of a telecommunications company with a suitable form of a phrase from **1**.

Developments in the telecommunications industry happen so fast, that we are always ¹___ _conducting surveys_ ___ to find out exactly what our customers want.
We ²_____ in the 21st century by offering quick and easy connections to Internet users. We have a call centre which is open 24 hours a day to
³_____ and we charge nothing for the call. We ⁴_____ by giving free local calls to customers who have been with us for more than two years.
We ⁵_____ by suggesting ways of reducing their phone bill to individual customers and this means we ⁶_____ from them.

3 Decide if the word in *italics* in each sentence is right (✓) or wrong (✗). Change the words which are wrong.

1 It was *possible* to contact the manager, so I sent him an email. ___✗ *impossible*___
2 We're very happy with our courier service because the drivers are so *reliable*. _____
3 The person on the phone was very *helpful*, so I made a complaint. _____
4 We ended our cleaning contract because we were *satisfied* with the service. _____
5 The bank gave us a special rate because we are *loyal* customers. _____

Business communication

1 Choose the correct answer in *italics* in sentences 1–6. Then match the sentences to responses a–f.

1 *What / How* do you think about that proposal?
2 *Are / Do* you agree that we should contact them now?
3 I think *you're / you have* right.
4 I don't feel we *should / shouldn't* do anything now.
5 *I'm not / I don't* agree with you.
6 *What / How* do you feel about closing the factory?

a Good. I'm glad you agree with me. ___
b I don't agree with it at all. _1_
c Yes, I do. ___
d I agree with you. It's too early. ___
e It seems like a good idea. ___
f Why not? ___

2 The participants in the meeting below are discussing ideas for improving phone skills. Sabina Dusek doesn't agree with the others. Complete the dialogue with phrases from the list.

I don't think   I think you're right
do you think   personally, I feel
do you feel   I don't agree at all
~~I think staff should~~   I agree

Albert If a customer has a complaint,
¹___ _I think staff should_ ___ say sorry immediately.
Sabina I'm sorry, but
²_____. If they say sorry, that means it's our fault.
Janek Oh, ³_____ so. We're just saying that we are sorry they have a problem. Customers like to hear that.
Albert ⁴_____ with you, Janek. In a survey we did recently, many of our customers said that the person they spoke to didn't understand the difficulties they were having.
Janek What ⁵_____ about this, Tomas?
Tomas Well, ⁶_____ there's something even more important here. Too many staff are telling customers that there's nothing they can do. They say the problem is the customer's fault. That's just not acceptable.
Albert Yes. ⁷_____.
How ⁸_____ about all this, Sabina? Don't you agree?
Sabina No, I'm afraid I don't. I think that some customers try to make us pay for their mistakes. But I agree that it's important to be polite and listen carefully first.

Language at work | Comparisons

Comparative and superlative forms

Form

1 Add *-er* or *-est* to one-syllable and some two-syllable adjectives.

> cheap   cheap**er**   the cheap**est**
>
> quiet   quiet**er**   the quiet**est**

If an adjective ends in *-y*, change the *-y* to an *-i* and add *-er* or *-est*.

> easy   eas**ier**   the eas**iest**

2 Double a consonant after a vowel at the end of short adjectives.

> hot   hot**ter**   the hot**test**
>
> big   big**ger**   the big**gest**

3 Some adjectives are irregular.

> good   better   the best
>
> bad   worse   the worst

4 Add *more* and *most* to two- or more syllable adjectives.

> expensive   **more expensive**   the **most expensive**

5 Add *than* after the comparative to compare two things / people.

> The Sales Manager is **more popular than** the Financial Manager.

Note: in the superlative form, you can also use *my, our, their,* etc. instead of *the*.

Use

1 Use the comparative to compare two things.

> Fridays are **better than** Mondays.

2 Use the superlative to compare one thing to many other things.

> Saturdays are **the best**.

3 To say something is the same, use *as* + adjective + *as*.

> My office is **as big as** yours.

4 To say something is different use *not as* + adjective + *as*.

> This machine **isn't as complicated as** the old one.

---

1 **Complete these sentences using the comparative or superlative form of the adjective in brackets.**

1 Our Managing Director is ____*younger*____ (young) than the Financial Director.

2 Our company was _____ (profitable) last year than this year.

3 We have seven factories; the _____ (large) one is in Mexico.

4 Hotels in London are _____ (expensive) than in Paris.

5 I think our new brochure is _____ (good) than our competitor's brochure.

6 Our _____ (famous) product is the VS520.

7 1995 was _____ (bad) year for our company ever.

8 Germany is _____ (big) country in the EU.

2 **A company is looking for a new office building. Read the information about the three possibilities. Tick (✓) the sentences which are true and correct the false sentences.**

Building	Master Tower	Edison Building	Soria Palace
Built	2000	2009	1989
Size	500m²	300m²	1,000m²
Cost	25,000 € / month	8,000 € / month	25,000 € / month
Distance from city centre	5km	20km	0km

1 The Master Tower is more modern than the Edison Building.

> *The Master Tower is not as modern as / is less modern than the Edison Building.*

2 The Soria Palace is larger than the Master Tower.

3 The Edison Building is the most expensive.

4 The Soria Palace is more difficult to get to from the city centre than the Master Tower.

5 The Master Tower isn't as modern as the Soria Palace.

6 The Edison Building is the largest of the three buildings.

7 The Soria Palace is more expensive than the Master Tower.

8 The Edison Building is further from the city centre than the Soria Palace.

Working with words

1 **Complete the sentences.**

1 Our __*flight*__ lands in Helsinki at 19.30.

2 I hope we will make our _____ to New York in Frankfurt.

3 What time does the train to the airport _____?

4 Would all passengers for Flight LH 129 go to _____ 16?

5 We have a _____ for a double room for two nights.

6 Exercise _____ in the hotel include a pool, a spa, and a gym.

7 How many pieces of hand _____ can I take on the plane?

8 Passengers with small children usually _____ the plane first.

9 We were late because our plane was _____ for an hour in Stockholm.

10 You can put valuables in the _____ in your room.

2 **Match 1–9 to a–i to make phrases. Then complete the sentences with the phrases.**

1	single *bed*	a	building
2	shuttle __	b	~~bed~~
3	departure __	c	trip
4	key __	d	bus
5	terminal __	e	desk
6	double __	f	room
7	one-way __	g	lounge
8	business __	h	card
9	check-in __	i	ticket

1 My hotel room was so small that there was only space for a ___*single bed*___.

2 We did some shopping in the _____ before we went to our gate.

3 She couldn't get into her hotel room because she didn't have her _____.

4 There's a _____ between terminals every five minutes.

5 Jack's wife accompanied him to Paris, so the company booked a _____.

6 The taxi dropped us off outside the _____.

7 He bought a _____ to Rome because he didn't know when to come back.

8 The manager of the office is away on a _____ this week.

9 They told us at the _____ that our flight was cancelled.

Business communication

1 **Match 1–8 to responses a–h.**

1 Did you have a good journey? _e_

2 Is this your first time in Tokyo? __

3 Did you see the palace? __

4 Do you often go away on business? __

5 Where do you usually go on holiday? __

6 Are you interested in water sports? __

7 What kind of music do you like? __

8 What did you think of the Dalí museum? __

a Yes, I am. I love windsurfing and jet-skiing.

b Oh, anything really. And I love going to concerts.

c I thought it was great.

d No, unfortunately I didn't get the chance.

e ~~Yes, it was fine thanks. Just a short delay in Paris.~~

f No, I came a few times when I was a student.

g I usually go to Greece with my family.

h Yes. I have two or three trips a month.

2 **Complete the conversation with a word from the list**

been   Did   go   kind   often   see   think   ~~trip~~

A Did you have a good ¹___*trip*___?

B It was a bit tiring actually. We were delayed for two hours at Heathrow.

A You must be fed up then. Have you ²_____ to Marrakech before?

B No, this is my first visit.

A Do you ³_____ travel abroad on business?

B No, hardly ever. I prefer going abroad on holiday.

A Really? Where do you usually ⁴_____?

B We go somewhere different every year. Last year we went to Thailand.

A Did you ⁵_____ the Reclining Buddha?

B Yes, I did. Bangkok was really interesting.

A ⁶_____ you visit the islands, too?

B Yes. We went to the island from the film 'The Beach'.

A What did you ⁷_____ of it?

B It was a bit disappointing really. There were too many tourists.

A What ⁸_____ of films do you like?

B I prefer action films really. And you?

A Me too. And thrillers.

Language at work | Countable and uncountable nouns

Nouns

Form

1 Nouns are either countable or uncountable. Countable nouns have a single and plural form. Uncountable nouns have one form.

Countable nouns: *room (rooms), bus (buses), city (cities)*
Uncountable nouns: *money, information, luggage*

2 Most plural countable nouns end in *-s* but some are irregular.

person → people   woman → women   child → children

3 Use *a* or *an* with singular countable nouns.

a reservation   an appointment

Use *some* with plural countable nouns and uncountable nouns.

some facilities   some information

4 Singular countable nouns use a singular verb form.

***Is there a shuttle bus** to Terminal 3?*

***My flight is** delayed.*

Plural countable nouns use a plural verb form.

***Are** there many **people** at the check-in desk?*

*The **tickets aren't** very expensive.*

Uncountable nouns use a singular verb form.

***Is there time** for us to look in the Duty Free shop?*

*Our **luggage is** already on the plane.*

Many / much

Use

1 Use *many* only with plural countable nouns.

***How many gates** are there in Terminal 1?*

*Not **many**.*

2 Use *much* only with uncountable nouns.

***How much money** did you spend?*

*Not **much**.*

3 *Much* and *many* are mostly used in questions or negative statements.

***How many** employees are there in your company?*

***How much** hand luggage have you got?*

*There **aren't many** people at the gate.*

*There **isn't much** time between our connecting flights.*

Language tip

Many nouns that are countable in a lot of other languages are uncountable in English.

Say: *information*

Don't say: ~~an information, informations~~

Other examples: *advice, equipment, accommodation*

---

1 **Write the words from the list in the correct place in the table.**

~~bill~~   flight   hotel   information   luggage
money   reservation   suitcase   travel   work

Countable	Uncountable
bill	

2 **Choose the correct answer from the words in *italics*.**

1 I don't need to take *much* / ~~many~~ luggage as I'm only staying for one night.

2 All my money *is* / *are* in the safe in my room.

3 There *is* / *are* a lot of traffic today.

4 How *many* / *much* people are waiting for the shuttle bus?

5 We got *a* / *some* bad news when we arrived at our destination.

6 My work *is* / *are* very near my house.

7 How *much* / *many* time have we got before we board?

8 The information the hotel receptionist gave us *was* / *were* wrong.

3 **A passenger is checking in for a flight. Complete the conversation with a suitable word.**

A Good morning. Can I have your passport, please?

B Hello. Yes, of course. Here you are.

A Thank you. How ¹ *many* suitcases have you got?

B Just this one. Can I have a window seat, please?

A I'm afraid there ²_____ any window seats, but I can give you ³_____ aisle seat.

B OK. That's fine.

A How ⁴_____ hand luggage are you carrying?

B I've got ⁵_____ laptop and a coat.

A That's fine. Now, here's your boarding pass.

B How much time ⁶_____ there before the plane takes off?

A Boarding will start in about an hour.

B OK, thank you. Just one more question. I need ⁷_____ money. ⁸_____ there any cash machines in the departure lounge?

A Yes, there are. They're just past the security check. Have a good flight.

Working with words

1 Choose the two possible correct answers from the words in *italics*.

1 I asked the company to give me *a quote / a delivery date / ~~an enquiry~~*.

2 The customer asked me for *a refund / an order / some prices*.

3 Jack called our supplier to make *some information / an enquiry / a complaint*.

4 We looked on the website to track the *shipment / delivery / refund*.

5 They were late paying their last *bill / goods / invoice*.

6 Eve confirmed the *order / price / complaint* by email.

7 Do you ever purchase *deliveries / goods / products* on the Internet?

2 Different customers are phoning suppliers in 1–8. Choose the correct answer from the words in *italics*.

1 Hello, I'm calling to ask about the goods we *~~quoted~~ / purchased* from your store last Monday. Can you tell me when you will *pay / deliver* them?

2 We'd like to *place / order* a hundred PDAs for customers, but we need them urgently. Could you *check / track* that you have enough in stock?

3 I'd like to *ask for / make* an enquiry about an order I recently made. I'm trying to *process / track* the shipment on your website, but it isn't working.

4 Can you *confirm / enquire* the price of the products we ordered from you? The price you *quoted / delivered* is different from the price on the invoice.

5 Good morning. I'm calling to *do / make* a complaint about your latest delivery. I'd like to *ask for / make* a refund because most of the products are broken.

6 Hello, I'm phoning to *cancel / enquire* my order. We've found another supplier who can *ship / track* the goods to us tomorrow.

7 Can I *place / purchase* an order for ten BlackBerrys, please? I'd also like to know if I can *confirm / change* the order if I decide I want something different.

8 How long does it take to *quote / process* an order? Also, how do you *confirm / check* the order – by email?

Business communication

1 Put these words in the right order to make suggestions.

1 we / team-building / a / Why / organize / don't / event
   Why don't we organize a team-building event?

2 about / we / order / think / Maybe / cancelling / the / should
   _____?

3 email / Head / sending / to / How / an / about / Office
   _____?

4 this / tomorrow / we / about / talk / again / Shall
   _____?

5 in / local / newspaper / We / the / could / advertise
   _____.

6 with / discuss / we / manager / this / I / the / suggest
   _____.

2 Complete the responses with a word from the list. Then match responses a–f to suggestions 1–6 in 1.

Fine   ~~great~~   Let's   sure   think   work

a That's a __great__ idea! Why don't we go paintballing? _1_

b I'm not _____ about that. Perhaps we should try to track it first. ___

c OK. _____ ask him what he thinks in our meeting tomorrow. ___

d Yes, I _____ you should call them right now and ask for a quote. ___

e I don't think that will _____. It's an internal problem, really. ___

f _____. I'll call you after lunch. ___

3 Three colleagues are discussing a recruitment problem. Put the dialogue in the right order 1–8.

a _1_ We've got too many orders right now. I think we need to take on a new person.

b ___ Yes, I agree. Why don't you make the phone call and we'll write the advert?

c ___ Good idea. That way we'll get local people. I suggest we call them right now.

d ___ Agencies are usually expensive. We could put an ad in the local paper. It comes out on Fridays.

e ___ I'm not sure about that. Most people who visit the website are interested in buying our products, not working for us.

f ___ What about placing an advert on our website? That way, people who are interested in the company will see it.

g ___ Well, we could contact a recruitment agency instead and get them to find some candidates.

h _8_ Fine.

Language at work | *will / going to / present continuous*

will

Form

Positive: *will* + verb
*I'll **meet** you at the reception desk in your hotel.*

Negative: *won't (will not)* + verb
*I **won't disturb** you.*

Questions: *will* + subject + verb
***Will you call** me later?*

Use

To make decisions at the moment of speaking.
A Can you let me have a number to contact you on?
*B Just a moment. I'll **give** you my business card.*

going to

Form

Positive: Subject + *am / is / are* + *going to* + verb
*I'm **going to look** for a new job after the holidays.*

Negative: Subject + *am / is / are* + *not* + *going to* + verb
*He **isn't going to work** late tonight.*

Questions: *am / is / are* + subject + *going to* + verb
***Are they going to look** for a new head of department?*

Use

To talk about a plan that we have already decided on.
*We're **going to move** to the new office in the spring.*

Present continuous

Form

See page 105.

Use

To talk about a future arrangement someone has made.
The arrangement usually has a fixed time or place.
*A What **are you doing** tomorrow after work?*
*B I'm **taking** my daughter to the dentist.*

Language tip

As well as the present continuous, we can often use *going to* for a future arrangement.

*The Managing Director's **visiting** the office tomorrow.*
*The Managing Director's **going to visit** the office tomorrow.*

---

1 **Choose the correct answer.**

1 There's no message. *I'm calling* / *I'll call* back later this afternoon.

2 It's her fiftieth birthday so *she's going to have* / *she'll have* a party.

3 You can call at any time because we *aren't going* / *won't go* out.

4 *I'm going to wash* / *I'll wash* my car tonight. It's really dirty.

5 He can't meet us tomorrow because *he'll visit* / *he's visiting* a client.

6 Don't worry about the taxi. It *won't be* / *isn't being* late.

7 I can't stand my job any longer, so *I'm going to look* / *I'll look* for a new one.

8 *She's playing* / *she'll play* tennis tonight, so she can't go to the dinner.

2 **Complete the mini conversations. Use *will*, *going to*, or the present continuous form of the verbs in brackets.**

1 A I can't hear you very well.
   B I'm sorry. I _____'ll speak_____ (speak) up a little.

2 A How are you getting on with that project?
   B We _____ (not finish) it on time.

3 A When are you going to talk to your boss about your timetable?
   B I _____ (meet) her tomorrow afternoon.

4 A When do we have to pay the invoice by?
   B I'm not sure. I _____ (ask) one of my colleagues.

5 A What are you doing tomorrow at 1 o'clock?
   B I _____ (have) lunch with a customer.

6 A Can you tell me when my order will arrive?
   B Just a moment. I _____ (check) with the driver.

7 A How did you get on at your job interview?
   B Really badly. I _____ (not get) the job.

Working with words

1 Complete these sentences with words from the list. You may need to change the form of the words.

offer	enter	share
~~promote~~	expand	launch
improve	discount	boost
attract		

1 Nobody knows our brand in this country. We need to _promote_ it.

2 If you have a loyalty card, we can _____ you a 5% discount.

3 We only have a small share of the European market and we need to _____ it.

4 We are _____ the new product in Asia next week.

5 The new bright colours for our product have _____ younger customers.

6 The very good summer helped to _____ our ice cream sales.

7 It will be difficult to _____ the Chinese market because we have no experience.

8 We have _____ our product range by introducing clothes for children.

9 If you have your student card, we can give you a _____ of 10%.

10 We need to increase our _____ of the European market.

2 Match the type of advertising to descriptions 1–6.

press ads	online adverts
outdoor advertising	~~direct mail~~
word-of-mouth	TV advertisements

1 I received this brochure in the post this morning. _direct mail_

2 Look at that billboard. They're advertising those running shoes again! _____

3 I love that ad! They've shown it three times this evening! _____

4 Let's go to that new Japanese restaurant. Rudi said it was very good. _____

5 They put our ad on page 10. There are so many other ads there, it's difficult to see it. _____

6 How much do we have to pay to put an ad on that website? _____

Business communication

1 Match 1–10 with a–j to make ten sentences you can use in a meeting.

1	We're here today _d_	a	... catch that.
2	I'm not ___	b	... you said?
3	I didn't ___	c	... with you.
4	What was that ___	d	~~... to discuss ...~~
5	Could you be ___	e	... to the next point?
6	We're getting off ___	f	... more specific?
7	We've covered ___	g	... what we've agreed?
8	We can come back ___	h	... the subject.
9	Can we move on ___	i	... everything ...
10	Can we sum up ___	j	... to that later.

2 Mike Thomson has called a meeting. One of the items on the agenda is the problem of wasting time in meetings. Complete the conversation with the sentences from 1.

Mike OK, can we start? [1] _We're here today to discuss_ how to make our meetings more effective. John, can you tell us about what you're doing in your department?

John Well, we've introduced the concept of the five-minute meeting. And it's working very well.

Pilar I'm sorry, [2] _____. Did you say a five-minute meeting?

John Yes, but it sometimes goes on for half an hour.

Hachirou Sorry, but [3] _____. Is it a five-minute meeting or a half an hour one?

John Well, the important thing is that it's short.

Mike [4] _____, John? How does the meeting work exactly?

John We meet every day after lunch and you inform everyone of where you are with your work and ...

Pilar Sorry, [5] _____?

John I said we meet every day after lunch for an update.

Sabine Why after lunch? Everyone's falling asleep then.

Mike I think [6] _____. Let's just talk about the idea itself. The time of day isn't important. If we have time, [7] _____.

(15 minutes later)

Mike OK, I think [8] _____ on the subject of the five-minute meeting. [9] _____ on the agenda: how to inform staff of decisions made in meetings?

(20 minutes later)

Mike So, very quickly, [10] _____ today? Sabine and Pilar are going to ...

Language at work | Modal verbs

Modal verbs

Use

1 To describe an action which is necessary, or a legal obligation, use *have to* or *need to*.

   You **have to** wear a seat belt when you are driving.

   We **need to** complete our tax form before 5th April.

2 To describe an action which isn't necessary, use *don't / doesn't have to* or *don't / doesn't need to*.

   We **don't have to** work at weekends in our company.

   The report **doesn't have to** be finished today.

3 For an action which is possible or permitted by law, use *can* or *be allowed to*.

   You **can** leave early today because we're not very busy.

   Companies **are allowed to** advertise alcohol after 10.00 p.m.

4 If the action isn't permitted, use *can't* or *am not / isn't / aren't allowed to*.

   Sorry, but you **can't** smoke here.

   Cyclists **aren't allowed to** use motorways.

Form

1 To ask a question with *have to* or *need to*, use *do* or *does*.

   Do I **have to** write this report now?

   Does the company **need to** have quality certification?

2 To ask a question with *be allowed to*, use *am / is / are*.

   Are cigarette companies **allowed to** advertise?

   Am I **allowed to** park here?

3 Questions with *can* begin with the word *can*.

   Can foreigners vote in national elections?

   Can I use my phone for personal calls?

1 Are these sentences true or false for your country? Correct them where necessary.

1 You're not allowed to drive a car if you don't have a licence.

2 Car drivers have to wear a seat belt.

3 Car passengers don't need to wear a seat belt.

4 You can't smoke in restaurants and pubs.

5 You're allowed to vote when you are 16 years old.

6 Products with lots of sugar need to carry a health warning.

7 Schoolchildren don't have to wear a uniform to school.

8 You can retire when you are 55 years old.

9 Advertisers aren't allowed to compare their products with their competitors.

10 Shops can open seven days a week.

2 Complete the missing words in this guide for new employees, using a suitable form of *have to*, *need to*, *can*, or *be allowed to*.

Working at FTC
Frequently Asked Questions (FAQs)

1 **Q** Where <u>*can I / am I allowed to*</u> park my car?

   A In the employee car park behind the main building.

2 **Q** _____ I _____ to wear formal clothes to work?

   A No, you don't. Jeans and a shirt are fine.

3 **Q** What hours do I have to work?

   A Everyone _____ _____ be in the company between 10 a.m. and 4 p.m. But you _____ _____ to choose when you start and finish work, e.g. 8 to 4, 10 to 6.

4 **Q** _____ I _____ to take my paid holiday when I want?

   A Yes, but you have to take at least three weeks in the summer.

5 **Q** Who do I see if I have a problem with my contract?

   A You _____ _____ speak to the HR Manager.

6 **Q** Can I use the Internet for personal research?

   A You _____ use it during your lunch break, but you _____ _____ to use it during office hours.

7 **Q** Am I allowed to use my office phone for private calls?

   A You can make local calls to landlines and you _____ _____ to pay for these. You _____ use the office phone for long-distance calls or calls to mobiles.

Working with words

1 Complete the sentences by finishing the words.

1 The new uniforms seem to be **p** _opular_ – everyone likes them.

2 Customer service has dealt with any problems in an **e**_____ way.

3 Our competitor has started producing environmentally **f**_____ telephones.

4 Our HR Manager wears very strange clothes – they're quite **u**_____.

5 Most customers found the new tracking system very **u**_____.

6 The manager has introduced a new **i**_____ to save energy in the office.

7 We have a special container in our office for **r**_____ ink cartridges.

8 Our new supplier is very **c**_____. Their warehouse is very near our factory.

9 That's the first time I've heard that idea. It's very **o**_____.

10 We got the new laptops at a good price – they were very good **v**_____ for money.

11 Our new furniture wasn't expensive. It was quite **a**_____ actually.

12 The **d**_____ of waste is a problem. We don't know where to throw it away.

2 Complete the conversations with a word or phrase from 1.

1 **A** Does your new hybrid car cause any pollution?
   B No, it's very _environmentally friendly_.

2 **A** Is the rent for your office expensive?
   B No, it's quite _____, actually.

3 **A** The new design of the AS982 is quite strange, isn't it?
   B Yes, it is. It's quite _____.

4 **A** How much did you pay for your new office furniture?
   B It was really cheap, but it's beautifully made. It was _____.

5 **A** Do you reuse plastic carrier bags?
   B Yes, we do. We believe in _____.

6 **A** How far do you live from your office?
   B Not far at all – I can walk to work. It's very _____.

7 **A** Who told you to turn off the lights at 6 o'clock?
   B It's an _____ from Head Office to try and reduce costs.

8 **A** The new ordering system seems to be working well.
   B Yes, it's quite _____, isn't it?

9 **A** What do people think of the new canteen?
   B Most people like it. I think it's very _____.

Business communication

1 Look at these sentences taken from a presentation about safety at work. Put the sentences in the order they come during the presentation.

a ____ That brings me to the end of my talk.

b ____ I'll talk about the annual medical checks later.

c ____ My name is Freya Branca and I work for the Safety Council.

d ____ Thanks very much for listening.

e ____ First of all, we're going to look at safety in the office.

f ____ Let's move on to safety off-site.

g ____ I'm here today to tell you about the new regulations being introduced next year.

h _1_ Good afternoon, everybody.

i ____ My next point is about general health issues.

j ____ As I said before, employees are going to have a compulsory medical check-up.

2 A representative from a green cleaning service is giving a talk about his company. Complete his presentation with phrases from the list.

I'll talk	Let's move on	~~Hello and welcome.~~
My next point	Thanks very much	as I said before,
That brings me	I'm here today	First of all,

1_____ _Hello and welcome._ _____ I'm Georgio Belatoni from Green Sheen. 2_____ to tell you about the advantages of contracting our cleaning service. 3_____ about the financial side of things later.
4_____ we're going to look at the benefits of employing Green Sheen to clean your offices. Well, the most important advantage is the clean and healthy working atmosphere we create by using only environmentally friendly products.
5_____ to our cleaning professionals. We choose our staff carefully, and you'll find our cleaners polite and friendly, a pleasure to have in the building. 6_____ is about your company image. By employing a green cleaning service, you will show your commitment to the environment, increase your appeal in the market, and attract more customers. Finally, let's talk about the cost of contracting Green Sheen. Our cleaning service is very good value for money, as we offer a personalized price. And, 7_____ you are likely to get more customers by going green.
8_____ to the end of my talk. 9_____ for listening. Now, are there any questions?

Language at work | The passive

Passive forms

Form

Verbs in sentences can either be active or passive.

The passive is formed with the verb *be* + past participle of the main verb.

Tense	Passive form
Present simple	The photocopier **is serviced** once a year.
	Our offices **are cleaned** in the evening.
Past simple	The meeting **was held** yesterday.
	The new computers **were installed** last week.

Questions

1 To make questions in the passive, put *is / are / was / were* + subject + past particple.

   Are the pipes produced abroad?

   Where were they made before?

2 To give a short answer to questions in the passive, use the subject + *is / are / was / were*.

   Were they delivered last week?

   Yes, **they were.** / No, **they weren't.**

Use

1 When the person who does the action is unknown.

   The flowers **are changed** daily.

   (I don't know who changes them.)

2 When the person who does the action is unimportant.

   The hotel **was built** in the 19th century.

   (It isn't important who built it.)

3 When the person who does the action is too obvious to mention.

   The books **were delivered** this morning.

   (It's obvious a delivery company brought the books.)

4 When we want to say *who* does something in a passive sentence, we use the preposition *by*.

   The party **was organized** by the social committee.

Language tip

Passive forms are usually used in formal written English more than in spoken English.

*Candidates for the job **are required** to speak fluent English.*

---

1 Correct these sentences.

1 Deliveries are make three times a week.
   _Deliveries are made three times a week_____.

2 The invoice sent yesterday.
   _____.

3 Over a thousand guests was invited to the event.
   _____.

4 The post collects at 10.00 a.m. every day.
   _____.

5 The software is wrote by our own engineers.
   _____.

6 The meeting was cancelling because of the strike.
   _____.

2 Choose the correct answer from the words in *italics*.

Outsourcing is when a company [1]*uses / is used* an external company to provide a service. The idea of outsourcing is not new; it [2]*first suggested / was first suggested* by Adam Smith in his book 'The Wealth of Nations', which [3]*published / was published* in 1776.

One of the main advantages of outsourcing is that it [4]*saves / is saved* a company money, resources, and energy. However, direct communication between a company and its customers [5]*is often lost / often loses* and customers can soon become dissatisfied.

3 Rewrite these sentences in the passive form starting with the words given.

1 They serve hot meals in the staff canteen.
   Hot meals are served in the staff canteen.

2 The HR Department sent an email to all employees.
   An email _____.

3 Someone stole the money during the night.
   The money _____.

4 The Heads of Department informed the staff about the decision.
   The staff _____.

5 We discuss salaries with employees individually.
   Salaries _____.

6 He keeps the key to the safe in his desk.
   The key to the safe _____.

Working with words

1 Put the letters in the right order to form a word and rewrite the sentence.

1 The **UPREPOS** of the trip was to motivate the new team.
   purpose

2 We held our last corporate **VETEN** at the America's Cup.
   _____

3 The **ENEUV** of the dinner was the top-class restaurant Triton in Prague. _____

4 Over 500 **TUSEGS** were invited to attend. _____

5 We were working to a **UTDEBG** of €50,000. _____

6 The **TOSH OYPCAMN** didn't provide transport, so we had to take a taxi. _____

2 Complete the sentences with a suitable form of the verb from the list.

accept	arrange	book
entertain	~~hold~~	reinforce

1 My company __*holds*__ a corporate event every June.

2 We invited our VIP clients to a luxury spa to _____ our relationship.

3 The host company _____ a trip to the Taj Mahal.

4 Our bank always _____ its clients at Roland Garros.

5 The venue we _____ last year was too small.

6 I couldn't _____ the invitation because the dinner was the same day as my daughter's graduation.

3 Complete the description of a corporate event with a suitable word from **1** and **2**.

The last corporate ¹__*event*__ I attended was a day at a Champions League Final. The ²_____ was a well-known publicity agency who wanted to ³_____ their VIP clients. The ⁴_____ of the event was to ⁵_____ the relationship between the company and their clients.

The event was ⁶_____ in the hospitality area of the Atatürk Olympic Stadium in Istanbul, which was a ⁷_____ I had always wanted to visit. Of course, I ⁸_____ my invitation as soon as it arrived!

Fortunately the company had a large ⁹_____, because the tickets were very expensive and they had invited more than a hundred ¹⁰_____. They had to ¹¹_____ the seats months in advance to make sure there was room for all of us. The football match was in the evening, so they ¹²_____ a trip to Topkapi Palace and Ayasofya in the afternoon where we had dinner before leaving for the stadium. Everyone had a great day, and the event was a complete success for the publicity agency.

Business communication

1 Put these words in the right order to make complete sentences.

1 very / you / kind / That's / of
   *That's very kind of you*____.

2 to / you / lunch / like / Would / join / for / us
   _____?

3 up / I / station / pick / the / Shall / you / from
   _____?

4 but / get / I'd / some / Thanks / rather / sleep
   _____.

5 you / book / like / table / me / Would / to / a
   _____?

6 water / you / of / Would / a / like / glass
   _____?

7 the / hungry / for / I'm / invitation / Thanks / but / not
   _____.

2 Rewrite these sentences with the word given.

1 Do you want something to eat? (like)
   *Would you like something to eat*____?

2 Shall we stop for a break? (like)
   _____?

3 Shall I meet you at the airport? (like)
   _____?

4 Would you like me to get some tickets? (shall)
   _____?

5 Shall we visit the new factory now? (like)
   _____?

3 Complete the mini conversations.

1 A __*Would*__ __*you*__ __*like*__ some water?
   B Yes, please. That would be nice.

2 A Would you like to join us for a drink?
   B _____ _____ _____ invitation, but I have to call my boss.

3 A Would you like me to find out what's on at the theatre?
   B Yes, please. That's _____ _____ _____ you.

4 A Would you _____ _____ _____ fax you the agenda?
   B Yes, please. That's very kind of you.

5 A Shall I call you a taxi?
   B No, _____. _____ _____ walk.

6 A Would you like to see the new sports facilities?
   B Yes, please. That _____ _____ _____.

Language at work | First conditional

First conditional

Form

There are two parts to a sentence in the *first conditional*, the condition and the result.

Positive and negative

if + present simple (= condition), *will / won't* + verb (= result)

> *If they **invite** me to the opera, I'll **accept** the invitation.*
>
> *If we **book** an expensive restaurant, we **won't have** any money for taxis.*

The sentence may begin with the condition or the result. Put a comma to separate the two parts when the condition comes first.

> *If I **work** late tonight, I'll **miss** the football.* (with comma)
>
> *I'll **miss** the football if I **work** late tonight.* (no comma)

Questions

1 The result usually comes before the condition in first conditional questions. The usual word order is *will* + subject + verb.

> *How **will you get** to Paris if you miss your plane?*
>
> ***Will the staff go** on strike if they don't get a pay rise?*

2 To give a short answer to *yes / no* first conditional questions, use the subject + *will / won't*.

> *Will you go to the conference if your boss agrees?*
>
> *Yes, **I will**. / No, **I won't**.*

Use

To talk about events that will probably happen in the future.

> *If the manager **resigns**, people **will be** very upset.*
>
> *If we **finish** the project by Friday, we **won't have** to work at the weekend.*

Language tip

We never use *will / won't* straight after *if*.

Don't say: *If I'll see her tomorrow, I'll tell her.*
Say: *If **I see** her tomorrow, I'll tell her.*

Don't say: *If he won't set his alarm, he won't get up on time.*
Say: *If he **doesn't set** his alarm, he won't get up on time.*

---

1 Choose the correct answer from the words in *italics*.

1 If they *won't plan / don't plan* the event carefully, they *go / 'll go* over their budget.

2 If the venue *is / will be* too small, we *don't book / won't book* it.

3 He *don't get / won't get* a good deal if he *'ll wait / waits* any longer.

4 If we *don't hold / won't hold* a corporate event this year, we *lose / 'll lose* some of our clients.

5 The manager *don't accept / won't accept* the invitation if she *won't like / doesn't like* the venue.

6 If we *'ll arrange / arrange* a trip to the Guggenheim, we *don't arrive / won't arrive* back at the hotel in time for dinner.

7 They *'ll cancel / cancel* the outdoor activities if it *rains / 'll rain* at the weekend.

2 Rewrite the sentences using the prompts.

1 if / the weather / be / bad / we / not go / sailing
   If the weather is bad, we won't go sailing   .

2 if / the singer / be / ill / they / cancel / the concert
   _____.

3 we / not go / to the show / if / it / finish / late
   _____.

4 how / they / travel / if / the airline / be / on strike
   _____?

5 he / call / the host company / if / he / not receive / an invitation
   _____.

6 what / you / do / if / it / snow / on the day
   _____?

7 if / she / not like / the food / she / order / something different
   _____.

3 Complete the sentences with the correct form of the verb in brackets.

1 If the guests _____*arrive*_____ (arrive) late, they _____*'ll be*_____ (be) too tired to attend a meeting.

2 If the budget _____ (not be) big enough, they _____ (go) somewhere different.

3 We _____ (complain) to the organizers if the food _____ (run out).

4 If the financial crisis _____ (continue), we _____ (not hold) an event this year.

5 They _____ (not find) the venue if we _____ (not give) them a map.

Working with words

1 Match 1–8 to a–h.

1	achieve _e_	a	responsible
2	manage ___	b	reputation
3	perform ___	c	the workforce
4	socially ___	d	performance
5	safety ___	e	~~your targets~~
6	diversity of ___	f	costs
7	good ___	g	record
8	environmental ___	h	well

2 Complete the mini conversations with phrases from 1 and choose the correct answer from the words in *italics*.

1 A Why do you say that my sales results are *disappointing / ~~satisfactory~~?*

   B Because you didn't _achieve your targets_ once last year.

2 A Did your _____ improve last year?

   B Yes, our results were *excellent / poor*. We only had three accidents all year, and none of them were serious.

3 A Did the team _____?

   B Well, much better than last week even though they didn't win.

   A Well, that was *encouraging / disappointing*.

4 A It's not *satisfactory / excellent* for a company just to make profits.

   B No, it must also be _____ and look after its staff.

5 A Why were your profits so *encouraging / poor* this year?

   B Because prices are rising and it's very difficult to

   _____.

6 A When you evaluated our _____, were the pollution levels acceptable?

   B Well, the results were *satisfactory / disappointing*, but they could be better.

7 A Has your company managed to increase the

   _____?

   B Yes, I would say that our performance here has been *encouraging / disappointing*. Now more than 50% of our workforce are women and 30% are from ethnic minorities.

8 A This article here says that we have a

   _____ for diversity: 20% of our employees are of Hispanic or Italian origin.

   B Well, that's *poor / encouraging*.

Business communication

Soft drinks sales in Europe

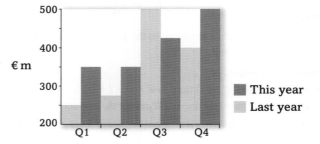

1 Look at soft drinks sales for last year and complete the presentation with prepositions from the list.

~~at~~   to   by   from   to   by   to

> Last year sales started the year [1] _at_ 250 million euros. They rose [2] _____ 250 million in the first quarter [3] _____ 275 million euros in the second quarter. In the next three months, they then increased [4] _____ 225 million [5] _____ 500 million euros. Unfortunately they then fell [6] _____ 100 million euros [7] _____ a final total of 400 million euros in the last three months of the year.

2 Look at the sales for last year and this year and choose the correct answer from the words in *italics*.

> As I said before, our sales [1] *rose / ~~declined~~* to 500 million euros in the third quarter of last year. Why did they go up so dramatically? This was thanks to the successful launch of our new sports drink 'Vitality'. But as you know, we then had that problem with the contaminated drinks can, and our sales [2] *grew / dropped* in the final quarter to 400 million euros.
>
> That contamination incident continued to have a negative effect on our reputation at the beginning of this year. As a result, sales [3] *decreased / increased* by 50 million euros in the first quarter. They then [4] *remained stable / grew* at 350 million euros for the next three months. However, since June our reputation has improved and our sales have [5] *risen / fallen* every month, [6] *increasing / decreasing* to reach 500 million euros at the end of this fourth quarter.

3 Are these sentences true for your country? Correct the sentences which are false.

1 House prices have fallen dramatically this year.

2 The price of petrol has risen in the last three months.

3 The number of unemployed people dropped last year.

4 Average temperatures have grown in the last 30 years.

5 The retirement age has increased in the last ten years.

6 Food prices have remained stable in recent months.

7 Jobs in production are declining.

8 The number of university students has decreased slightly in the last twenty years.

Language at work | Present perfect (2) with *for* and *since*

Present perfect (2)

Form

See page 111.

Use

1 To talk about an action that started in the past and is continuing now.

I've worked for this company for ten years.

2 We use *for* with a period of time.

She's had this job for a month / two years.

3 We use *since* with a precise date or point in time.

They've been here since 2007 / August / this morning.

Language tip

1 *How long ...?* and *for* (+ period of time) are used with the present perfect and the past simple.

Present perfect	Past simple
How long have you had your present job?	*How long did you do your last job?*
I've had it for six months.	*I did it for five years.*

2 Sometimes we use different verbs to describe the start of the action (past simple) and the action itself (present perfect).

Present perfect	Past simple
He's worked for this company since 2004.	*He joined this company in 2004.*
I've been here for an hour.	*I arrived here an hour ago.*
He's known her since January.	*He first met her in January.*
They've lived here for six months.	*They moved here six months ago.*

Name: Angela LeMero

DOB: 1 June 1975

Qualifications

1998	Degree in Business Administration from University of Portland, Oregon

Work Experience

2005–present	Portland Running Company – Manager Day-to-day management of two shops Responsible for sales growth and cost management
2002–2005	One Step Fitness Club – Assistant Manager Responsible for developing customer activities
1998–2002	Sun Sports Clothing – Sales Assistant

1 Look at Angela LeMero's curriculum vitae and correct sentences 1–7.

1 I've got a degree from Portland University in 1998.

2 I worked as a Manager at Portland Running Company since 2005.

3 I've been responsible for cost management since several years.

4 I have been an Assistant Manager at One Step Fitness Club for three years.

5 At One Step Fitness Club I've developed customer activities.

6 I have worked as a sales assistant for four years.

7 I've left One Step Fitness Club in 2005.

2 Complete the questions with the present perfect or past simple using the information from Angela LeMero's curriculum vitae.

1 How long / Angela / work / Portland Running Company

How long has Angela worked for Portland Running Company ?

2 When / she / join / One Step Fitness Club

_____?

3 How long / she / be / Assistant Manager / One Step Fitness Club

_____?

4 How long / she / be / a manager

_____?

5 Where / she / work / 1998–2002

_____?

6 How long / she / be / responsible for sales growth

_____?

7 How long / she / work / Sun Sports Clothing

_____?

8 How long / she / be / sports and fitness industry

_____?

Working with words

1 Use a word from A and a word from B to complete the sentences.

A	B
oil	supply
economic	~~crisis~~
population	energy
world	growth
renewable	demand
global	shortage
~~energy~~	development

1 People will take the __*energy*__ __*crisis*__ more seriously when they can no longer afford to run their cars.
2 The _____ _____ of oil and gas is running out.
3 Where there is _____ _____ the financial situation of a country improves.
4 Wind and water are sources of _____ _____ .
5 _____ _____ means that there will be nine billion people living on the planet by 2050.
6 More countries need more oil these days so the _____ _____ has increased.
7 Governments are hoping to find new oil fields to avoid an _____ _____ .

2 Complete the text with the correct form of a verb that means the same as the words in brackets.

Population growth and economic development are also having a devastating effect on the world's water supply. The situation is [1]*deteriorating* (getting worse) rapidly and experts [2]_____ (think) that two-fifths of the people in the world already face water shortages. A Swiss bank [3]_____ (predicts) that by 2025 around 60% of the population will not have enough water to live on.

The problem is not that water is [4]_____ (coming to an end), but that there are more of us to share it. One of the solutions lies in [5]_____ (making better) the management of water distribution. If everyone takes a more responsible attitude to how they use this resource, disaster may be avoided.

Business communication

1 Put these words in the right order.

1 find / the / Is / likely / solution / to / government / a
   ___*Is the government likely to find a solution*___ ?
2 I / have / we / factory / close / won't / hope / to / the
   _____
3 staff / support / will / The / decision / definitely / the
   _____ .
4 you / successful / think / will / the / Do / strike / be
   _____ ?
5 probably / oil / start / shortage / until / The / won't / 2015
   _____
6 world / unlikely / supply / water / The / is / to / of / increase
   _____

2 Rewrite these sentences with the words given.

1 Will the manager listen to our demands? (likely)
   ___*Is the manager likely to listen to our demands*___ ?
2 Will they find a substitute for oil? (likely)
   Are they _____ ?
3 The plastics industry is likely to notice the effects first. (probably)
   The plastics industry _____ .
4 Petrol prices will probably rise dramatically. (likely)
   Petrol prices _____ .
5 They're sure the oil supply won't last forever. (definitely)
   The oil supply _____ .
6 I hope they'll invest more money in renewable energy. (hopefully)
   _____ in renewable energy.

3 A and B are discussing climate change. Complete their conversation with words from the list.

Hopefully	likely	are
probably	will	~~think~~

A So, do you [1]__*think*__ climate change is serious?
B Yes, I do. The polar ice caps have already started to melt and many coastal areas [2]_____ likely to be flooded in the future. [3]_____ , governments [4]_____ take measures to protect the people living in cities by the sea because if they don't, some of them will [5]_____ die.
A What can we do to help?
B Well, the best way is to help cut carbon emissions. Global warming is more [6]_____ to slow down if companies and individuals reduce their carbon footprint. The next few years will be crucial to the future of the human race.

Language at work | Future predictions

will / won't

Form

See page 117.

Use

Use *will* to talk about something that is certain to happen.

> In the future more people **will work** from home.

Use *won't* to talk about something that is certain not to happen.

> Employees **won't stay** in the same job all their working life.

may / might (not)

Form

may / might (not) + verb

Use

1 Use *may* or *might* to talk about something that will possibly happen.

> Office buildings **may look** completely different in the future.

> Employees **might have** to share a desk with their colleagues.

2 Use *may not* or *might not* to talk about something that possibly won't happen.

> In the future people **may not retire** until they're 70.

> Workers **might not commute** so much because of the oil crisis.

3 *May* and *might* both have the same meaning and are used in the same way.

Language tip

Going to is also used to make predictions, but only when the prediction is based on visible evidence.

> *Be quiet! The speaker **is going to start**.* (She's going towards the microphone.)

> *Look out the window. It**'s going to rain**.* (There are a lot of black clouds.)

---

1 **Rewrite the sentences with *will, won't, may / might*, or *may not / might not*.**

1 Perhaps / the CEO / visit the office this afternoon

   The CEO may visit the office this afternoon .

2 I'm sure / we / finish the report today

   _____ .

3 Perhaps / the manager / not in her office right now

   _____ .

4 Perhaps / your secretary / know when the meeting is

   _____ .

5 I'm sure / I / not / get the job I applied for

   _____ .

6 Perhaps / they / not give us a pay rise this year

   _____ .

7 I'm sure / he / not go on any more business trips

   _____ .

2 **Complete the dialogue with *will, may / might, may not / might not*, or *won't* and the verb in brackets.**

A Do you think you'll be working for the same company in ten years' time?

B I'm not sure. I ¹_____ *may look for* _____ (look for) a different job, if I'm still earning the same salary. It depends on my promotion prospects, too. I hope I ²_____ (be) a manager by then, and I certainly ³_____ (feel) very satisfied with my job if I'm still in the same position. How about you?

A I don't think my company ⁴_____ (exist) in ten years' time. We make the plastic casing for mobile phones, but without oil, we can't manufacture the plastic. I'm not sure, but I ⁵_____ (lose) my job once there's an oil shortage.

B Why don't you try to find a new job now while you've got the chance?

A I'm thinking about it, but I still haven't decided. I ⁶_____ (apply) for a new job until I'm really sure my company is going to close. I've seen a lot of R & D jobs on the Internet, so I'm sure I ⁷_____ (find) it difficult to change companies.

Working with words

1 Match 1–8 to a–h to make complete sentences.

1 Computer shortcuts usually allow you to _f_
2 I have to meet ___
3 At weekends I don't have ___
4 My job is 60km from my home, so I ___
5 It's important to ___
6 You should allow ___
7 My train never arrives ___
8 Multitasking isn't very efficient, it just ___

a … yourself time to take a break each day.
b … enough time to see friends.
c … plan your work schedule carefully.
d … spend a lot of time travelling.
e … on time.
f … save time.
g … wastes time.
h … deadlines in my job.

2 Complete the advertisement from Dream Holiday Planners with words from the list.

time	enough	allow	save	time
plan	don't	on time	spend	schedule

If you ¹___don't___ have ²_____ time to plan your perfect holiday, contact us. You can ³_____ a lot of ⁴_____ by allowing us to organize everything for you. Send us your destination, your interests, and your budget and we will ⁵_____ your holiday ⁶_____ for you. We will ⁷_____ you enough time to visit the sights and relax. You will just ⁸_____ your ⁹_____ enjoying the holiday and not worrying about the small details. So, just send us your requirements right away and we'll send you your dream holiday plan within a week. All you have to do is arrive at the airport ¹⁰_____.

Business communication

1 A swimsuit buyer, Sue Taylor, is negotiating the conditions of a new contract with a supplier, Franco Nebulo. Put their conversation into the correct order 1–10.

a _1_ **Sue** We have a problem with your quotation.
b ___ **Franco** I think you'll find they sell quickly. But at that price, we would need payment within 30 days.
c ___ **Franco** Well, if you ordered 100 suits or more, we could offer you a price of £12.
d ___ **Sue** OK, then. We have a deal. I'll fax you the order right away.
e ___ **Franco** Oh dear. What seems to be the problem exactly?
f ___ **Sue** I think we could order that quantity. But what if we didn't sell them all?
g ___ **Franco** Great! I'll wait to hear from you.
h ___ **Sue** What if we agreed to pay within 60 days? That would allow us to sell more swimsuits before we pay you.
i ___ **Sue** Basically, £15 per suit is too expensive. If we agreed to work with you, could you reduce your price?
j ___ **Franco** Yes, I suppose we could accept those payment terms.

2 A restaurant ordered 50 ducks and the supplier sent chickens by mistake. Put the words into the right order to complete the conversation.

Restaurant We / latest / delivery / your / have / a / with / problem
We have a problem with your latest delivery.

Supplier dear / problem / the / exactly / Oh / What's
¹_____?

Restaurant ducks / Basically, / ordered / but / fifty / sent / I / me / chickens / you.
²_____.

Supplier sorry / chickens / Would / agree / to / keep / you / the / I'm ³
_____?

Restaurant I'm / that / be / acceptable / wouldn't / No / afraid ⁴_____.

Supplier ducks / be / we / Would / sent / today / if / it / too / the / late ⁵
_____?

Restaurant that / have / the / allow / No / me / to / weekend / them / would / for
⁶_____.

Supplier them / OK / send / I'll / today
⁷_____.

Language at work | Second conditional

Second conditional

Form

Positive

1 *If* + past simple, *would / might* + infinitive (without *to*)

If they **dropped** *their prices, we* **would (we'd) buy** *their products.*

2 The word *if* can also appear in the second part of the sentence.

We **would (We'd) send** *them a catalogue if we* **had** *their address.*

3 You can replace *would* with *might*. In this case *might* means *perhaps*.

If they offered me the job, I **would** *accept it.* (I'm sure I would accept it.)

If they offered me the job, I **might** *accept it.* (Perhaps I would accept it.)

Negative

If + past simple negative, *would not (wouldn't)* + infinitive

If he **didn't love** *city life, he* **wouldn't live** *there.*

Use

1 To talk about things which will probably not happen and the results of these things.

If there **was** *a new job in New York, I'd* **apply** *for it.* (But there probably won't be a job available.)

2 To talk about impossible or hypothetical situations and their results.

If oil **didn't exist**, *we* **wouldn't have** *all these pollution problems.*

3 The second conditional is different from the first conditional.

First conditional: **If I have time, I'll call you.** (It's possible or probable that I'll have time.)

Second conditional: **If I had time, I'd call you.** (But I probably won't have time.)

Language tip

Note that the past simple in a second conditional sentence refers to the present or the future. It doesn't refer to the past.

If they **offered** *me the chance to work abroad* **(now / next year)**, *I'd accept it.*

---

1 Look at this book review and complete 1–9 with phrases from the list.

might they do	they could start
could only read	didn't know
they would give	~~you lost your job~~
would you think about	found themselves
we would recommend	

What would you do if you were 50 years old and [1] _you lost your job_? If you [2] _____ where your next pay cheque was coming from, [3] _____ setting up your own business? Journalist Matthew Colbert talked to twenty successful entrepreneurs who started their own companies after being made redundant in their 50s. He asked them what advice [4] _____ to people if they [5] _____ in the same situation. If [6] _____ their businesses again, [7] _____ things differently?

'20 Lives That Began At 50' is a fascinating collection of interviews for anybody over 50 who's thought of starting their own company. If you [8] _____ one business book this year, this is the one [9] _____.

2 Choose the correct word in *italics* to complete these sentences.

1 I *would / ~~will~~* travel around the world if I *has / had* enough money.

2 What part of your job *do / would* you delegate if you *had / would have* an assistant to help you?

3 If you *were / would be* me, *were / would* you sign the contract?

4 If we *would give / gave* them more money, they *worked / might work* during their holiday.

5 We *would finish / finished* on time if the electrician *worked / would work* faster.

6 *Would / Did* we receive the goods tomorrow if you *sent / would send* them today?

7 He *wouldn't / didn't* work late if you *wouldn't pay / didn't pay* him so well.

8 I *might buy / might bought* a flat if I *earned / would earn* more money.

9 Where *do / would* you go if you *don't get / didn't get* the promotion?

Working with words

1 Match 1–8 to a–h.

1	give _g_	a	employees
2	promotion ___	b	skills
3	improve ___	c	goals
4	develop ___	d	a step back
5	take ___	e	prospects
6	set ___	f	performance
7	achieve ___	g	~~feedback~~
8	motivate ___	h	goals

2 Complete these sentences with a word or phrase from **1**.

1 If you always arrive late at work, this won't improve your _promotion prospects_ .

2 The best way to _____ _____ is to discuss the positive points about an employee first.

3 Doing training courses is a good way to _____ your _____.

4 I took a month's holiday this year. It really helped me to take a _____ _____ from my job.

5 Our boss doesn't _____ _____ for the team, so we don't know where we are going.

6 One way to _____ employees is to give them an annual bonus for good results.

7 It can be difficult to _____ your goals if they're too ambitious.

8 I've just done a course on time management. It has helped me to _____ my performance at work.

3 Jan Olsen has just had his annual appraisal with his line manager and is talking to his colleague, Anja Lund. Complete the conversation with a word or phrase from the list.

> set the goals   improve my promotion prospects
> motivate   achieve   develop my skills
> ~~appraisal~~   give them feedback

Anja How did your ¹_appraisal_ go then?

Jan It was OK. She told me I should ²_____ my team better and ³_____ more often.

Anja Really? I mean, she's not great at doing that herself, is she?

Jan I know, but I can't tell her that. She also said that I needed to do more in-company training and especially IT training to ⁴_____.

Anja Yes, but did she ⁵_____ which you need to ⁶_____ in the next year?

Jan Yes, she did and apparently, if I manage to do this, it will ⁷_____ for next year.

Business communication

1 Choose the correct word in *italics*.

1 A They've asked me to change the schedule again.
   B I know how you *think* / *feel*. It's not *easy* / ~~right~~ for you.

2 A The deadline's next Thursday and we still don't have an answer.
   B I *follow* / *see*. So what are you going to do about it?

3 A I don't know how I'm going to finish this work on time.
   B Don't *worry* / *be worry*. I'm sure there's *a solution* / *an issue*.

4 A So they're coming next week.
   B *I agree* / *Right*. And how long are they staying?

5 A It's difficult when you have customers complaining every day.
   B I understand *really* / *totally*. But it's not your *fault* / *responsible*.

6 A Why don't you *talk* / *talking* to your boss?
   B No, I *can't* / *don't* do that.

7 A Have you *think* / *thought* of *contact* / *contacting* a recruitment agency?
   B Yes, that *can* / *might* be possible.

8 A Perhaps you could *take* / *to take* a short holiday.
   B Yes, that's a good *point* / *idea*.

2 Mariana is a production manager. She's talking to a colleague, Pete, about a problem she has. Choose phrases from **1** to complete their conversation.

Pete You look stressed.

Mariana We haven't got enough staff at the moment.

Pete ¹_____ _But it's not your fault_ _____.

Mariana I know it isn't, but we're already behind schedule.

Pete ²_____.

Mariana Mmm. Yes, but what solution?

Pete ³_____ of employing some temporary staff?

Mariana No, ⁴_____. It will take too long to train them.

Pete Well, ⁵_____ you ask some people to work overtime?

Mariana ⁶_____, but I don't think the company will agree to pay the extra hours.

Pete ⁷_____ offer the staff extra holiday in return for unpaid overtime.

Mariana Yes, ⁸_____.

Language at work | Modal verbs for giving advice

must, mustn't, should, shouldn't, and *could* + infinitive

Use

These modals are used to give advice.

1 Use *must* or *mustn't* for something that is very important or necessary.

> *You look ill. You **must** see a doctor.*
>
> *You **mustn't** tell my boss I have a new job.* (It's very important you don't tell him.)

2 Use *should* or *shouldn't* for something that is or isn't a good idea.

> *You **should** stop smoking.* (It would be a good idea.)
>
> *You **shouldn't** drink alcohol at lunchtime.* (It's not a good idea to do this.)

3 Use *could* for something that is a possible solution, but maybe not the best.

> *You **could** speak to your boss about the problem.*

Form

Positive: There is no change in the form of modal verbs.

> *I / You / He / She / We / They **must** make a decision soon.*

Negative: Add *-n't* to the modal verb. There is no *don't* or *doesn't*.

> *You **mustn't** do that.* (Not ~~You don't must.~~)
>
> *He **shouldn't** call so late in the evening.* (Not ~~He doesn't should.~~)

Questions

1 To ask a question with *should* or *could*, use *should / could* + subject + verb.

> ***Should I accept** that new job?*
>
> ***Could I ask** him to come later?*

When we ask for advice, we often prefer to begin the question with *Do you think ...?*

> ***Do you think I should** accept that job?*
>
> ***Do you think I could** ask him to come later?*

2 We do not usually make questions with *shouldn't*, *must*, or *mustn't*. Use *have to* instead of *must*.

> ***Do I have to** apply for promotion?*

Language tip

1 When giving advice, we often begin the sentence with *I think ...*

> *I think you **must / should / could** email him.*

2 Do say: *I **don't think** you **should** ...*
   Don't say: ~~I think you shouldn't~~ ...

---

1 Match problems 1–7 to the advice a–g and choose the correct modal verb in *italics*.

1 Our competitor's new product is cheaper than ours. _f_
2 Our salary costs are too high. ___
3 The new job is less interesting and it pays less. ___
4 Our restaurant is losing customers. ___
5 They've asked me to work abroad. ___
6 I'm stressed at work. ___
7 I've made a big mistake in the accounts. ___

a You *should / shouldn't* ask for language lessons.
b You *could / mustn't* change the menus.
c You *could / mustn't* work such long hours.
d You *mustn't / must* recalculate your figures.
e I *think / don't think* you should accept it.
f You ~~*shouldn't*~~ / *could* reduce your price for the first three months.
g You *should / shouldn't* recruit any more people.

2 Aleksander is giving Natalia advice about writing a good CV. Three of the verbs in **bold** are correct, but five are incorrect. Find the five incorrect verbs and correct them.

Dear Natalia

You asked for help with writing your CV. Here are some ideas to help you.

Obviously, you [1]**should** _mustn't_ forget your contact details (address, phone, etc.) and you [2]**must** _____ include your education, work experience, and skills. You [3]**must** _____ include a photograph if you want, but it's not absolutely necessary.

It's a good idea to write quite a short CV, so you [4]**must** _____ write more than two pages, and don't forget, you [5]**should** _____ start with your most recent job first.

I think you [6]**should** _____ also write short sentences, and use verbs with impact, for example, 'achieved my goals', 'improved my performance', etc.

Finally, you [7]**shouldn't** _____ check that you haven't made any spelling or grammar mistakes – and most importantly – you [8]**could** _____ always tell the truth!

Hope this is useful.

Best wishes,
Aleksander

Working with words

1 Put the stages of Vladimir's career in the right order 1–9.

a ___ At this point he decided to help the runner and his career path changed direction.

b ___ When he injured his knee during a race, his career plans changed.

c ___ He gave up his job to go back to university and study physiotherapy.

d ___ His ambition was to become a professional runner.

e ___ He made the decision to become an economist instead of an athlete.

f ___ He completed an economics degree and started work in a big multinational.

g _1_ Vladimir's greatest strength was his fitness.

h ___ While he was working he spent all his evenings training other runners.

i ___ One day, the best athlete on the team suffered a similar knee injury to Vladimir.

2 Complete these sentences with a suitable word or phrase.

1 Rita wants to *make the right decision*, so she's taking her time.

2 She left her job to _____ on her writing.

3 I _____ five years at university and then I couldn't get a job.

4 They want to _____ their jobs in the city and go and run a hotel in the country.

5 My _____ is to become an airline pilot.

6 I'm looking forward to the _____ of learning a new language.

7 Atsushi decided to change _____ and become a taxi driver.

8 When he failed his final exams, all his _____ plans had to change.

9 I'm going to do some voluntary work when I _____ my degree.

10 Anna's greatest _____ is her personality – she gets on with everyone.

11 The first stage of her career _____ was to get a law degree.

12 My only _____ is my handwriting – nobody can read it!

Business communication

1 Choose the correct answer from the words in *italics*.

1 *In my previous role / ~~In my current role~~* I was head of the Paris office.

2 *Recently / At the moment* he's designing some new software for the Planning Department.

3 *From 2000 to 2005 / Up to now* she's been in charge of Human Resources.

4 Our sales figures nearly doubled *last year / over the last year*.

5 *Up to now / Over the next year* we'll do more tests on the new design.

6 I was the CEO of a small company *in my previous role / over the last year*.

7 She's been responsible for contacting new clients *recently / at the moment*.

2 Complete the sentences with a suitable word.

1 _Over_ the next year we hope to open a new office in Asia.

2 In my _____ role, I'm in charge of the Marketing Department.

3 _____ he's been promoted to Chief Accountant.

4 She worked in South America _____ 2002 to 2005.

5 _____ to now I've given advice to six major companies.

6 _____ the moment she's working on her thesis.

7 In the _____ she'll be responsible for the restructuring of the company.

3 Complete this presentation with phrases from the list.

| at the moment | In the future | ~~In my previous role~~ |
| Last year | Up to now | Over the next week |

Right then, before I start, I'll tell you a bit about myself and my organization. My name's Amjad Kazalbash and I run the Star School of Management. [1] *In my previous role* I was a manager in a successful electronics company. Later I decided to open a school to train future managers. [2]_____ my colleagues and I have given courses in nearly a hundred different companies, and all of our clients have gone away satisfied. [3]_____ I took on five new trainers which means there are twenty highly qualified professionals working at my school [4]_____. [5]_____ we hope to develop even more training courses. But, for now, I hope you'll find the sessions useful. [6]_____ I will be supervising the course and answering any questions you may have about the material. So now, let me introduce you to your trainer . . .

Language at work | Revision of tenses

Present time

1 Use the *present simple* to talk about general facts or regular actions.

> He **works** for a multinational company.
> He **doesn't** usually **drive** to work.
> How often **does** he **go** away on business?

For form see p103.

2 Use the *present continuous* to talk about an action happening at the time of speaking or a temporary project.

> She's **making** a phone call.
> She **isn't interviewing** anyone this week.
> Where **is** she **going**?

For form see p105.

Past time

1 Use the *past simple* to talk about finished actions in the past.

> We **launched** the new snack bar in 2005.
> It **didn't sell** well at first.
> Where **did** you **advertise** your new product?

For form see p109.

2 Use the *present perfect* to talk about past actions where the time includes the present.

> He's **worked** for the same company for twenty years.
> He **hasn't had** a holiday since 1995.
> **Has** he ever **thought** about changing his job?

For form see p111.

Future time

1 Use *will* to make a decision at the moment of speaking or to make a prediction.

> I'll **find** out the price for you.   **Will** you **call** me back?
> Don't worry, I **won't forget**.   When **will** oil **run** out?

For form see p117.

2 Use *going to* to talk about a plan that's already decided.

> We're **going to deliver** your order on Friday.
> We **aren't going to pay** the invoice until we're satisfied.
> What time **is** the delivery **going to arrive**?

For form see p117.

Language tip

We usually use the *present continuous* to talk about arrangements in the future with a fixed time or place.

> I'm **visiting** a client **tomorrow morning**.
> I'm **not travelling** to New York **next week**.
> **Are** you **having** lunch with the manager **later**?

---

1 Complete the text about Richard Branson with a suitable form of the verb in brackets.

London-born Richard Branson is one of Britain's most well-known entrepreneurs. At school he ¹*didn't perform* (not perform) well due to his dyslexia, but that ² _____ (not stop) him from starting two business ventures by the time he was 15.

In the 1970s and 1980s Branson ³ _____ (find) fame and fortune through his record business, comprising a chain of record stores and his record label Virgin Records. Since then he ⁴ _____ (launch) over 300 companies under the Virgin brand, including Virgin Atlantic and Virgin Trains. In addition to running businesses, Branson ⁵ _____ (make) several attempts in his life to break world speed records, such as the fastest Atlantic Ocean crossing.

On 25 September 2004, Branson ⁶ _____ (sign) a deal to create a new space tourism company called Virgin Galactic. In the future this company ⁷ _____ (take) people on a flight into space for the modest sum of $200,000.

One of Branson's current ventures is Virgin Fuels, a company which ⁸ _____ (invest) in research into providing an alternative fuel for cars. Branson ⁹ _____ (hope) to offer cheaper fuels to airlines in the near future too.

2 Complete the questions using the information in **bold** to help you.

1 _____*How often do they hold*_____ a corporate event?
   They hold a corporate event **twice a year**.

2 _____ the new product?
   We'll advertise the new product **in the media and on the Internet**.

3 _____ this year's conference?
   The London office is going to arrange this year's conference.

4 _____ our next meeting?
   We're having our next meeting **next Monday**.

5 _____ his boss?
   He's known his boss **for many years**.

6 _____ for the new office furniture?
   They paid nearly **€100,000** for the new office furniture.

7 _____ your office?
   The last person leaves my office **at 9.00 p.m.**

Irregular verb list

Verb	Past simple	Past participle	Verb	Past simple	Past participle
be	was / were	been	let	let	let
become	became	become	light	lit	lit
begin	began	begun	lose	lost	lost
break	broke	broken	make	made	made
bring	brought	brought	mean	meant	meant
build	built	built	meet	met	met
burn	burnt / burned	burnt / burned	pay	paid	paid
buy	bought	bought	put	put	put
catch	caught	caught	read	read	read
choose	chose	chosen	ride	rode	ridden
come	came	come	ring	rang	rung
cost	cost	cost	rise	rose	risen
cut	cut	cut	run	ran	run
do	did	done	say	said	said
draw	drew	drawn	see	saw	seen
dream	dreamt / dreamed	dreamt / dreamed	sell	sold	sold
drink	drank	drunk	send	sent	sent
drive	drove	driven	set	set	set
eat	ate	eaten	shine	shone	shone
fall	fell	fallen	show	showed	shown
feed	fed	fed	shut	shut	shut
feel	felt	felt	sing	sang	sung
fight	fought	fought	sit	sat	sat
find	found	found	sleep	slept	slept
fly	flew	flown	speak	spoke	spoken
forget	forgot	forgotten	spell	spelt / spelled	spelt / spelled
freeze	froze	frozen	spend	spent	spent
get	got	got	stand	stood	stood
give	gave	given	steal	stole	stolen
go	went	gone / been	swim	swam	swum
grow	grew	grown	take	took	taken
have	had	had	teach	taught	taught
hear	heard	heard	tell	told	told
hide	hid	hidden	think	thought	thought
hold	held	held	throw	threw	thrown
keep	kept	kept	understand	understood	understood
know	knew	known	wake	woke	woken
lead	led	led	wear	wore	worn
learn	learnt / learned	learnt / learned	win	won	won
leave	left	left	write	wrote	written
lend	lent	lent			

File 01 | Unit 1

Activity, page 11

Rules

1 You need two counters or small coins. Player A, place your counter or coin on the Player A, Start square. Player B, place your counter or coin on the Player B, Start square.

2 Player A, move down to the next square in one of three directions.

On a blue square, answer the question.

> *Example: Blue Square: Where are you from?*
> *Player A: I'm from Korea.*

On a yellow square, give a question to the answer there.

> *Example: Pink Square: I'm a sales manager.*
> *Player A: What do you do?*

3 If you are correct, move down one square.

If you are not correct, move left or right.

4 Now Player B plays.

5 If you arrive on a 'Joker' square, you will either hear a question from your teacher or on the audio. The first person to answer correctly moves down to the next square.

The other player moves back one square.

File 02 | Unit 2

Case study, Discussion, Exercise 2, page 17

The company used the media to warn the American people not to use the medicine.

They recalled 31 million bottles from shops at a cost of $100 million.

They stopped all production of the medicine and designed new packaging to protect this and other medicines from contamination.

They offered a special reduction of $2.50 to people buying the medicine.

More than 2,250 sales reps made presentations to doctors to encourage them to use the product again.

File 03 | Unit 2

Case study, Task, Exercise 1, page 17

Student A

1 You are the Area Manager for the cosmetics company. Call your Production Manager at Head Office to inform him / her of this problem and suggest that the company stops production of the product.

2 You receive a call from a journalist. He / She wants to know more about the problem moisturizer. Answer his / her questions and say you'll call him / her back when you have more information.

File 04 | Unit 3

Business communication, Exercise 6, page 22

Student A

Look at the information in the slide below.

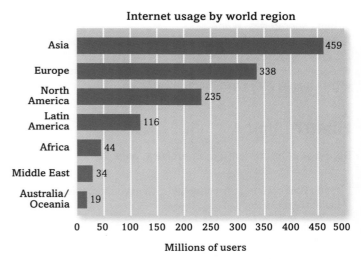

Internet usage by world region

Copyright © 2007, www.internetworldstats.com

File 05 | Unit 15

Business communication, Exercise 7, page 94

Student B

1 Listen to your partner's problems and make suggestions.

2 Now describe the problems below and respond to your partner's suggestions. If you reject a suggestion, give your reasons.

   a Tomorrow is your annual appraisal. You want to talk about your promotion prospects. But every year, your boss talks non-stop for 45 minutes and there's no time to discuss other things.

   b You want to work part-time for two years to give you time to do an MBA (Masters in Business Administration). But until now you've always worked 60 hours a week, and you know that the 25-year-old son of the CEO is very interested in your post.

File 06 | Unit 4

Language at work, Exercise 6, page 27

Student A

Ask questions to complete the missing information about Martin Cooper, using the question words in *italics*. Do **not** include the information highlighted in yellow in your question. Then answer Student B's questions.

  Example: Where was Martin Cooper born?

Martin Cooper was born in _____, in 1928. *Where?*
He studied _____, at the Illinois Institute of Technology. *What?*
In 1954 he started working for _____, where he helped develop portable products. *Who?*
At that time Motorola was in a race with Bell Laboratories to make _____. *What?*
The first private tests of the phone were in Washington and the first public demonstration was in New York on _____. *When?*
Cooper made the first call by cell phone to _____, at Bell Laboratories. *Who?*
In 1983 a smaller version of the phone went on sale for _____. *How much?*
Cooper became the _____ before he set up his own company called Arraycom. *What?*

File 07 | Unit 4

Business communication, Exercise 1, page 28

> If you find camping uncomfortable, then you've obviously never slept in a Podpad.
>
> Podpads are the latest in outdoor accommodation. A portable wooden house with beds, curtains, electricity point, and solar panel, they make tents look positively primitive!
>
> And that's not all.
>
> When you arrive at the campsite, you will find your Podpad waiting for you; transported by us, built for you.
>
> What could be easier?
>
> To book your Podpad now, log onto www.podpads.com
>
> Podpads for comfortable camping.

File 08 | Unit 4

Business communication, Exercise 5, page 28

Student A

You have researched the Energypod from Metronaps. Read the notes and give a report on your research.

Purpose:
• Find best place for employees to have a 20-minute sleep.

Why?:
• Employees work better in the afternoon after a short sleep.
• Metronaps can be installed anywhere.

What I did:
• Decide where to install one – R & D Department.
• Order one from Metronaps on trial.
• Organize interviews with employees.
• Speak to employees who used it and who didn't use it.

Result:
• Easy to sleep in, but want to be in another building.

File 09 | Unit 4

Case study, Discussion, Exercise 4, page 29

In December 2001 Meridian Delta Ltd. proposed a plan to develop housing, shops, and offices on the land around the Dome, as well as to relaunch the building itself as a sports and entertainment centre. They put Anschutz Entertainment Group (AEG) in charge of running the new building. AEG then signed a sponsorship deal with the mobile phone company O2, and the building became known as The O2.

The O2 opened on 24 June 2007 as a major new sports and entertainment venue. The new building consists of a central 23,000-capacity indoor arena for live music or sports events, surrounded by a wide boulevard known as Entertainment Avenue. This contains a mixture of leisure attractions including an 11-screen cinema, exhibition space, a smaller live music venue, restaurants, bars, and cafés. The summer launch included a free concert by Bon Jovi followed by sell-out performances by Prince and Barbra Streisand in the O2 Arena. The O2 is now one of London's top entertainment venues and forms part of the London experience for tourists.

File 10 | Unit 4

Case study, Task, Exercise 1, page 29

Options

- an aquarium
- a shopping centre
- a multi-purpose indoor arena
- a theme park
- a business park
- an industrial estate
- a conference centre

Possible benefits

- provide employment
- bring more business to city
- improve image of city
- attract visitors
- provide entertainment

Factors to consider

- cost
- size of site
- transport
- benefit to local residents of different ages

How you did the research

- email
- phone
- letter
- door-to-door
- in the street

Who you talked to

- the local government / town council
- the national government
- local residents – what age groups, and families or single people?
- local business people and companies

File 11 | Unit 5

Case study, Discussion, Exercise 4, page 35

Oxfam introduced an e-recruitment solution.

- All applications are monitored online.
- All unsuccessful applications can be stored in a talent bank.
- Applicants can update their skills in this bank.
- When there is an emergency, applicants are contacted through email.
- Money is saved because jobs are not advertised in national newspapers.
- Paper applications are put onto the system.
- The site is in four different languages, which helps recruitment abroad.
- Applicants can find out about the charity on the website.

File 12 | Unit 5

Case study, Task, Exercise 1, page 35

Student A

Look at the situation with the recruitment process six months ago and the progress made.

Six months ago	Progress made
Jobs were advertised in the national press every three months.	Had one meeting to discuss problems.
Hundreds of applications.	Talked to a company about an e-recruitment package.
Many candidates were unsuitable.	
Cost of advertising was very high.	Agreed what the budget is.
Only one part-time HR manager.	

File 13 | Unit 6

Case study, Task, Exercise 1, page 41

Company 1 – Nothing quite like home

I bought some furniture from this company. When I went into the shop, they offered me some coffee and there was a sofa to sit on. When I paid for the furniture, they gave me an envelope which had two balloons inside. They asked me to blow up the balloons on delivery day and put them outside my house. They said it would help the driver find my house and deliver on time. Ten days later they sent me some vouchers for that company to thank me for helping the driver.

Company 2 – Gizgets

I bought a gadget from this company. The first thing that happened was that they sent me the wrong product. I rang them and they sent me another one immediately, but it was more expensive and better quality. Then, unfortunately, a few days later, I dropped it and broke it. It was my fault, but when I phoned the company asking for a replacement, they were so friendly and offered to give me another free one. It arrived the next day.

Company 3 – Poochworld

I bought some products for my dog from this online company. A couple of weeks after they arrived, I got an email from the owner of the company asking me how my dog was getting on. I was also asked to send in a photo of my dog to go onto their website. People can visit the website and vote for their favourite dog each month. The winner receives a special bag of dog biscuits. I felt as if the company really wanted to get to know me and my dog.

Company 4 – TV news

I went to this shop one day looking for a new flat-screen TV. I couldn't decide which one to buy, but the owner of the shop said I could take two of them home and try them. There was no time limit and I did not have to pay for them. I rang the shop at the end of the first week and said that I wanted to buy one of the TVs and so I paid for it over the phone. I offered to come straight back in with the other TV. However, they told me to bring it back when I was next in the area. When I went back to the shop, I was given a cup of coffee and treated as if I was a friend.

File 14 | Unit 6

Case study, Discussion, Exercise 4, page 41

The awards can be given in different categories including teams, individual, and innovation. However, the WOW award is the only category where the winner is nominated by the customers. Companies which win an award can use it to promote their businesses.

One recent winner of the WOW award was I Want One Of Those (IWOOT), an online company which sells gadgets, gifts, and toys, ideal for people who do not actually *need* anything. This company received 300 nominations for the award in seven months. Some of the comments from satisfied customers included '… the delivery time was so quick and hassle free', '… helpful and friendly' staff, '… lovingly packaged by Kamal', '… you keep me informed of every step of my order', with a '… good means of tracking the parcel'.

File 15 | Unit 7

Working with words, Exercise 5, page 43

Student A

Have conversations with your partner for these situations.

1 You are checking out of a hotel. Student B is the receptionist. Ask
   - to check out
   - for your bill
   - if you can book a room for next month (two nights)
   - for the receptionist to call a taxi to take you to the airport (Terminal 4).
2 You work in the ticket office of an airline at your local airport. Student B is a passenger. Respond to his / her questions. Invent your answers.

File 16 | Unit 7

Language at work, Exercise 8, page 45

Student A

1 You are a receptionist at the hotel in Hong Kong where Student B is staying. Use this information to answer his / her questions.

   Transport: You recommend the Airport Express train service, which is quicker than a taxi and there is no problem with the traffic.

   23-minute journey to the airport. Costs HK$100. Trains every 12 minutes. First train at 05.50.

   Check-in: You recommend the flight check-in service at Hong Kong railway station. This is for passengers using the Airport Express service (seven check-in desks for Cathay Pacific). Open at 5.30 a.m.

   Shops at airport: Cartier, Gucci, Hermès, Muji to Go, Omega, etc.

2 You are looking for a luxury hotel in Portugal for a future conference. Phone the Dom Pedro Palace Hotel in Lisbon and find out the following information.

   Location: Where? How far from airport / railway station? Free airport shuttle bus?

   Facilities: Number of rooms? Air conditioning in rooms? How much space for meetings? Any restaurants? Business centre with computers / fax machines etc.? Other facilities or services?

   Leaving and arriving: Check-in and check-out times?

File 17 | Unit 8

Case study, Task, Exercise 2, page 53

Student A

Look at the information below about Interglobal Ltd.

Company history:	Global carrier since 2000
Type of company:	International
Price:	€6 per package. Discount starts at 1,000 packages
Collection:	Twice daily
Speed:	Three working days
Delivery options:	10.30 delivery / 15.30 delivery (only weekdays)
	Call and collect service
First time delivery rate:	75%
Tracking facilities:	Via call centre

File 18 | Unit 9

Case study, Task, Exercise 1, page 59

Student A

These are the ideas that you have for promoting the 3C card and their costs.

- Adverts on a search engine popular with young users. Advert appears when you type 'cool', 'money', or 'cash'. *€100,000*
- Adverts on a (legal) music download site. When the page opens, the image of the 3C card 'floats' across the screen. *€70,000*
- Adverts on a popular IM (instant messaging) service between 5.00 p.m. and 11.00 p.m. *€100,000*
- Interview with a young manager from your bank on a late-night TV programme about money issues for young people. *€40,000*

File 19 | Unit 10

Business communication, Exercise 6, page 64

Student A

You work for a green office cleaning company. Give a presentation to Student B about your service, using the notes below.

> ### Advantages of using a green cleaning company
>
> - improves working conditions of staff – cleaning products non-toxic
> - receive personalized service – same team are always sent
> - creates green image of company – environmentally friendly products are used
> - helps local industries – small company

File 20 | Unit 10

Case study, Task, Exercise 1, page 65

Group A

Your issue is transport. You think that employees should be encouraged to reduce their use of private cars and air travel by 40%. These are some of the measures your company could take:
- carpooling – *how? when?*
- using hybrid cars – *who? how? cost?*
- having incentives for using public transport – *what? cost?*
- reducing number of business trips – *how? alternative?*

File 21 | Unit 11

Case study, Task, Exercise 1, page 71

Group A

Italian experience

Guests travel to Italy to spend a cultural weekend in the beautiful city of Verona. They spend two nights at the luxury five-star Hotel Baglioni and go out for a traditional seafood dinner the first evening. The next morning is spent following the Romeo and Juliet trail before travelling to the ancient Roman amphitheatre to watch Verdi's opera *Nabucco* in the evening.

File 22 | Unit 12

Business communication, Exercise 6, page 76

Student A

1 Describe BMW's sales. Your partner will mark them on his / her graph.
   Example: In January, sales were just over 75,000. In February, they rose to about …
2 Listen to your partner's description of Mercedes' sales, and mark them on your graph.

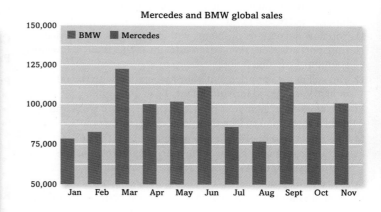

Mercedes and BMW global sales

File 23 | Unit 14

Case study, Task, Exercise 3, page 89

Student A

You are the Project Manager for Phoenix Office Design. If you don't meet the deadline of 31 December, you will have to pay your client Odensa $1,000 for each day that construction is delayed. Your objective is to try and limit your extra costs.

File 24 | Unit 12

Activity, page 77

1 Good for your reputation, and now you have a cheap source of recycled plastic. Score three points.

2 An important sales argument. Outdoor furniture needs to resist the weather – and vandalism! Score three points.

3 You earn a good reputation for promoting equal opportunity policies. Score three points.

4 Your web pages will mainly be read by potential employees or future customers. Not a very public way to promote your image. Score one point.

5 This works for six months, but now you're at full capacity again and there's no more space to expand. Score one point.

6 A good choice. Local salaries won't be too high because of the employment situation. Score three points.

7 Recycling is an important part of environmental protection. But in general, plastic isn't good for the environment. Score one point.

8 Your market share remains stable because your competitors have had to increase their prices too. Score three points.

9 A good socially responsible gesture. It will also make you more popular with your local council customers. Score three points.

10 Not a socially responsible action, but you'll be sure to have a good team. If you want the best, your wage bill may be high, though. Score one point.

11 You now have many problems with delays in delivery. Also, transport costs are rising dramatically. Is this really a low-cost solution? Lose one point.

12 You sell at a good price, but your association with the oil industry isn't good for your image. Lose one point.

13 The workers accept your proposal, preferring to work four days a week than to lose their jobs. Score three points.

14 The safest way to prevent any more accidents. Your customers are very happy with your socially responsible gesture, and your ex-supplier agrees to pay half the cost. Score three points.

15 After six months, your customers start complaining that the quality of your furniture isn't the same as before. Lose one point.

16 The local council say they don't want another factory in their beautiful town. Lose two points. Read the question again and choose another option.

17 Your customers are very disappointed – this doesn't solve the problem. What happens if somebody gets seriously injured? Lose two points.

18 Your good reputation is damaged when the press hear about your sexist policies. Lose three points.

File 25 | Unit 13

Case study, Discussion, Exercise 3, page 83

Productivity

Invested money – more robots on production line
Introduced flexible working – 3 shifts every day, 7 days a week → more production hours

Logistics

Three main suppliers relocated to near factory + 60% components now delivered from UK → less time and money wasted

Relations with workforce

Workers organized into teams of 8–15 people responsible for solving their own problems on production line → improved relations with management

Environmental concerns

Minis for European market transported by rail

Customer satisfaction

Customers offered personalized car and can choose extensive range of options even after order is placed.

File 26 | Unit 13

Case study, Task, Exercise 1, page 83

Problems at Textiles Inc.

Productivity
- low productivity
- high production costs
- inefficient

Logistics
- factory in rundown area on outskirts of town
- no public transport links

Relations with workforce
- largely female part-time employees
- high level of dissatisfaction
- high staff turnover

Environmental concerns
- textiles and factory very old-fashioned
- fined recently for not conforming to environmental legislation

Customer satisfaction
- poor – textiles do not meet customers' needs
- many goods returned

File 27 | Unit 14

Language at work, Exercise 8, page 87

Student A

1 Read the questions below and answer them for yourself.
2 Ask your partner the same questions, starting with *If …*
   Example: *If you wanted to call a colleague at home, what would be the latest possible time to phone: 9.00 p.m., 10.30 p.m., or it doesn't matter?*
3 Compare your answers and say why they are the same or different.
4 Check your score in File 57 on page 146.

1 Imagine you want to call a colleague at home. What's the latest possible time you would phone?
   a 9.00 p.m.?   **b** 10.30 p.m.?   **c** it doesn't matter?
2 Imagine a customer asks you for a quotation by the end of the week. When would you email it?
   a Thursday?   **b** Friday?   **c** when you find the time?
3 Imagine you're in a meeting which started at 9.00 a.m. It's now 1.00 p.m. Would you
   a suggest stopping for lunch?
   b look at your watch every five minutes?
   c not worry about it?
4 Imagine your friends and family advise you to slow down and work less. Would you
   a say it's not possible because there's too much to do?
   b try to follow their advice?
   c say you're surprised – your work isn't stressful at all?

File 28 | Unit 14

Business communication, Exercise 5, page 88

Student A

You work for Sigma Supplies. You have asked Pixel Printing to print your new catalogue for next year, but you now want to change the details of the order. Phone the company, explain the situation, and negotiate the new conditions.

	Original order	You now want
No of pages	300	350
No of catalogues	5,000	6,000
Delivery	By 15 Dec	By 15 Nov
Price per catalogue	€3.00	The same price

Notes
You think you should pay the same price per catalogue as you are increasing your order.
Pixel Printing is a good quality supplier with reasonable prices.

File 29 | Unit 11

Case study, Task, Exercise 1, page 71

Group C

The French Connection

Guests are taken on a trip to the Champagne region of France to taste the exquisite wines of the area. They stay in a private castle where the food is prepared by famous French chefs. The first morning is spent playing golf or enjoying the relaxing spa in the castle. Then guests are taken on a tour of an exclusive vineyard by a leading wine expert and they try a number of different champagnes.

File 30 | Unit 14

Case study, Task, Exercise 2, page 89

Who / what	Time	Notes
Internal walls	3 weeks	Internal walls must be finished first.
Plumbers	1 week	Can work at same time as electricians.
Electricity	2 weeks	Internal walls must be finished first.
Floor	2 weeks	Building must be empty first week.
Decorators	2 weeks	On holiday last week in December. Might work then if offered enough money.

File 31 | Unit 3

Business communication, Exercise 6, page 22

Student B

Look at the information in the slide below.

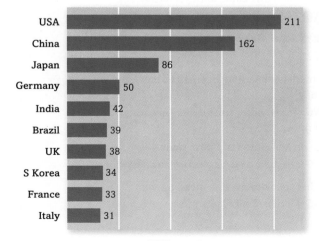

20 Top Countries in Internet Usage

Country	Millions of users
USA	211
China	162
Japan	86
Germany	50
India	42
Brazil	39
UK	38
S Korea	34
France	33
Italy	31

Millions of users

Copyright © 2007, www.internetworldstats.com

File 32 | Unit 15

Business communication, Exercise 7, page 94

Student A

1 Describe the problems below and respond to your partner's suggestions. If you reject a suggestion, give your reasons.

  a Your company has paid for you to do a one-week training course. When you arrive at the training centre on the first day, you discover you've made a mistake. In fact, the course is next week, which is also the first week of your summer holiday.

  b Once a year your company organizes an English test for employees who want to work in the International Division. You're really interested in a new post in the USA, and you have a good level of English. But on the day of the test you don't feel well, and you only score 52%. To work abroad, you need a minimum of 65%.

2 Now listen to your partner's problems and make suggestions.

File 33 | Unit 16

Language at work, Exercise 5, page 99

Student A

Sentences	Points
1 This hotel is the cheaper I could find. *WRONG: This hotel is the cheapest I could find.*	
2 If I will go to Jaime's party, I'll see you there. *WRONG: If I go to Jaime's party, I'll see you there.*	
3 They gave me some good advice. *RIGHT*	
4 You must to finish the report today. *WRONG: You must finish the report today.*	
5 English is speaking all over the world. *WRONG: English is spoken all over the world.*	
6 The parcel didn't came until yesterday. *WRONG: The parcel didn't come until yesterday.*	
7 Look at John. He's wearing jeans again! *RIGHT*	
8 The manager has sent an email to our suppliers yesterday. *WRONG: The manager sent an email to our suppliers yesterday.*	
9 I'll go on a business trip next week. *WRONG: I'm going on a business trip next week.*	
10 I didn't speak to my line manager yet. *WRONG: I haven't spoken to my line manager yet.*	

File 34 | Unit 15

Business communication, Exercise 4, page 94

Student A

You work in the IT Department. These are your problems.

- Virus in computer system
- 25 calls from users
- Only five people in IT department

File 35 | Unit 16

Business communication, Exercise 4, page 100

Student A

Look at the information on Paolo Ricci and prepare a short presentation about him.

Paolo Ricci *(male)*	Computer Science degree – Rome Master's degree – New York
Previous employment	Programmer – Karpinsky Ltd. Head Programmer – Panda Software
Recent experiences	Helped develop new software for advertising industry Designed new program for Spot-on Advertising Inc.
Present role	Head of IT Media Strategy Group Developing new software for planning department
Plans for the future	Introduce new software Develop new program for Accounts

File 36 | Unit 2

Case study, Task, Exercise 1, page 17

Student B

1 You work at Head Office as the Personal Assistant to the Production Manager. Your boss is in a meeting at the moment. Take a message.

2 Now you are a journalist. You want more information about this crisis. You call the Area Manager of the local branch. You want to know how many people have been affected, how badly they are affected, and what the company is going to do about it.

File 37 | Unit 4

Language at work, Exercise 6, page 27

Student B

Answer Student A's questions about Martin Cooper. Then ask questions to complete the missing information, using the question words in *italics*. Do **not** include the information highlighted in yellow in your question.

Example: When was Martin Cooper born?

Martin Cooper was born in Chicago, USA in _____. *When?*

He studied electrical engineering at _____. *Where?*

In 1954 he started working for Motorola, where he helped develop _____. *What?*

At that time Motorola was in a race with _____ to make the first cell phone. *Who?*

The first private tests of the phone were in _____ and the first public demonstration was in New York on 3 April 1973. *Where?*

Cooper made the first call by cell phone to Joel Engel at _____. *Where?*

In _____ a smaller version of the phone went on sale for $3,500. *When?*

Cooper became the Corporate Director of Research and Development for Motorola before he set up his own company called _____. *What?*

File 38 | Unit 4

Business communication, Exercise 5, page 28

Student B

You have researched the Yelocab in the Yelo complex opposite your office building. Read the notes and give a report of your research.

Purpose:
- Find best place for employees to have a 20-minute midday sleep.

Why?:
- Employees work better in the afternoon after a short sleep.

What I did:
- Choose ten employees to try it out.
- Rent a Yelocab for one month.
- Put it outside the main office building.
- Interview these ten employees on different days.

Result:
- Yelocabs are very relaxing, but employees are not happy about paying for them themselves.
- Speak to Sales Director to negotiate a deal for all employees.

File 39 | Unit 5

Case study, Task, Exercise 1, page 35

Student B

Look at the situation with retaining staff six months ago and the progress made.

Six months ago	Progress made
85% of employees – women under 35. Average length of stay in organization – 18 months. Benefits – 20 days paid holiday a year. Full pay for women on maternity leave for six weeks.	Now 20% men. Extended full pay for women on maternity leave to 20 weeks. Increased holiday to 25 days a year.

File 40 | Unit 7

Working with words, Exercise 5, page 43

Student B

Have conversations with your partner for these situations.

1 You are a hotel receptionist. Student A is a guest. Respond to his / her questions. Invent your answers.

2 You are a passenger at an airport and you need to fly to Oslo urgently. Student A works at the ticket office. Ask
   - for the time of the next plane to Oslo
     Example: What time does the next plane to Oslo leave?
   - for a one-way ticket   • what time the plane lands
   - which terminal the plane lands at.

File 41 | Unit 7

Language at work, Exercise 8, page 45

Student B

1 You are staying at a hotel near Hong Kong station. You have a flight home from Chek Lap Kok Airport tomorrow morning at 10.30 a.m. Find out the following information.
   Transport: Best way to get there? Time needed to get there? Cost? Number of trains per hour? First train in morning?
   Check in: Where? Check-in desks for Cathay Pacific? Opening time of check-in desks?
   Shopping: Presents for family – any good shops at airport?

2 You are a receptionist at the Dom Pedro Palace Hotel in Lisbon. Student A will call you to ask for information. Use this information to answer his / her questions.
   Location: In centre of Lisbon, 7 km from Lisbon International Airport. Low-cost minibus to hotel.
   Facilities include: 263 rooms (all air-conditioned with Internet access), 20 meeting rooms, Italian restaurant, cocktail bar, sports and health facilities, shops.
   Other business facilities: Business centre on 2nd floor.
   Leaving and arriving: Check out before midday, check in after 2.00 p.m.

File 42 | Unit 8

Case study, Task, Exercise 2, page 53

Student B

Look at the information below about Stable & Sons.

Company history:	30 years in the business
Type of company:	National
Price:	€10 per package
	Discount starts at 500 packages
Collection:	Daily
Speed:	Four working days
Delivery options:	Daily delivery (including Saturdays)
	Early morning and late evening special service
First time delivery rate:	80%
Tracking facilities:	Via email

File 43 | Unit 9

Case study, Task, Exercise 1, page 59

Student B

These are the ideas that you have for promoting the 3C card and their costs.

- Outdoor advertising on buses taking young people to school and university. *€80,000*
- National competition for best photo taken by a mobile phone. Photos posted on your bank's website. 100 winners get a 3C card and $300 in cash. *€80,000*
- Ten 30-second TV adverts on popular youth music channel. *€90,000*
- Free concert tickets for the first 1,000 people to take out cash with the card on a particular date. *€60,000*

File 44 | Unit 10

Business communication, Exercise 6, page 64

Student B

You work for a company of green consultants. Give a presentation to Student A about your service, using the notes below.

Advantages of using a green consultancy company

- expert advice from experienced consultants
- receive list of green contacts
- kept up-to-date on any changes in law
- improves company image – shows you are serious about environment.

File 45 | Unit 10

Case study, Task, Exercise 1, page 65

Group B

Your issue is resources. You think that the company could reduce its consumption of paper and water by 25%. These are some of the measures your company could take:

- cutting paper wastage – *how?*
- more recycling – *what?*
- conserving and recycling water – *how? where?*
- reducing waste in the canteen – *how?*

File 46 | Unit 11

Case study, Task, Exercise 1, page 71

Group B

The Boat Race

Guests are given the pieces of a full-size boat which they have to build and brand in teams using their own imagination. They then have the opportunity to race in their boat against the other teams to see whose boat is the fastest. At the end of the race, the winners celebrate their victory with a bottle of champagne. The day ends with a fantastic barbecue and buffet-style dinner with a free bar.

File 47 | Unit 12

Business communication, Exercise 6, page 76

Student B

1 Listen to your partner's description of BMW's sales, and mark them on your graph below.
2 Describe Mercedes' sales. Your partner will mark them on his / her graph.

   Example: In January, sales were about 65,000. In February, they rose to just over …

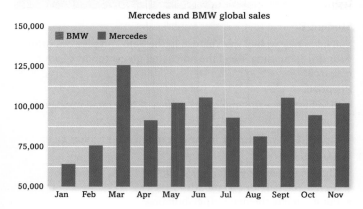

File 48 | Unit 14

Language at work, Exercise 8, page 87

Student B

1 Read the questions below and answer them for yourself.
2 Ask your partner the same questions, starting with *If* …
   Example: *If some friends invited you for Sunday lunch at 1.00 p.m., what time would you arrive – 1.00 p.m., 1.30 p.m. at the latest, or any time before 3.00 p.m.?*
3 Compare your answers and say why they are the same or different.
4 Check your score in File 57 on page 146.

1 Imagine your boss invites you for Sunday lunch at 1.00 p.m. What time would you arrive?
   a 1.00 p.m.?   **b** 1.30 p.m. at the latest?
   c any time before 3.00 p.m.?
2 Imagine you're travelling to work and your train stops between stations because of problems on the line. What would you do?
   a get really irritable?
   b look at your watch?
   c read a book or listen to music?
3 Imagine you have a three-day business trip that starts tomorrow. Would you
   a write a list of things to take?
   b have a list in your head of what you need?
   c have no list at all?
4 Imagine you're in the supermarket on Saturday and you have ten items to pay for. All the checkouts are very busy. Would you
   a leave the items and go out without paying?
   b find the shortest queue and hope it doesn't take too long?
   c go to the nearest queue and relax – it's the weekend?

File 49 | Unit 14

Business communication, Exercise 5, page 88

Student B

You work for Pixel Printing. Sigma Supplies have asked you to print their new catalogue for next year. They will phone you to ask for some changes. Complete the table below and decide what conditions you can accept or offer using the notes to help you.

	Original order	Sigma now want
No of pages	300	
No of catalogues	5,000	
Delivery	By 15 Dec	
Price per catalogue	€3.00	

Notes
You are very busy in November.
For a print order of 5,000–6,000 catalogues, the normal price is €1 per 100 pages.
Sigma Supplies is a very good customer.

File 50 | Unit 14

Case study, Task, Exercise 3, page 89

Student B

You are the Project Manager for Metropolis Construction. You want Phoenix Office Design to pay these costs.
1 $1,000 for an additional electrician.
2 $600 a day more for the decorators to work in the last week of December.
3 $4,000 to cover the salaries of the builders who were unemployed for three weeks in September / October when work stopped.

File 51 | Unit 15

Business communication, Exercise 4, page 94

Student B

You work in the Sales Department. These are your problems.
- Computer virus – lost important document (customer proposal)
- Boss threw away only paper copy by accident
- Customer needs proposal tomorrow

File 52 | Unit 16

Language at work, Exercise 5, page 99

Student B

Sentences	
1 My colleague's girlfriend work in logistics. *WRONG: My colleague's girlfriend works in logistics.*	
2 Where you went on holiday last year? *WRONG: Where did you go on holiday last year?*	
3 He works here since ten years. *WRONG: He's worked here for ten years.*	
4 Your mobile phone isn't as small than mine. *WRONG: Your mobile phone isn't as small as mine.*	
5 The goods were delivered this morning. *RIGHT*	
6 He'd get the job if he would speak German. WRONG *He'd get the job if he spoke German.*	
7 How many informations are there in the book? *WRONG: How much information is there in the book?*	
8 We don't can receive personal calls at work. *WRONG: We can't receive personal calls at work.*	
9 I may be late for the meeting tomorrow. *RIGHT*	
10 The company will close if they won't solve the problem. *WRONG: The company will close if they don't solve the problem.*	

File 53 | Unit 16

Business communication, Exercise 4, page 100

Student B

Look at the information on Asami Takahashi and prepare a short presentation about her.

Asami Takahashi (female)	Psychology degree – Tokyo University Master's degree in Human Resources Management
Previous employment	HR Department Sanyo 2001–2004 Assistant HR Manager Sony 2004–2007
Recent experiences	Gave courses on staff motivation Introduced procedures to improve employee-management relations
Present role	Head of HR Developing plan to restructure departments
Plans for the future	Discuss problems with heads of department Make changes to improve staff morale

File 54 | Unit 8

Case study, Task, Exercise 2, page 53

Student C

Look at the information below about Nova Solutions.

Company history:	Founded last year
Type of company:	National
Price:	€8 per package Discount starts at 100 packages
Collection:	On demand online
Speed:	Two working days
Delivery options:	Every day delivery (including Sundays) Notification of delivery service (by text to customer)
First time delivery rate:	90%
Tracking facilities:	On website

File 55 | Unit 9

Case study, Task, Exercise 1, page 59

Student C

These are the ideas that you have for promoting the 3C card and their costs.

- Adverts at bottom of emails at times when young people use email most (9.00–12.00 a.m., 6.00–9.00 p.m.). Users can click on a link to the 3C website. *€60,000*
- Adverts on most popular national TV channels between 9.00 p.m. and midnight. *€80,000*
- Direct mailing to all school and university students. *€50,000*
- Adverts on popular social networking site used by young people between 8.00 p.m. and midnight. *€100,000*

File 56 | Unit 10

Case study, Task, Exercise 1, page 65

Group C

Your issue is energy. You think your company should reduce its energy consumption by 40%. These are some of the measures your company could take:

- cutting electricity consumption – *how? where?*
- finding alternative renewable sources of energy – *what? cost?*
- motivating employees to save energy – *how? what?*
- replacing old systems and machines – *which?*

File 57 | Unit 14

Language at work, Exercise 8, page 87

Mostly 'a's Doing things on time is very important for you. You need to live in a 'clock time' culture.

Mostly 'b's You would probably be happy in a 'clock time' or 'event time' culture.

Mostly 'c's You're very relaxed! An 'event time' culture would be very good for you.

File 58 | Unit 11

Case study, Task, Exercise 1, page 71

Group D

MotoGP

Guests are invited to spend a day in the hospitality area of the MotoGP. They will enjoy a full day of delicious food and plenty of drinks in a marquee which is in the middle of the action. All marquees have a magnificent view of the start / finish line so that guests can see the most exciting moments of the race. The event includes a guided visit to the pit lane where mechanics will give a demonstration of a wheel change.

Unit 1

01

James Which company do you work for?

Fiona It's called Besam. B-E-S-A-M. You probably don't know it.

James No, I don't. What does the company do?

Fiona We specialize in automatic door mechanisms. But we're a subsidiary of Assa Abloy. Perhaps you know that name?

James No, sorry. I don't.

Fiona It's a Swedish group. It makes locks and security systems. I'm sure you know some of our products. Yale locks … or Chubb … or Vachette, for example?

James No, I'm afraid I don't. Is it a very big group, then?

Fiona Yes, it is. There are about 30,000 employees.

James That is big.

Fiona And annual sales of about three billion euros.

James So are you mainly in the European market?

Fiona No, we operate in 40 different countries worldwide. There are 150 different companies in the Assa Abloy group.

James Who are your main competitors, then?

Fiona The Eastern Company …? Ingersoll-Rand …? Master Lock?

James Well, I think you can see now that I know nothing about the security business.

Fiona So who do you work for?

James Microsoft.

Fiona And what does your company do?

James We make … Ah, that's a joke, right?

02

The Nestlé Company was created in 1866 by Henri Nestlé. The first Nestlé product was baby milk. The company still produces baby products today, but this is just one in a wide range of food and beverage products, including bottled water, breakfast cereals, and ice cream. It's a very successful company with sales last year of more than 107 billion Swiss francs.

Nestlé is a truly global company. Its Head Office is in Vevey in Switzerland, but it manufactures in 780 factories around the world, and sells on all five continents. For this, it depends on its 276,000 employees. Nestlé believes that it is important to invest in its employees. Training is an important part of its philosophy. In 2002, 65% of its employees received some form of training. That's one reason why less than 5% of employees leave every year.

Nestlé also invests in people outside the company, giving money and help to local communities. The company offers education in nutrition, and health programmes, and gives free food. It also plays a role in protecting the environment, by using less water, less energy, and less packaging. Stay tuned for more, in *Nestlé in Focus*, right after the break.

03

1

A Could I speak to you for a moment?

B Yes, of course.

2

A Can you tell me your name?

B Sure. It's Woody Neilson.

3

A Can I have another drink, please?

B Certainly. Same again?

4

A Could you call me again tomorrow?

B I'm afraid I'm on holiday.

5

A Would you repeat that, please?

B Yes, sorry. The reference is 1256 K.

6

A Could you help me for a moment?

B Sorry, but I'm very busy. Can it wait?

04

Gianluca Excuse me. Is this seat free?

Jana Yes, it is. Go ahead.

Gianluca Thanks very much. Can I introduce myself? I'm Gianluca Donatelli.

Jana Nice to meet you. I am Jana Frkova.

Gianluca Nice to meet you too, Jana. Where are you from?

Jana I am from the Czech Republic. But I work all over Europe.

Gianluca And who do you work for?

Jana I don't work for a company. I am self-employed.

Gianluca Oh really? And what do you do?

Jana I am a journalist. I write articles for consumer magazines.

Gianluca So why are you at this conference?

Jana I am here to research an article on Internet service providers.

Gianluca That's interesting. A friend of mine works for an Italian service provider. Can I introduce you to him?

Jana Yes, of course. That would be nice.

Gianluca Roberto. Can you come here for a minute? This is … Sorry, what's your name again?

Jana Jana. Jana Frkova.

Gianluca Roberto. This is Jana. She's writing an article on Internet service providers.

05

1 Excuse me. Is this seat free?

2 Thanks very much. Can I introduce myself? I'm Gianluca Donatelli.

3 Nice to meet you too, Jana. Where are you from?

4 And who do you work for?

5 Oh really? And what do you do?

6 So why are you at this conference?

7 That's interesting. A friend of mine works for an Italian service provider. Can I introduce you to him?

8 Roberto. Can you come here for a minute? This is … Sorry, what's your name again?

9 Roberto. This is Jana. She's writing an article on Internet service providers.

06

1

Gianluca What do you do?

Jana I am a journalist. I write articles for consumer magazines. What about you? What do you do?

Gianluca I'm a sales manager.

2

Gianluca Why are you at this conference?

Jana I'm here to research an article on Internet service providers. What about you? What are you here for?

Gianluca We want to find new customers in the European market.

07

Joker question 1 This Internet services company has its Head Office in Mountain View, California. If you're looking for information on the Internet, go to this company's page first. What's the name of the company?

Joker question 2 This car manufacturer is based in the UK, but it's a subsidiary of the German company BMW. It's well known for its luxury cars, but it also makes engines for the aeronautic and marine industries. What's the name of the company?

Joker question 3 This Japanese company specializes in audio, video, and communications products. It has around 160,000 employees. One of its most well-known products is PlayStation. What's the name of the company?

Joker question 4 This American company has its Head Office in Seattle, Washington. Its products include the 737, 747, 767, and the new 787. It's the main competitor of Airbus. What's the name of the company?

Joker question 5 This company specializes in tyres for cars, but it's also well known for its calendars. It's a competitor of Michelin and Goodyear, and it's based in Italy. What's the name of the company?

Joker question 6 This Northern European company produces mobile phones, multimedia systems, and wireless networks. In the mobile phone market, its main competitors are Ericsson and Motorola. What's the name of the company?

Joker question 7 This French group is a world leader in dairy products, including yoghurts, cheese, and desserts. It's the number two in bottled water, and it also produces biscuits. What's the name of the company?

Unit 2

08

Interviewer Where do you work?
Sang Chun In the Technical Support Department.
Interviewer So what do you do exactly?
Sang Chun Basically, my job consists of answering calls from customers who are having problems with their software. But it also involves working with sales reps from time to time. We visit new customers together.
Interviewer Do you develop software too?
Sang Chun We aren't involved in developing *new* programs. But when programmers are preparing new versions of *old* products, we take part in the discussions. We speak to customers every day, so we know the technical issues very well.
Interviewer So what sort of problems do you have to solve?
Sang Chun Oh, the usual. We deal with installation issues, password problems, bugs, things like that.

09

1
A Technical Support. Aidan speaking.
B Hi, Aidan.
A Who am I speaking to?
B Sorry, this is Nadira. I'm trying to access my customer files, but the computer isn't accepting my password.
A Yes, I think you're the fifth or sixth person to tell me that. There's a problem with the server.
B Is somebody working on it at the moment?
A Yes, *I* am. But it's not easy, because I'm on my own here. Everybody else is having lunch. Try again in half an hour.
B OK, Aidan. Thanks.

2
A Excuse me, Carlos.
B Yes, what's the problem? Can it wait? I'm having a meeting in here!
A Who are you talking to?
B A supplier. We're discussing new prices for this year. Why are you disturbing me?
A It's just that somebody is asking to use the room.
B But I use this room every Monday. I always have a meeting here.
A Yes, but you know that the Sales Director always has priority.
B Yes, I know. Is he waiting there now?
A Yes, he is.
B OK, OK. I'm leaving.

10

1 The code for England is double oh double four.
2 My mobile number is oh double seven, double oh, nine, double oh, three, four, seven.

11

1
A Could you give me your contact details?
B Sure. My name's Geoff Eccleston. That's E-double C-L-E-S-T-O-N.
A Eccleston. With a double C?
B That's right.
A And your first name, Geoff … Is that Geoff with a G or Jeff with a J?
B With a G. G-E-O-double F.
A OK, I've got that.

2
A Can I have your name, please?
B Yes, it's Briony Rhys. That's B-R-I-O-N-Y …
A B-R-I-O-N-Y. And your surname? Rhys, did you say?
B Yes, that's R-H-Y-S.
A R-H-Y-S. OK.

12

1
A Ackers and Shipton. How can I help you?
B Is Mrs Ackers there, please?
A Speaking. Who's calling, please?
B This is Simon Ilago from AOS – Ace Office Supplies.
A What can I do for you, Mr Ilago?
B I'm calling about a special price on our printers, Mrs Ackers.
A I'm sorry, but I can't discuss this now. I have a meeting in five minutes.
B Can I call you back tomorrow?
A Sorry, but I'm out of the office tomorrow. But thanks for calling. Goodbye.
B Er … You're welcome. Goodbye.

2
A BFC Consulting. Ralf Gustuvson speaking.
B Hello. Could I speak to Leo Keliher, please?
A I'm afraid he's out of the office at the moment.
B Could I leave a message?
A Yes, of course. Could I have your name, please?
B This is Natalie Kent, from NT Consulting. Could you ask Leo to call me back? It's quite urgent.
A Yes, sure. Could you tell me what it's about?
B Yes, I'm phoning to offer him some sub-contracting work.
A OK. I'll give Leo the message.
B Thanks for your help. Goodbye.

Unit 3

13

1
In our department we do reports at the end of each month which show all the money going into and out of the company. It takes a really long time. I have a meeting today with Anna Neves, who's responsible for our software. She's coming to show me a new program she wants to buy. She says it will help us a lot with all our financial reporting.

2
Our company is divided into three business units: Home, Industrial, and Public Services. I work in the Industrial Business Unit. I organize all the transport from suppliers to our factories, and from our factories to customers.
Today I have a visit from Ralf Ehrling. He's the person in charge of buying for the whole group. He wants to use just three or four big international transporters for all three of our business units. He thinks it will cost less to have a small number of suppliers.

3
I have contact with a lot of training organizations. We have a lot of people learning English here. We're also organizing a lot of IT courses this year, because we're changing our marketing software at the moment. I report to the HR Director. She's coming here for a meeting today. We're employing a lot of new people this year, and she thinks they have special training needs. We're talking about what courses we can offer them.

14

1
A Here on the first floor we have all the administrative offices. This is the CEO's office, just here on the right. He's not here today.
B How often does he use this office?
A Oh, he's here about one day a week …
B Where does he come from? He's American, isn't he?
A Yes, he's from New York.

2
A This is our HR Manager, Carla Brookes. Carla, this is Robert Sielicki. He's interested in doing some marketing work for us in Poland.
C Ah, that's good news. Nice to meet you, Mr …
B Sielicki. But please call me Robert. Nice to meet you too, Carla.
C How long are you staying here, Robert?
B Just two days – today and tomorrow.
C And who do you want to see while you're here?
B Well, one or two people in Sales and Marketing. But I'd also like to see *you* later, if possible. I'm very interested in the training programmes you have here.

3
A We're now going into the new part of the building. This is where we have our new call centre for customers from all over the world.
B When did it open?

A Just two months ago. In January.
B And how many calls a day do you receive?
A I think it's about 500 a day. Let's ask the Customer Service Manager.

4

A Can I introduce you to Alex Fenton? Alex is responsible for new business in Northern Europe. He's on the road most of the time, talking to new customers.
B Hello, Alex. So which countries do you visit?
D Sweden and Denmark mostly. But we're also very interested in Poland.
B How much do you know about the Polish market?
D Not very much. I think we have a meeting this afternoon to talk about it.

15

1

A Welcome to Freebird.
B Thanks very much. It's nice to be here.

2

A Did you have a good trip?
B Yes, thanks. It was fine.

3

A And did you find your way here all right?
B No problem. Your secretary sent me a very good map.

4

A That's good. Where are you staying?
B At the Continental Hotel.

5

A So how long are you here for?
B Just three days.

6

A Would you like something to drink before we start?
B Yes, please. A coffee would be nice.

7

A OK, I'll fix that for you. Now, did you get the programme I sent you?
B Yes, I did thanks.
A Good, so perhaps we can get started.

16

A Welcome to Freebird.
B Thanks very much. It's nice to be here.
A Is this your first time in Lisbon?
B Yes, it is.
A Did you have a good trip?
B Yes, thanks. It was fine.
A What time did you arrive last night?
B Oh, I was at my hotel at about eight o'clock.
A That's good. Not too late, then. And did you find your way here all right?
B No problem. Your secretary sent me a very good map.
A That's good. How did you get here – by car?
B Yes, I rented a car at the airport.

A Where are you staying?
B At the Continental Hotel.
A And is it comfortable enough for you?
B Yes, thanks. It's very comfortable.
A I'm pleased to hear that. So how long are you here for?
B Just three days.
A And will you have time to look around Lisbon while you're here?
B Yes, I hope so.
A Well, I'm sure we can arrange something. Would you like something to drink before we start?
B Yes, please. A coffee would be nice.
A How do you like it?
B Black please, no sugar.
A OK, I'll fix that for you. Now, did you get the programme I sent you?
B Yes, I did, thanks.
A And would you like to make any changes?
B No, everything seems fine.
A Oh, good, so perhaps we can get started.

17

This pie chart gives you the breakdown of Lenovo's sales worldwide. Can everybody see that OK? As you can see, 27.6% of sales are in the Americas, but notice that China represents 37.5% of worldwide sales.
This graph shows the change in market share in the last two or three years. As you can see, in 2006 Lenovo's market share was 35.8%. After a bad start in 2007, it went up again to 36.1% in the second half of the year. It went down again at the end of the year, but rose again in 2008. However, the important thing here is that Lenovo is still the market leader in China, with about a third of all PC sales.
This diagram summarizes the company's main operations. So sales are based in Beijing where there are also facilities for manufacturing, research and development, and after-sales. But note that the company has operations in many different cities. There are R & D centres in five different cities, and production units in the same number of locations. Our call centre operates 24 hours a day, and we have more than 3,000 technical support engineers to deal with customer problems.

Unit 4

18

A So, how did Fat Face start?
B Well, we had the original idea one night in 1988. We were both working in a bar in a ski resort called Meribel in the French Alps. We were working at night so that we could ski all day, but the late nights and early mornings were too much. We needed to find another way to pay for our skiing, so we hit upon the idea of selling T-shirts.

A I suppose you didn't think of doing any market research at the time.
B No, we just ordered 100 T-shirts and were incredibly surprised at how quickly we managed to sell them.
A Who designed the T-shirts then?
B We did. We decided to create our own, so that they would be more original. We got a manufacturer in the UK to print them for us and then send them over to Meribel. We did product trials by seeing which designs sold the quickest.
A So why the name Fat Face?
B When we decided to open our first shop, we obviously needed a name. Fat Face comes from one of our favourite ski slopes in Val d'Isere called 'La Face'.
A How would you describe your clothing?
B Practical and stylish at the same time. People associate our brand with an active, outdoor lifestyle. At the same time, the designs are interesting and attractive.
A When did you actually launch Fat Face Ltd?
B The shop opened in 1993, and sales were quite slow to start with, but they soon got better, especially at the beginning of the year 2000. Sales are now extremely good, so we've come a long way since our skiing days in Meribel!

19

Presenter Welcome to our new series *Business Foundation* where we're going to take a look at the inventors who have made our lives so different today. People like Sabeer Bhatia, one of the founders of Hotmail, who launched his online email service in 1996; Martin Cooper, who made the first mobile phone call in 1973; Tim Berners-Lee, who developed the World Wide Web in 1991; and Otto Wichterle, who made the first contact lens in 1961 in what was then Czechoslovakia. Today we've got IT expert Neil Harris in the studio to tell us the story of Sabeer Bhatia. Neil, when did Sabeer come to the USA?

20

Presenter Neil, when did Sabeer come to the USA?
Neil Well, Sabeer arrived in the USA in 1988 when he got a place to study electrical engineering at CalTech, the California Institute of Technology. After that he went on to do a master's degree at Stanford University.
Presenter What did he do then?
Neil Well, he didn't finish his doctorate at Stanford because he decided to take up a job offer with Apple. Here he met Jack Smith, and later the two of them joined a start-up company called Firepower Systems Inc. At this point Sabeer and Jack started working together on new ideas for the Internet.
Presenter So how did they get the idea for Hotmail?

Neil Actually, it was Jack Smith who thought of it first. He was frustrated because he couldn't send an email privately at work. He called Sabeer on his cell phone with an idea for a private email service. Sabeer told Jack to hang up because someone might hear their conversation. When Sabeer got home, the two discussed the idea in more detail and then Sabeer came up with a business plan.

Presenter How did they decide on the name?

Neil They tried all kinds of names ending in the word 'mail'. In the end they decided on Hotmail because it contained the letters HTML, the coding on all web pages.

Presenter When did Sabeer and Jack launch Hotmail?

Neil Well, first they had to get funding, but they didn't want to tell too many people about their idea because someone might copy it. Eventually, a sponsor agreed to invest $300,000 in the idea. Sabeer and Jack launched Hotmail on July 4th, 1996, Independence Day, and in less than six months they had one million users.

Presenter What about the offer from Microsoft?

Neil Well, Microsoft soon realized how well Hotmail was doing and in the autumn of 1997 they made their first offer for the company. It took them two months to negotiate an agreement with Sabeer, who finally sold Hotmail on December 30th for around $400 million. It was agreed that Sabeer would continue as CEO of Hotmail, but he only stayed for about a year.

Presenter Why did he leave Microsoft?

Neil Nobody knows, but he's still busy in the world of IT. He has great plans for his home country – he wants to develop a similar location to Silicon Valley in India.

Presenter Let's hope he makes it then. Neil Harris, thank you for joining us.

21

A Did you have a good weekend?

B Yes, it was great! We went away for a change.

A Did you? Where did you go?

B We went to Monte Carlo.

A That's interesting! To see the car racing?

B Yes, that's right. It was really exciting!

A Was it? I've never been to Monaco.

B It was my first time, actually. I really enjoyed it and the weather was fantastic.

A Oh really? It rained here all weekend. I think you went to the right place!

22

I'm here to report on our experiment with Podpads at the Summerhouse festival last month. The purpose of our research was to find the most comfortable place for visitors to stay during outdoor festivals. We wanted to find out which accommodation would keep people dry in bad weather.
Why did we choose Podpads? Because they are much stronger than tents. The makers also have an installation team who put up the Podpads before the event and take them down again afterwards.
First, we contacted Podpads.com and ordered 50 Podpads for the Summerhouse festival. Then on our website we offered free accommodation to 50 visitors if they took part in our research.
We spoke to our Podpad residents after one night and then again after a second night. All of them said they would consider hiring a Podpad at the next festival they went to, depending on the price.
Finally, we visited the farmers who let us use their land. We asked them for their opinion of the company. They commented on the efficiency of the team who put up the Podpads and then took them down as soon as the festival was over. I think we can say that the Podpads were a huge success. We found that they were popular with both visitors and farmers, and, more importantly, they will protect the people using them from bad weather.

Unit 5

23

Anna I'm a mother with two young children. I took this job because it offered me flexible hours. I get to work at eight in the morning, but then I can leave at four in the afternoon to get the children from school. I also have six weeks paid holiday, which is very useful in the summer when the schools are closed. I get private healthcare for all the family, and that saves me a lot of money. I don't plan to have any more children, but the maternity leave is also good here – six months on full pay.

Mark I travel a lot because I'm in sales. So I get a company car with the job. I can use it at weekends too, which is great as I get cheap petrol. They also give me a laptop for doing all my reports and a mobile phone. I can use the phone for personal calls too, which is useful. And the kids can use the laptop at weekends. I also get free gym membership. A lot of people go to the gym in the lunch hour and after work. But it's not much good for me, because I'm always on the road.

Valerie What interested me first about this job was the training courses they offered me. I've done courses in management, teamwork, and customer service. And the company also offers subsidized childcare. I had a baby last year, so that's been really useful for me. We also have a very good company pension scheme, but I'm only 28, so that's not really important now. What interests me more at the moment is the annual bonus. That means more money for Christmas presents in December … if the company's results are good.

24

A Have you ever seen a video CV?

B No, I've never seen one, but I have heard of them. In fact, I read an article about them a few days ago. It said that people have started making video clips as part of their job applications. And some companies have already started offering video CV services.

A Well, someone has emailed me a CV today, and there's a link to a video on her blog, but I haven't watched it yet.

B Well, shall we have a look at it now?

25

Interviewer So when did you start working in the non-profit sector?

Naomi When I left university in 1998.

Interviewer And er … have you ever worked for a big organization?

Naomi No, I haven't. But I've worked for three smaller ones with operations in Africa. So I've already had a lot of experience in the field.

Interviewer And have you been to Africa in the last year?

Naomi Yes, I have. This year I've been to Tanzania. I spent six months working on a construction project.

Interviewer What did you do there exactly?

Naomi Well, my job was to supervise the building of a new school. It opened in June.

Interviewer And were you happy with the results?

Naomi Yes, I was. The school was ready two months early. And that saved us $10,000 on the construction costs.

26

Paula Antonio, I need you to make a list of participants for tomorrow's training course.

Antonio OK, I'll do that right now.

Paula And please include all their mobile phone numbers.

Antonio I'm not sure I can do that. I haven't got a list. Do we have one somewhere?

Paula Yes, just look in the green file on my desk. And I'd like you to phone the Sales Director for me this afternoon.

Antonio No problem.

Paula Can you tell him that the welcome party is at six thirty this evening?

Antonio Yes, of course. Anything else?

Paula Yes. Could I ask you to go to the party too? I know it's late, but I can't be there because I have a meeting.

Antonio I'm afraid I can't, Paula. I've got a train to catch at six.

27

Natasha Ben, I wanted to talk to you about the SNT project.

Ben Ah yes. Where are we with recruitment exactly?

Natasha Well, we've already shortlisted twenty candidates.

Ben That's good. Can you give me their CVs?

Natasha I emailed them to you last week. Have you looked at your emails?

Ben No, sorry Natasha. I've been very short of time this week.

Natasha Well, time's running out. I need to call the candidates early next week to arrange the interviews.

Ben Well, I'll read everything this weekend. Don't worry. Leave it with me.

Natasha And what about the interviews at the end of the month? I'd like you to tell me when you're free. I'll need you for two or three days.

Ben Well, I'm not sure at the moment. I've got one all-day meeting at SNT that week, but I haven't heard what date yet.

Natasha Look, Ben, the interviews are very soon. Can you let me know by Monday morning at the latest?

Ben OK, OK, I'll do it. By the way, have you finished the job description yet?

Natasha No, I haven't had time. I want to work on it this afternoon. I also need to speak to the MD about salaries and benefits. It seems that you and he don't agree.

Ben I'm having a meeting with him this afternoon.

Natasha OK, so can you deal with the salaries issue when you see him?

Ben No problem.

Natasha Thanks, Ben. So that's salaries to discuss this afternoon, CVs to read this weekend, and your availability for interviews by Monday morning. You won't forget all that?

Ben No, I won't.

Unit 6

28

1

Last year I bought a book about the painter Degas from a local bookshop. When I got home, I found the book was in Spanish, not in English. I went back to the shop, but they didn't have the English version in stock. They said it was impossible to give me a refund. Actually, they weren't at all helpful.

2

I booked a taxi to go to the airport to catch an early flight. The taxi arrived at my house almost an hour late and I missed my flight. I'm not going to use that taxi company again because they're so unreliable.

3

We bought a new executive chair for our office, but after just a week a wheel came off. I phoned the company to complain and they said they would send another immediately. In the end, it took nine phone calls and nearly two months to get a new chair. We've been loyal to the same company for years. However, we were dissatisfied with the service this time, so we've changed to a different company.

29

And the final story on Consumer News tonight is about customer service and the Internet. Broadbase Software conducted a survey into how online customers are treated. It asked people to buy a product from an online retailer and then return it as soon as they received it. They were also asked to try and make contact with the retailer.

The results of the survey are generally encouraging for consumers. They can contact all the companies either by email or through a call centre, and, with 89% of them, customers can choose how to return goods. But 29% of companies take more than two business days to answer emails. This means that if customers want a quicker response, they have to spend more money by making a telephone call.

The results show that the returns policy of online retailers is getting better, but Broadbase Software believes it is still not absolutely satisfactory.

30

Ludmila So, can you tell us something about the results of this survey into the use of the Internet, Petr?

Petr Well, first of all, let's look at the different age groups. There is still a large difference between the number of young and older people who access the Internet. 90% of those in the 16–24 age group have used the Internet in the last three months, whereas the percentage in the 65+ age group is only 24%.

Ludmila That's not that surprising though, is it? After all, young people have grown up with the Internet.

Petr That's true. And also, as you might expect, the most popular activity is searching for information about goods or services, which takes up 86% of our time online. The second most popular activity is sending and receiving emails at 85%. Generally, men use it more than women, but one of the few activities that women are more interested in than men is looking for health-related information. 31% used the Internet for this as opposed to 24% of men.

Ludmila What about where we access the Internet? Do we spend a lot of time at work online when we should be working?

Petr No, actually, 87% log on from home, whereas only 44% access it from work. 52% of Internet users say that the most important reason why they don't use the Internet more is because they don't have time, but only 10% worry about the security and their privacy.

Ludmila OK. One last question. Which products have the highest sales?

Petr Films and music. 51% say that they have bought films, music, or DVDs recently, whereas 46% say that they have purchased travel, accommodation, and holidays.

31

1

Supplier Can I help you?

Customer Yes, I'm calling because you've sent me 20 colour ink cartridges instead of 20 black ones.

Supplier I see. Can you give me your order number, please?

Customer Yes, it's WJ92745.

Supplier Yes, I'm very sorry about that. I'll send somebody round tomorrow with the black cartridges. Is that OK?

Customer Yes, thank you.

2

Customer Hello. I'm calling because there is a mistake with my invoice. It says $1,000 instead of 100.

Supplier Oh right. Can you give me the number on the invoice?

Customer It's RF007/24.

Supplier Yes, it's our mistake. I'm terribly sorry. I'll send you a new invoice.

Customer Thank you.

3

Supplier Optimum Office Supplies. How can I help you?

Customer Hello. I'm calling because I ordered some paper a week ago and it still hasn't arrived.

Supplier That is a problem. When was the delivery date?

Customer Yesterday morning.

Supplier I do apologize for that. We're having a problem with our delivery agents. I'll call them to find out what has happened.

Customer Don't worry. I think I'll cancel the order. It's not the first time this has happened.

32

Cris Right, let's start. The reason we're here today is to discuss how we can improve our customer service. As you've seen from my email, we've had far too many complaints in the last three months. First of all, let's look at our sales staff. Customers say they're rude and they don't know anything about our products. Jeanne, let's hear your idea.

Jeanne Well, I think we should change the profile of our sales staff. I don't feel we should employ so many young people, because they don't know how to deal with customers.

Kirsten I don't agree. All we need to do is give our sales staff a week's training before they start.

Cris How do you feel about that, Sven?

Sven I agree with you, Kirsten. A training course would teach our sales staff how to deal with customers as well as giving them some information about the company. They would be happier in their jobs and so they'd be more polite to customers.

Cris I think you're right, Sven. OK, so let's move on to our refunds policy. Customers have complained that it's too strict, and we've lost a lot of business recently. What do you think, Kirsten?

Kirsten Personally, I feel we should give all customers their money back if they're not satisfied with their purchase.

Jeanne I don't agree at all. Think of the expense! I don't think we should give refunds to customers if they can't produce a receipt.

Kirsten Well, perhaps we should exchange the product if there's no receipt. Do you agree?

Jeanne That sounds better.

Sven Yes, that's much better.

Cris OK then …

Unit 7

33

1

This is a flight announcement for flights scheduled to leave Terminal 1 in the next hour.

Flight BA7293 to Singapore at 14.45 has been delayed until 16.30. Passengers are asked to wait in the departure lounge and watch the screens for further information. Flight BA7293 to Singapore delayed until 16.30. Passengers should wait in the departure lounge.

Flight UA0472 to Boston is now boarding at Gate J13. Flight UA0472 to Boston now boarding at Gate J13.

2

Customer Oh, hello. Can you tell me what time I have to check out, please?

Receptionist Yes. You have to leave your room by twelve and return your key card to reception.

Customer Would it be possible to leave my suitcase here until I have to go to the airport?

Receptionist Yes, of course. But please don't leave anything valuable in it.

Customer No, of course not. I'll take my valuables out of the safe and put them in my bag. Can I pay my bill by credit card?

Receptionist Yes, of course.

3

Passenger Oh, good morning. I need to get to Copenhagen as soon as possible.

Ticket clerk Well, Flight EX3465 departs at 13.00. Shall I see if there are any seats free in economy class?

Passenger Yes, please.

Ticket clerk Yes, that's fine. Would you like a one-way ticket or a return?

Passenger Only one way, please. I don't know when I'm coming back.

Ticket clerk OK. That's £44.99, please.

Passenger Can you tell me what time the flight lands in Copenhagen?

Ticket clerk Yes. It lands at 15.45.

Passenger And at which terminal?

Ticket clerk Terminal 2.

Passenger Thanks a lot.

34

The two best train services to the airport are the Narita Express and Airport Narita (Rapid Service) and the journey takes about an hour. A more expensive option is to take a taxi. Fares start at 14,000 yen.

There are five private shower rooms in Terminal 2 which come with shampoo, bath towels, and hairdryers. They can be used by passengers arriving at or departing from the airport. A 30-minute session costs 500 yen.

Passengers can exchange money at the many banks in the airport. Cash machines are available in the Check-in area of Departures, but there are none in the departure lounge.

Passengers can leave luggage in the airport for a maximum of three days. The lockers cost 300 yen per day for a small bag and can be found in both terminals.

A number of different companies offer mobile phones to rent in the airport. Passengers should go to the information desk in Departures to find out where their chosen company is located.

35

1

Receptionist Good morning. Can I help you?

Customer Yes. I want to see Susana Kechel.

Receptionist Can I have your name, please?

Customer Jim. Jim King.

Receptionist Do you have an appointment, Mr King?

Customer Yes.

Receptionist OK. Which company are you from, Mr King?

Customer Flying High Ltd.

Receptionist Thank you. Please sign here and I'll see if Ms Kechel is available.

2

Receptionist Good morning. Can I help you?

Customer Yes. Hello. My name's Helen Edwards and I'm from Citibank. I have an appointment with Susana Kechel at 11 o'clock.

Receptionist OK, I'll call Susana Kechel and tell her you're here. Could you tell me your name again, please?

Customer Yes, it's Helen Edwards.

Receptionist Thank you. Would you like to take a seat while you're waiting?

Customer Yes. Thanks.

Receptionist Susana will come and meet you in about five minutes.

Customer Do I need to sign in?

Receptionist Yes. Can you just sign here, please?

Customer Of course.

Receptionist Thank you. And here's your security pass.

Customer Thank you very much.

36

Dan Excuse me. Are you Jozef Dropinski?

Jozef Yes, I am. And you must be Dan Ford.

Dan That's right. Pleased to meet you, Jozef.

Jozef Nice to meet you, Dan.

Dan OK, then. Let's go and get a taxi.

Jozef Right. I'll follow you.

Dan OK, the taxis are outside, about two minutes' walk from here. So, did you have a good flight, Jozef?

Jozef Hmm, it was delayed for half an hour, but apart from that, everything was fine.

Dan Well, I suppose half an hour isn't so bad. Do you often travel abroad on business?

Jozef Probably about once a month, really. Last month I was in Granada.

Dan Really! Granada's beautiful isn't it?

Jozef Yes, it is. Have you been there, then?

Dan Yes, I went there with my wife for a weekend a couple of years ago. Did you see the Alhambra?

Jozef Yes, fortunately we had time to do a bit of sightseeing, so I went to have a look.

Dan What did you think of it?

Jozef I thought it was beautiful. And really peaceful too. In fact, I loved it.

Dan The architecture is amazing, isn't it? Are you interested in architecture, Jozef?

Jozef To be honest, I don't really know much about it, but I do enjoy visiting new places when I can. What about you?

Dan Yes, me too, but I've only got time to travel during the holidays. When do you usually take your holiday?

Jozef I usually have a fortnight in the summer and a week in early spring. How about you?

Dan I always go skiing for a week in February.

Jozef Do you? Where do you usually go?

Dan To Andorra. There are some excellent ski slopes there. Can you ski?

Jozef Yes. I really enjoy it. Last year we went to Slovenia in March. It was brilliant, and there was plenty of snow.

Dan Well, here are the taxis. Let's get in the queue.

Unit 8

37

It all starts when a potential customer phones us or emails us to make an enquiry about our products. We provide them with the information, then quote them a price, normally within 48 hours, if they want a standard product. The customer then places the order, and we begin to process it. Obviously, we check first of all that the product or products are in stock, and then we confirm the order with the customer and give them a delivery date. If they agree with the date, we package the goods and ship them to the customer. Our customer can track the progress of their order at any moment, in real time, using our online tracking service. We then deliver the shipment to the customer, hopefully to the right address, with the invoice attached. We then ask them to pay the invoice within 30 days. Fortunately, most of them do.

38

Supplier JPH printing. How can I help you?
Customer Hello. This is Houghton Consulting here. H-O-U-G-H-T-O-N. I'm calling about an order for some business cards. I'd like to know when we can expect them.
Supplier Could I have the order number please, madam?
Customer Yes, it's 762/29B.
Supplier One moment, please. I'll just check. Right, here it is. 762/29B, you said?
Customer Yes, that's right. The delivery date was Monday the 26th of February, but the business cards didn't arrive then.
Supplier Yes, there's a note on the order. I'm afraid there's been a problem with the quantity you ordered. We're going to deliver the cards next Thursday morning instead. That's the 8th of March.
Customer Oh no, that's too late. We're attending the company conference in Toronto on the 5th of March and we need the business cards to take with us.
Supplier So, when is the latest we can deliver the cards?
Customer On Friday the 2nd of March at the latest.
Supplier OK. I'll speak to the manager and see if we can change the delivery date. As soon as I've spoken to him, I'll call you back. OK?
Customer Yes, thank you. I'll expect your call very soon then. Thanks.

39

Fenola Hello. Is that Michael Wan?
Michael Speaking.
Fenola Hello, Michael. It's Fenola Young here from GW Architects.
Michael Hello, Fenola. How can I help you?
Fenola I'd like to meet you some time next week to discuss our ideas for the new software application.
Michael Yes, of course. When are you available?
Fenola Does Tuesday morning suit you?
Michael I'm afraid I'm not available on Tuesday. Shall we say Wednesday at 11 instead?
Fenola Yes, that suits me. Thank you so much.
Michael Thank you. So that's Wednesday at 11, then.

Fenola Yes. Goodbye.

40

Fenola Hi. Sven?
Sven Hi, Fenola. How's it going?
Fenola Not too bad. Listen. Can we meet for lunch next week?
Sven Great idea. When are you free?
Fenola Is Tuesday OK for you?
Sven Sorry, I can't make it on Tuesday. How about Thursday at 12.30 instead?
Fenola Sounds good. Same place as usual?
Sven Yes. Same place at 12.30. See you then.
Fenola See you on Thursday. Bye.

41

Heather OK, then, let's start, shall we? We're here to decide on a new logo for the company. Any ideas?
Tony Well, personally, I quite like the old one. Why don't we just change the colours, make it look a bit more modern, and leave it at that?
Heather I don't think that'll work, Tony. We want something really new here. A state-of-the-art design that shows how far we've come since we started.
Ingrid Maybe we should change the name of the company, too. I mean 'Rollinson's Audiovisual Solutions' is quite long, isn't it?
Karl Yes, I think we should shorten it. We could just have the initials R-A-S in the logo.
Ingrid That's a great idea, Karl! 'R-A-S'. That sounds good, doesn't it? How about changing our name to R-A-S?
Heather I'm not sure about that, Ingrid. One thing is the company logo and another thing is the name. I suggest we use the initials R-A-S in the logo, but keep our name so that people still know who we are. What do you think?
Karl Fine. I think that makes sense.
Heather Good. Now, let's move on to the question of who's going to design the logo.
Tony Well, if we want a complete change, we'll need to find a different designer. Shall we ask a few local designers to send us a sample of their work, and take it from there?
Heather OK. Let's look at some local companies first and see what sort of work they produce. Tony, will you look into that?
Tony Yes, of course. No problem.
Heather Right then. What about style? What are we actually looking for here …

42

One of the most obvious considerations for an online retailer when choosing a delivery company is the price of the service. However, a low-cost company is only a good choice if the service is fast. Customers want the products they order as soon as possible and so a next-day service is the most popular. They also like to know

where their goods are, so an efficient online tracking system is essential. It's important that your delivery company offers a number of different delivery options, like early morning or late evening, to make the delivery convenient for the customer. Some companies send a text message or an email to their customers to tell them when to expect their goods. This obviously improves their first time delivery rate. If you have to deliver the same product more than once, the delivery is more expensive for the retailer. Finally, the speed of the delivery can also be improved if the goods are collected from the retailer daily, twice daily, or on demand.

Unit 9

43

1
I know that companies have to advertise to sell their products. But you don't need to have big billboards everywhere. They're really horrible and they get bigger and bigger every year. I think the Mayor of São Paulo was right to do what he did.

2
I think you need to have laws on advertising. You have to stop companies advertising products which are bad for you. In my country, you aren't allowed to advertise cigarettes, for example.

3
I think some advertising laws are really stupid. Where I live, you are allowed to advertise beer and alcohol on TV, but you can't do it before 8.00 p.m. The idea is to protect children, but most children watch TV until at least 10.00 p.m.

4
Some people say there's too much advertising online. But when we use the Internet, we usually don't have to pay to get the information we need. That's because many website owners make their profits from advertising, so we can use their websites for free. I agree that there are a lot of ads online, but you don't have to look at them.

44

A I don't agree at all. I think it's wrong to close all these factories and move production to low-cost countries.
B Sorry, but when you produce goods in China, for example …
A Can I just finish?
B Sorry, go ahead.
A I mean, it's all happening so quickly. Factories are closing and there are no new jobs for factory workers here.

B Can I just say something here? Relocating to low-cost countries helps to reduce prices for us in the West. And those countries …

A Yes, but if you don't have a job, you don't have any …

B Please let me finish. It's the low-cost countries like China or India which will be the big markets in the future. If you produce there, it's a good way to attract future customers and earn market share.

A Yes, but companies need to boost sales here too. And if people don't have jobs …

45

Sonya So, we're here today to talk about Central Europe. We need to discuss our new marketing campaign.

Anton So, who's going to start?

Sonya Maybe you, Anton. Can you tell us about the advertising budget?

Anton Yes, OK. To support the new sales campaign, we have to spend more on advertising this year. Last year our spending in Central Europe was 28.6 million euros. This year we have decided on a budget of 37.5 million.

Edward Sorry, I didn't catch that, Anton. What was that you said?

Anton Yes, sorry. Our spending last year was 28.6 million euros. And this year our budget is 37.5 million euros. We want to spend the extra money on a big outdoor advertising campaign.

Sonya Yes, that's definitely a good idea.

Anton OK, if we now look at the budget for Western Europe, we see that last year we had …

Edward Er, sorry, Anton, but I think we're getting off the subject here. Can we come back to that later?

Anton Yes, OK. But I really think we need to discuss Western Europe too.

Edward OK, I think we've covered advertising. Can we move on to the next point?

Sonya Sure. Do you want to talk about sales now, Edward?

Edward All right. Well, we forecast a 7–10% increase in annual sales for this year, and we are looking for a similar figure for the two following years. That's in the markets where we have a stronger presence.

Sonya Sorry, Edward, I'm not with you.

Edward What do you mean?

Sonya Could you be more specific? Which countries are we talking about?

Edward I mean Poland, Hungary, and the Czech Republic.

Sonya OK, thanks.

Edward Well, anyway …

Anton Can I just say something? As I said before, I really feel we need to review the budgets for Western Europe.

Sonya OK, Anton, I agree, but I think we need to have another meeting about that

on another day. Edward, did you have anything else to say?

Edward No, I think that's everything. Can we sum up what we've agreed?

Sonya Sure. So, Edward, you're going to prepare a detailed sales forecast, country by country, and Anton, you're going to …

Unit 10

46

1

We've got some rather unusual drinks machines in our office which recycle bottles and cans. They're called reverse vending machines. When you've finished your drink, you put the can back into the machine. They're quite popular actually, as our office produces less waste and you feel as if you're helping the environment.

2

We didn't do much to help the environment in my office until someone started an initiative to turn the lights off. It's a really effective way to save energy and cut costs.

3

The most environmentally friendly area in my company is probably the canteen. Most work canteens use plastic knives and forks, but the ones we use are biodegradable, and so are the cups. I think it's a useful way of teaching people about green issues and at the same time making rubbish less harmful.

4

We've started a carpooling system in my office, so that we don't all drive our cars to work every day. The idea is quite popular, actually, and about 60% of the staff take part. At least two people travel in each car, which means we're cutting our carbon emissions by more than half. It's also useful because we don't arrive so late at the office!

47

Blanca So, Tony, what services does your advertising agency outsource?

Tony Well, cleaning for a start. We contract a private cleaning service to clean our offices because the building is so big.

Blanca Aah. That wouldn't work for us. You see, the machines in the factory need to be cleaned by professionals, so we employ our own cleaners.

Tony Really? And how about maintenance?

Blanca We outsourced this until last year, but now we employ three technicians. We need experts to look after the machines.

Tony Right. We outsource to a maintenance company.

Blanca Do you?

Tony Yes, it costs us less to contract a private company than to employ our own maintenance people.

Blanca What about IT? Who looks after your computers?

Tony We've got our own IT department because the programs are so specialized. How about you?

Blanca No, we outsource to a local IT company. We haven't got enough computers to need our own technicians.

Tony How about human resources?

Blanca We've only got about 50 employees, so we've got an agency which finds new staff for us when we need them. I suppose you employ your own staff?

Tony Absolutely. The HR Department is quite big, so it can do all the employing itself. We outsource the training, though, because there's so much of it.

Blanca We outsource training too, because we don't need it very often.

Tony What else? I know, the canteen. Have you got your own cooks?

Blanca No, the catering is outsourced to another company because only a few employees use the service. And you?

Tony Yes, we outsource, too, so that we get a better service. Talking of food, I'm hungry. Do you fancy going out for lunch?

48

Teresa Hello, Guido. You said you wanted to talk to me.

Guido Yes, come in, Teresa. I wanted to talk to you about the green initiatives proposed by Head Office. Which proposals do you think would be most effective?

Teresa Do you mean in my department, or in the whole company?

Guido I mean in the whole company. Head Office wants us to cut our carbon emissions by 10% before the end of the year.

Teresa Sorry, did you say by the end of this year? I thought the proposals said by the end of next year.

Guido Yes, you're absolutely right. We've got until the end of next year. I've been looking through the ideas, and I think it would be really easy for us to keep the windows closed when the heating is on.

Teresa So, are you saying we should tell people they can't open the windows?

Guido Yes. At least not when the heating's on. Also, perhaps we could turn the heating off for part of the day.

Teresa What do you mean by part of the day?

Guido Just a couple of hours in the afternoon, between 2.00 and 4.00, let's say.

Teresa Well, I suppose that might work. The office does usually get very warm then.

49

Hello and welcome. I'm Christoffer Jonsson from Carbon Reductions and I'm here today to tell you about the advantages of going green. If you take action now, you'll be ready for the government's new green laws. I'll talk about the new regulations later. First of all, we're going to look at the benefits of a clear green policy. Well, the most important advantage of becoming more environmentally friendly is an increase in your company profits. Just by turning off machines when you're not using them and turning the heating down in warm weather, you can reduce your electricity bill. If you pay 20% less for energy, your business will get a 5% increase in profits.

Let's move on to the question of your company image. An increasing number of consumers and business customers today will only buy from or invest in companies who help protect the planet. By showing you are trying to reduce carbon emissions, you will increase your appeal in the market and attract more customers.

My next point is about your reputation as an employer. If you make a commitment to the environment, you will encourage more people to come and work for you. People don't just want to buy from responsible businesses, they also want to work for them.

There is one more important result for your business if you start adopting environmental policies now. In the near future, governments are planning to bring in new regulations for dealing with climate change. Being prepared for these will save you time and money when the new rules are introduced. And, as I said before, you'll make bigger profits if you start saving energy right now.

That brings me to the end of my talk. Thanks very much for listening. Now, are there any questions?

Unit 11

50

1

Last January a large electronics company in Spain held a corporate event for its leading dealers and I was lucky enough to be invited. The purpose of the event was to reinforce the relationship between the company and its clients, and the venue was a five-star hotel in Brazil. They arranged a few trips for us, including a visit to the beautiful city of Salvador da Baía, and an afternoon riding quad bikes along the deserted beach. I had a great time.

2

The best corporate event I've ever attended was a visit to Italy. One of the big banks in Germany decided to entertain its VIP clients by inviting them to the opera. The venue they booked was the world-famous opera house La Scala. The invitation was actually addressed to my boss, but he was

unable to go, so he asked me to go in his place. I accepted the invitation and flew to Milan two months later. The event was the opening night of *Tristan and Isolde*. It was wonderful and after the performance we had a tour of the building. The evening finished in the most exclusive restaurant in Milan where we talked business over a delicious five-course meal accompanied by the best wines.

51

Francesca Where do you think we should take them?

Jacquie Well, Benito's is good. I went there last week.

Francesca How much is it per person?

Jacquie Er, about €35–40.

Francesca Sounds good. What do you think, Luigi?

Luigi Well, actually, I think we should go to that new seafood place – La Galette?

Jacquie It's expensive though, isn't it?

Luigi Yes, it's about €60 a head. But if it's nice, we'll be able to sit outside.

Jacquie Yes, but there'll be five of us, so if we choose La Galette, it'll cost us about €300, including the wine. Benito's will be about half that.

Luigi Anyway, which evening shall we go?

Francesca How about Friday?

Luigi Mmm, but if we go to La Galette on Thursday, there'll be live jazz.

Jacquie Well, there's a singer at Benito's nearly every evening.

Francesca So what time does Benito's open?

Jacquie At seven, I think.

Francesca And do we have to book a table?

Jacquie No, I don't think they take bookings. But it won't be full if we get there for just after seven.

Francesca OK. Let's go to Benito's, then. Is that OK with you, Luigi?

Luigi Yes, fine.

52

Teo I don't know what to have, Anita. What do you recommend?

Anita Well, you must try the Parma ham. It's absolutely delicious!

Teo OK, that sounds good. I'll have the ham as a starter.

Anita Perhaps we can share the ham and order a salad, as well?

Teo Good idea, and then we can each order a main course.

Anita Right. What do you fancy?

Teo I'm not really sure. Er, what are the pizzas like?

Anita Well, they're not bad, but I recommend the pasta. It's excellent here – they make it themselves.

Teo Mmm, delicious. What are you having?

Anita I think I'll have the lasagne. What about you?

Teo I'll have the spaghetti carbonara.

Anita OK. Shall we order a bottle of wine?

Teo Yes. Why not?

Anita Red or white?

Teo I prefer white, if that's all right with you.

Anita That's fine. Waiter!

53

1

A So, here we are. This is your hotel.

B Thanks very much for picking me up at the airport.

A My pleasure. Just before you go, some of us are meeting for dinner tonight. Would you like to join us?

B Thanks for the invitation, but I'm exhausted. I think I'll just get something in the hotel and then have an early night. I'll see you tomorrow. Good night.

2

A Please take a seat.

B Thanks.

A Shall I get you a glass of water?

B Yes, please. That would be nice.

3

A Hello. Samantha, isn't it?

B Yes, that's right.

A Hi. I'm Filip. Would you like a coffee?

B No, thanks. I'd rather have tea.

4

A Did you know the Chinese State Circus is in town?

B No, I didn't. Oh, I love them. I've seen them three times.

A Well, would you like me to book a ticket for you?

B Yes, please. That's very kind of you.

Unit 12

54

1

It's not how they described it to me. At the interview they said that their target was to have 45% of management positions filled by women. But five years later, I'm still here in the same office and two men who arrived at the same time as me have been promoted above me. It's very disappointing – I really thought I had a big future here.

2

We've reduced the number of accidents in the plants by 20%. We haven't achieved our target of less than 100 accidents per year, but we're getting there. Last year was encouraging, because the number of serious injuries went down dramatically.

3

We've had a really excellent year, much better than we expected. We're the darlings of the stock market at the moment. If you want to buy shares in the company, I think you should do it now before the price goes up too high.

4

The last three years haven't been very good. First, there was that pollution incident in our biggest factory. Then, there was all that media criticism for not using electric vehicles. It's been a very poor performance – I don't like to tell people who I work for.

5

Well, it hasn't been easy in the last twelve months. The new CEO told us to reduce our costs by 10%. In the end, we only managed to reduce them by five. But then it was quite a good year for business. I suppose I could say we've had a satisfactory year.

55

Raul When did you start selling here in Dubai, Lionel?

Lionel We, um, opened our first sales office in 2004.

Raul And how long did it take to get your foot in the market?

Lionel Well, we had disappointing results for the first two years. But since 2006, our market share has gone up to nearly 5%. What about you, Raul? How long have you worked here?

Raul I've been in Dubai for three years now, actually.

Lionel Do you have a family here?

Raul Yes, my wife and children moved here last year. What about you?

56

1 one point three nine per cent
2 nought point oh three three
3 one hundred and two
4 seven thousand four hundred and sixty-seven
5 nine hundred and six thousand five hundred and seventy

57

It's 5.55 p.m., and here's the world stock market summary.
In Tokyo this morning, the Nikkei closed at 13,688.28, that's 2.84% up on yesterday's closing figure. The FTSE 100 was 38.6 points up, at 5,932.2. The DAX also finished the day slightly up, at 6,904.85. That's a rise of just 0.07%.
At midday New York time, the Dow Jones was down by 69.85 points to 12,357.41. And the Nasdaq was also down by 10.19 points to 2,316.91 – that's a fall of 0.44% since the start of trading.

58

Have a look at this graph. It shows the number of cars produced in China compared with the other three major world producers – the USA, Japan, and Germany. Let's start with Japan. As you can see, passenger car production fell at the end of the nineties. But since the beginning of this century, production has risen from eight million to around ten million. In the USA production also dropped at the end of the nineties. But since then, the number of cars has continued to decrease. In fact, new car production has fallen by two million since 1997.
The performance of the German car industry has been less disappointing than the USA. Car production grew from five to five point five million at the end of the nineties. Since 1999, it has remained stable at just under six million vehicles per year. So let's turn to China. As you can see, in the first four years, the number of new cars increased to just over half a million vehicles. But in the last ten years, it has grown dramatically. Car production rose to three million in 2005, and since then, it has increased by one million vehicles a year.

Unit 13

59

Presenter Welcome to 'Eye on the Environment', and today analyst Judy Collins is here to tell us about the effects of the oil crisis. Judy, how will the oil crisis affect the economy?

Judy Collins Well, Andy, economists estimate that a 5% reduction will cause the price of oil to rise by more than 400%. And customers will have to pay more for consumer goods, too.

Presenter Can you explain?

Judy Collins Well, oil-based substances are used to make plastic and so all plastic goods will become more expensive as the oil starts to run out.

Presenter And, obviously the car industry will be one to suffer.

Judy Collins Yes. Not many people know that over 20 barrels of oil are used to make one single car. And then the cars need oil as fuel. Experts forecast that only a few people will be able to run cars in the future.

Presenter What effect will that have on the workplace?

Judy Collins Fortunately, recent advances in technology will improve working conditions for many employees as companies will have to introduce teleworking schemes. Air travel will also be limited because of the cost of fuel and so more business will be conducted internationally by videoconferencing. The situation will deteriorate until a substitute for oil is found, which won't be an easy task as oil is used in so many different ways.

Presenter Judy Collins, thank you for talking to us.

60

In 2020 more women will work than ever before and the working population will be older in general. Many working women will be mothers, so they will occupy the increasing number of part-time jobs available. There won't be many management positions as employees will work together in self-managed teams. In addition, work will be more flexible and colleagues might not see each other often as most people will work from home. Companies will still have office buildings, but they will be much smaller and there won't be many offices. Instead the buildings might contain the company gym and a bar area, or cafeteria, for social events.
Finally, employees may not stay with only one company in 2020, and so employers will have to offer much better working conditions. More employees may take career breaks, but in the future, they will be able to rejoin their company in the same position and with the same salary they had before. In general, companies will have to fight hard to keep their staff, and so employees will be in a much better position.

61

Luis So, Gina, what are we going to do about our problems with staff turnover?

Gina I think we should organize a team-building weekend.

Luis Yes, that might work, I suppose. But it could get expensive.

Gina Well then, how about holding a weekly departmental meeting where people could talk about their problems?

Luis I'm not sure about that. I think everyone is too busy to spend a couple of hours a week in another meeting.

Gina OK. So, why don't we offer employees some specialized courses in languages or IT skills?

Luis That's a good idea. We could see how much it would cost. Any other ideas?

Gina Well, we could give everyone a pay rise!

Luis No, I'm not happy about that at all. There are people who deserve it and people who don't.

Gina OK then. What about introducing a bonus system, so the people who stay longer get paid more? Would that work?

Luis I think that's a great idea! Let's try it and see what happens.

62

Jean So, let's start, shall we? As you know, the object of the meeting is to answer any questions you have about the new teleworking scheme we're introducing from next month. Hiroko, would you like to start?

Hiroko Yes, thank you, Jean. I wanted to ask about money. I understand that teleworking will reduce costs for the company. Just how much are we likely to save?

Jean I can't tell you the exact figures right now, Hiroko, but the new scheme will definitely save the company a lot of money, especially in heating, lighting, and office space.

Rebecca So is our office building likely to close?

Jean No, the office is unlikely to close completely, although we won't need such a big building any more. We may look into the possibility of moving to a new building, or we might rent out some of the office space we don't need.

Ivan I wanted to ask about productivity. Do you think people will do more work from home?

Jean I hope employees will feel more motivated when they can organize their own time. Teleworking is a sign that we trust our workers to do their work independently without someone standing over them all the time. It probably won't be easy for some people to start with, but I'm sure people will be happier working from home.

Ivan But are you expecting an increase in productivity?

Jean Yes, I am. Apparently, most companies report an increase of 10–40%, so hopefully productivity won't decrease because of the new scheme. Next question?

Hiroko I wanted to ask about the employees. What advantages will they get from the scheme?

Unit 14

63

Franca Hi, Silvia. So you're back from New York. How was it?

Silvia Good. It's a great city to visit. And I met some really interesting people at work. But I'd go crazy if I lived in the USA.

Franca Why's that, then?

Silvia Well, it's the pace of life there. Everybody's always running. No time to stop and think. Do you know what I mean?

Franca Yes, of course. So what would you do if they offered you a job there? It's quite possible. They're looking for new people all the time.

Silvia Well, if it was only for a year or two, I might say 'yes'. It would be good for my CV.

Franca But only for a short time?

Silvia Yes. If they wanted me for longer, I wouldn't accept it. It would be too stressful.

64

1

A Can you finish the report by Friday?

B Well, I'm not sure. There's a lot to do on it.

A Well, within a week then.

B Listen. I'll do it before the end of next week, I promise. Would that be OK?

A Well, I suppose so.

2

A When do we need to send the quotation?

B They asked for it as soon as possible.

A OK, I'll start working on it right away.

B Do you think it'll be ready on Monday?

A Yes, I think so.

B Oh, just one other thing – can you send me your hours for June when you have time?

A Yes, sure.

65

Luca Hi, Hans-Peter. It's Luca. I'm calling because we have a problem with delivery.

Hans-Peter Oh, tell me more.

Luca Well, basically, we've got a lorry drivers' strike here. They're blocking all the major roads. I can't guarantee that we can deliver today's order on time.

Hans-Peter Oh no! We need those parts by tomorrow.

Luca Yes, I know. But I have another solution. Would it be OK if we sent them by train?

Hans-Peter Yes, that would be possible. But could you get them to us in time?

Luca Yes, I've checked. They'd arrive at about 6.00 p.m. tomorrow.

Hans-Peter Six o'clock! But we need to start production mid-afternoon.

Luca Ah, I didn't know that. Well, what if we transported them by train to the border? Could you send a lorry to pick them up?

Hans-Peter Yes, I think we could do that. What time would the driver need to be there?

Luca The train gets in at ... er, 5.35 in the morning.

Hans-Peter OK, good. That would allow us to get the parts to the factory on time.

Luca Of course, rail transport is more expensive than road. Would you agree to pay the extra cost?

Hans-Peter No, sorry, Luca, that wouldn't be acceptable. This lorry drivers' strike is your problem, not ours.

Luca OK, I understand.

Unit 15

66

1

Scott Hello, Thierry. Come in and take a seat.

Thierry Thanks.

Scott Now, this isn't easy for me to say, Thierry. Basically, I've been very disappointed with your performance this year in Eastern Europe. I was hoping for much better results in that region.

Thierry Well, I'm surprised, Scott. You asked us to boost sales and we achieved that. 3% up on last year.

Scott Yes, but I really wanted to see 10%.

Thierry Well, you never told me that when we spoke this time last year.

2

Scott OK, everybody, we have ten minutes left. Can we talk about the South American market? Er ... Pilar, you were at the trade show in Mexico City last week. Can you tell us how it went?

Pilar Scott, I didn't go to Mexico. I had to go to Spain last week. I told you about it in our meeting two weeks ago. Don't you remember?

Scott No, sorry, I don't. Never mind. Um ... Roberto. Didn't you do a report on the South American market a few weeks ago?

Roberto Yes, but I didn't know we were talking about that today. I don't have the figures here. They're on my computer at home.

3

Maria Hi, Scott. Is there enough for me there?

Scott Yes, help yourself. The sugar's right there.

Maria So, have you finished looking at that proposal?

Scott Not yet. I've got to about page 10.

Maria It's just that I need your signature on it. I have to send it this evening.

Scott Sorry, Maria. I've got so much to read at the moment. The sales managers have just emailed me their monthly reports. I think I'll be here all weekend!

Maria Well, before looking at them, could you just finish reading the proposal, Scott? It's only about fifteen pages in all.

67

First, think about where the appraisal will take place. If possible, you shouldn't use your own office, because employees sometimes find it difficult to talk easily. The next thing to remember is that this is a two-way conversation between you and the employee. So you mustn't do most of the talking, even if the person in front of you is very quiet or shy. If you know something about the employee's personal life, you could begin by asking them about their family or a recent holiday, for example. This will create a positive atmosphere. Now, when you begin to talk about your employee's performance, you shouldn't start with negative feedback. First, you should look at their personal goals for last year, and let them say how they have or haven't achieved them. And if they haven't achieved them all, you must discuss why this hasn't happened and offer real solutions.

68

1

First, I think Marek should try to take a week or two of holiday and spend some time with his wife and children. It'll also give him time to take a step back and think about the reasons for his poor performance.

When he returns to work, he needs to work on his management skills. First, he must learn to manage his own work better. He should ask for training in time management and managing people. It might be an idea to hire a personal coach.
Then he really must talk to his team. He should set clear goals for them, and each person should know that they are responsible for meeting their own deadlines. If they can do all that between 9.00 a.m. and 5.00 p.m., that's fine. If not, they will have to consider making the team bigger.

2

Klaudia is young and successful. Maybe her boss, the Sales Manager, is afraid of her. Or perhaps he just doesn't want to lose his best sales rep. Klaudia should talk to him first because she needs his help to get a better job in the company. She could ask him what she can do to improve her promotion prospects. If it's a question of training, he should offer it to her.
The other possibility is to speak to the CEO. She shouldn't do this immediately because her boss won't be happy. But if her boss doesn't help her, she should tell the CEO that after five years in the same job, she would really like management experience. She could say that she would prefer to stay with the same company, but if it's not possible, she will leave.

69

1

A Hey, I just opened my email and saw your message. How did you know?
B Well, last time we met, you told me you'd be 40 on the first of June.
A I don't remember that at all. Well, it was very nice of you to think of me.
B You're welcome.

2

A Well, that was good.
B Yes, it was. Thanks very much. Next time you come, it's on me.
A No problem. It was great to hear all your news.

3

A Do you think you'll be OK with it now?
B Yes, that's great. I think I can manage by myself now. Thanks for helping me.
A That's OK. Call me if there's anything else you need to know.

4

A So, well done, you've done a great job. And I'll speak to the HR Manager about your training needs.
B Great. Well, thank you for all your help and advice. It's been really useful.
A Not at all. And let me know if there's a problem with that training course.

70

Glen You look stressed. What's happened?
Marisa Well, Tom asked me to work late again tonight.
Glen Is that for the annual report?
Marisa Yes, but I said no.
Glen Right. Why's that?
Marisa Because I have a meeting at my son's school this evening.
Glen I see.
Marisa And tomorrow's Friday, and I have to leave at six because I'm going to the theatre. I don't know why I feel so bad about it. I haven't been home before nine o'clock once this month.
Glen I know how you feel. Sometimes I think it might be an idea to have a bed here!
Marisa The worst thing is – I don't understand this new software we're using. That's why this report is taking so long.
Glen I understand totally.
Marisa I mean, I've asked three times for IT training this year, but they always say they don't have the money for it.
Glen I know. It's not easy for you. When's the deadline for the report?
Marisa Next Monday.
Glen Listen, it's not your fault. The company should let you do that training course.
Marisa Yes, but the report still has to be done. And Tom says that when there's a deadline to meet, work comes first. And he's right.
Glen Listen, I'm sure there's a solution. Let's go for a coffee and think about it. And don't worry.

71

Glen Perhaps you could go to your son's school, then come back to the office later in the evening.
Marisa No, I can't do that. He'll want to talk to me about his teachers after the meeting. I can't just tell him I'm going back to work.
Glen Have you thought of coming in at the weekend?
Marisa Well, that might be possible. But Tom has to be there too. I think he's got a wedding on Saturday, or something. And I'm not free on Sunday.
Glen But as Tom says, when there's a deadline to meet, work comes first.
Marisa That's true.
Glen So why don't you tell Tom that you can work on Saturday? If he can't, that's his problem.
Marisa Yes, good idea.

72

1

I've applied for three jobs in the International Division. I had the right experience for the job, but each time I was rejected because my English wasn't good enough. But in my six years with the company, they've only given me one 30-hour English course.

Oh, and another thing ... those three jobs I applied for ... I saw them all advertised in the national press. They don't advertise jobs here in the company until very late, or sometimes not at all.

2

It's difficult to know what project managers really think of your performance. They only tell you if things are going badly. We have a system of annual appraisals, but managers don't always do them. They say there's no time, but I don't think they like doing them. Actually, I think some of them are just not very good at communicating with people.

3

When I first joined the company, I had one week of technical training. After that, I was on my own. I don't see my colleagues very much, because we're usually with customers. After six months here, I have so many questions to ask. It's difficult when each project is so different – at the moment I'm working on a new motorway, a bridge, and a petrol station. There are lots of consultants with experience in those fields, but they never have time to answer your questions.

4

We work on the same projects, but we don't really work together. If something goes wrong, it's always somebody else's problem. We have an 'Employee of the Month' award here. Each month, the Project Managers can choose one employee whose performance has been exceptional. The winner receives three hundred pounds more in his pay packet. I really don't think it's a good idea – it just encourages employees to think about themselves, and not about others.

Unit 16

73

1

I was working for a European airline when I decided I needed a career change. I was 45 and tired of the low salary and antisocial hours in the airport. I applied for a job with a travel agency, where I could use my strengths in dealing with the public. I got the job, which pays much better than my previous one, but I'm finding it very stressful. Unfortunately, my greatest weakness is time management, so I've always got too much work. I don't know how long I'll stay here.

2

When I left school at 16, I had no career plan, so I went straight into the army. By the time I was 28, I realized that I didn't want to spend my whole life there, so I decided to leave. I went to night school to get the qualifications to go to university and study maths because I wanted to go into teaching. Now I'm Head of Maths at a secondary school and I think I made the right decision to leave the army.

3

Fifteen years ago I left my job in the civil service so that I could have children. When they were old enough to go to school, I started looking for part-time work so that I would be home in time to pick them up in the afternoon. The only jobs available were in the local supermarket, but I wanted more of a challenge. I decided to do a course in human resources at the local college, and now I run the Human Resources Department of a local company. I really love my job.

4

Last year I decided to give up my high-powered banking job and move to the country to concentrate on my painting. It had always been my ambition to hold an exhibition of my own pictures, but I'd never had enough time to paint. Unfortunately, I didn't realize how much I would miss my old life. I don't enjoy painting now that I do it full-time, so I'm thinking about calling the bank and asking for my old job back.

74

… and it's not just pop stars who give their money to good causes; sports personalities are getting involved too. Let's look at the case of international footballer Ulises de la Cruz. Several times a week he sends money back to his hometown in Ecuador. Ulises grew up in a very poor village in the Chota valley and experienced extreme poverty when he was young. As an adult, he spends much of the €900,000 he earns per year trying to improve life in the community. When Ecuador reached the World Cup Finals for the first time in 2002, Ulises paid for a new system providing water for the village instead of buying a fast new car. Since then he's set up a medical centre, and he's provided the school with books and a new roof. He pays the salaries of the doctor, the nurse, and the dentist in the medical centre, and he buys breakfast and lunch for all the children who go to school in the village.
Ulises' current project is focused on something which is very important to him: sport. At the moment he's building a sports and community centre for his village. He says he'll open it at the end of the season if it's finished in time. Life for the 200 families in the village has improved greatly thanks to the footballer, but Ulises hasn't finished yet. Next he's going to build 40 new homes for the villagers. The village is going to have a complete facelift and the man responsible for that is Ulises de la Cruz.

75

1

A Well, it's half past five. Time to go home. Shall I wait for you?
B No, don't worry. I'm going to stay and finish off this report.
A OK. Bye then. See you on Monday.
B Bye. Have a good weekend.

2

A Well, that was interesting, wasn't it?
B Yes, it was. But I really must go now.
A Right. Well, it was nice meeting you.
B And you, too. See you next time.

3

A Bye, Sue, I'm off.
B Bye, Brian. See you tomorrow.

4

A Well, here's your taxi.
B Right. Thank you for everything.
A You're welcome. Goodbye. Have a good trip.
B Thanks and goodbye, Dylan.

76

1

Good morning and welcome to the annual conference of Wired 2 Play Entertainment Ltd. My name is Thorsten Richter and I'm Head of the European Division.
I've been with the company for fifteen years, and last year I was promoted to this position. In my previous role I ran the Creative Department in Bonn where we developed the best-selling games 'Riders in the Storm' and 'Kingdom Come'.
Over the last year I've met with all the country managers to discuss our falling sales figures. At the moment we're working together with a consultant, Amy Chang, to analyse our main problems. In the future we may have to target a different market to increase sales. I'd be grateful for any ideas you might have here.
So, that's enough about me. Let me tell you about those sales figures I mentioned …

2

Right then, before I start, I'll tell you a bit about myself. My name's Amy Chang and I'm a freelance consultant. I studied economics and business at Beijing University from 2002 to 2005 and after doing my MBA, I joined PricewaterhouseCoopers. I left Price when I had the opportunity to go freelance. Recently I have worked on several successful cases with clients of yours, which is how I came into contact with your company. Up to now I've managed to find solutions for all the companies I've worked with.

In my current role as consultant to your company, I'm looking to improve your sales figures and reduce your costs. Over the next year I'll spend two weeks in each department before I sit down and write my recommendations report. I'm looking forward to working with all of you.

OXFORD
UNIVERSITY PRESS

Great Clarendon Street, Oxford OX2 6DP

Oxford University Press is a department of the University of Oxford.
It furthers the University's objective of excellence in research, scholarship,
and education by publishing worldwide in

Oxford New York

Auckland Cape Town Dar es Salaam Hong Kong Karachi
Kuala Lumpur Madrid Melbourne Mexico City Nairobi
New Delhi Shanghai Taipei Toronto

With offices in

Argentina Austria Brazil Chile Czech Republic France Greece
Guatemala Hungary Italy Japan Poland Portugal Singapore
South Korea Switzerland Thailand Turkey Ukraine Vietnam

OXFORD and OXFORD ENGLISH are registered trade marks of
Oxford University Press in the UK and in certain other countries

© Oxford University Press 2009

ISBN: 978 0 19 474810 0   (Book)
ISBN: 978 0 19 473938 2   (Pack)

Printed in China

This book is printed on paper from certified and well-managed sources.

ACKNOWLEDGEMENTS

*The authors and publisher are grateful to those who have given permission to
reproduce the following extracts and adaptations of copyright material*: p 8 The Nestle
company name and image is reproduced with the kind permission of Société
des Produits Nestlé S.A. p 22 from Lenovo Group Limited, 2007/08 Q1 Results.
Copyright Lenovo, 2008. All rights reserved. Reproduced by permission.
p 24 fictitious interview with Fat Face. Reproduced by permission. p 35 from
www.onrec.com online recruitment magazine. Reproduced by permission.
p 66 'Corporate Entertaining' from Business Focus Teacher's Club website.
© Oxford University Press. Reproduced by permission. p 90 from 'Special
Report: Coaches can make you a real superhero', www.timesonline.co.uk,
10 April 2005. Reproduced by permission.

Sources: www.assaabloy.com; http://lsb.scu.edu; www.wrigley.com;
www.india-today.com; www.wikipedia.com; www.podpads.com;
www.swissmasai.co.uk; www.about.com; www.statistics.gov.uk;
www.thewowawards.co.uk; www.iwantoneofthose.com; www.yotel.com;
www.narita-airport.jp; www.ups.com; www.microsoft.com;
www.greencitizen.com; www.riskybusiness.wordpress.com;
www.worldcarfans.com; www.newyorker.com; www.lsi.com;
www.telegraph.co.uk; www.bbc.co.uk; www.bostonworks.com

*We would also like to thank the following for permission to reproduce the following
photographs*: Alamy pp 6 (Gazprom/Caro), 6 (Pirelli/idp oulton park bike
collection), 6 (UNICEF/vario images GmbH & Co.KG), 9 (Nestlé/Nick Chaldakov),
24 (Fat Face/ilian travel), 25 (electric razor/Fergus McNeill), 25 (light bulb/
bluemagenta), 25 (bag/Paddy McGuinness), 29 (Millenium Dome/Aflo Co.
Ltd.), 30 (creche/Picture Partners), 38 (woman at laptop/bilderlounge/Claudia
Göpperl), 40 (Image Source Black), 44 (Ian Leonard), 48 (UPS/David R. Frazier
Photolibrary, Inc.), 52 (Andrew Holt), 55 (direct mail/Paddy McGuinness), 55
(men talking/Hill Street Studios), 61 (car pool sign/Dennis MacDonald), 72
(bobhdeering), 77 (bottles/A Room With Views), 83 (cars/Roger Bamber), 84
(clock/CW Images), 84 (clock/CW Images), 98 (Ulises de la Cruz/Associated
Sports Photography); Axiom p 96 (yacht); Tim Branch p 14 (signs); Corbis
pp 6 (Mitsubishi/Brian Booth/Transtock), 41 (opening door/Fancy/Veer), 42
(Lisbon/Atlantide Phototravel), 53 (delivery van/Martyn Goddard), 54 (peacock/
Craig Tuttle), 61 (biodegradable cup/Ramin Talaie), 136 (Mike Segar/Reuters);
Getty Images pp 6 (Volkswagen/Jean-Christophe Verhaegen/AFP), 7 (man and
woman/Digital Vision), 11 (athletics track/David Madison), 12 (golf/Scott
Spiker), 12 (Sara/Purestock), 12 (Benjamin/Hola Images), 12 (Heidi/Stephan
Hoeck), 15 (woman on the phone/Ghislain & Marie David de Lossy/Cultura),
17 (microphones/Jon Feingersh), 18 (birds/Charles McRae), 18 (meeting/
Thomas Barwick), 20 (Ryan McVay), 21 (walking down corridor/Stockbyte),
24 (paper boat/Ashley Karyl), 25 (chairs/altrendo images), 32 (John Lund/Marc
Romanelli/Blend Images), 33 (man and woman/Jose Luis Pelaez), 35 (Oxfam/
AFP), 36 (flower stall/Karim Sahib/AFP), 36 (customer survey/Sparky/The Image
Bank), 37 (angry man/Medioimages/Photodisc), 37 (call centre/Colin Gray), 47
(Prague/Livio Sinibaldi/Photodisc), 48 (apples/Roderick Chen), 49 (warehouse/
Michael Rosenfeld), 50 (Bambu Productions), 54 (Carrefour/AFP), 55 (billboard/
AFP), 59 (student/David Deas), 60 (computers/Jonathan Kingston), 65 (pylons/
Sam Robinson/Digital Vision), 66 (balloons/altrendo images), 66 (Sumo
wrestling/Koichi Kamoshida), 66 (golf/Chris Condon), 68 (Ghislain & Marie
David de Lossy), 74 (Gavin Hellier), 78 (solar energy/Lester Lefkowitz), 78 (oil
well/Seth Joel), 86 (Mitchell Funk), 87 (café/Gary Yeowell), 90 (Tai Chi/Bruno
Morandi), 90 (business coach/UpperCut Images), 92 (PhotoAlto/Eric Audras),
101 (ladder/Otmar Thormann); iStockphoto p 11 (joker/Joe Peragino); Courtesy
of Greg Mortensen p 96 (Greg Mortensen); PA Photos p 8 (AP Photo/Keystone/
file/Fabrice Coffrini); Photolibrary.com pp 30 (leaf cutter ants/David M Dennis/
Animals Animals), 60 (trees/Christine Schneider/Cusp), 71 (glasses/Jonnie Miles/
age fotostock), 80 (IBID); Courtesy of www.podpads.com p 28; Punchstock
pp 30 (gym /Zefa RF), 61 (office building/Digital Vision); Reuters pp 6 (VW
distribution centre/Christian Charisius), 23 (visitors/Denis Balibouse), 26
(Sabeer Bhatia/Arko Datta), 26 (Martin Cooper/Steve Marcus), 72 (dragon boat
races/Kin Cheung), 89 (Ryugyong Hotel), 98 (hometown footballers/Guillermo
Granja); Courtesy of Reverse Vending Corporation p 61 (reverse vending
machine); Rex Features pp 6 (AOL/Mimi Mollica), 9 (Nestlé and Nesquik/Eric
Vidal), 26 (Tim Berners Lee/Jaakko Avikainen), 42 (Yotel room), 62 (Sipa Press),
75 (hotel); Still Pictures pp 95 (engineers/Knut Mueller/Das Fotoarchiv); Tony
de Marco p 56; Courtesy of www.yelony.com p 143

Images sourced by: SuzanneWilliams/Pictureresearch.co.uk

Cover photo: Chris King

*The authors and publisher would also like to thank the following individuals for their
advice and assistance in developing the material for this book*: Gareth Davies, Pat
Allen, Lucy Adam, Jill Prewett, David Rose, and Lynne White.